CONCENTRATE Q&A
TORT LAW

CONCENTRATE
Q&A
TORT LAW

Dr Karen Dyer

Formerly Senior Lecturer in Law,
University of Portsmouth

OXFORD
UNIVERSITY PRESS

OXFORD
UNIVERSITY PRESS

Great Clarendon Street, Oxford, OX2 6DP,
United Kingdom

Oxford University Press is a department of the University of Oxford.
It furthers the University's objective of excellence in research, scholarship,
and education by publishing worldwide. Oxford is a registered trade mark of
Oxford University Press in the UK and in certain other countries

Published in the United States of America by Oxford University Press
198 Madison Avenue, New York, NY 10016, United States of America

British Library Cataloguing in Publication Data
Data available

Library of Congress Control Number: 2019935756

ISBN 978–0–19–874529–7

Printed in Great Britain by
Bell & Bain Ltd., Glasgow

Contents

Guide to the Book

Every book in the Concentrate Q&A series contains the following features:

ARE YOU READY?

Are you ready to face the exam? This box at the start of each chapter identifies the key topics and cases that you need to have learned, revised, and understood before tackling the questions in each chapter.

DIAGRAM ANSWER PLAN

Not sure where to begin? Clear diagram answer plans at the start of each question help you see how to structure your answer at a glance, and take you through each point step by step.

KEY DEBATES

Demonstrating your knowledge of the crucial debates is a sure-fire way to impress examiners. These at-a-glance boxes help remind you of the key debates relevant to each topic, which you should discuss in your answers to get the highest marks.

SUGGESTED ANSWER

What makes a great answer great? Our authors show you the thought process behind their own answers, and how you can do the same in your exam. Key sentences are highlighted and advice is given on how to structure your answer well and develop your arguments.

QUESTION

Each question represents a typical essay or problem question so that you know exactly what to expect in your exam.

LOOKING FOR EXTRA MARKS?

Don't settle for a good answer—make it great! This feature gives you extra points to include in the exam if you want to gain more marks and make your answer stand out.

CAUTION

Don't fall into any traps! This feature points out common mistakes that students make, and which you need to avoid when answering each question.

TAKING THINGS FURTHER

Really push yourself and impress your examiner by going beyond what is expected. Focused further reading suggestions allow you to develop in-depth knowledge of the subject for when you are looking for the highest marks.

Guide to the Online Resources

Every book in the Concentrate Q&A series is supported by additional online materials to aid your study and revision: www.oup.com/uk/qanda/

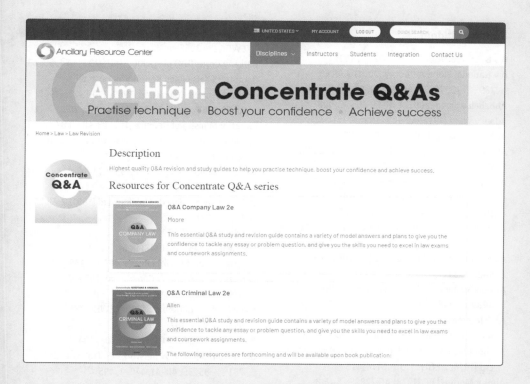

- Extra essay and problem questions.
- Bonus questions to help you practise and refine your technique. Questions are annotated, highlighting key terms and legal issues to help you plan your own answers. An indication of what your answers should cover is also provided.

- Online versions of the diagram answer plans.
- Video guidance on how to put an answer plan together.
- Flashcard glossaries of key terms.
- Audio advice on revision and exam technique from Nigel Foster.

Table of Cases

Table of Legislation

European Directives

International Instruments

Exam Skills for Success in Tort Law

Students frequently ask, 'how do I achieve a good grade for my law exam?' It comes as a surprise to students to discover that lecturers are delighted to award high marks to them for their exam papers; but it should come as no surprise that the basis for a good grade in tort law is a detailed understanding of the law of tort. As a significant portion of tort is common law, you will need to read several key judgments during your studies, if you wish to do well.

The second stage is to develop a systematic approach to using your knowledge of law to answer examination questions. High marks are awarded to answers which exhibit legal precision, systematic structuring, clear communication, and enjoyment in answering the question set. These are not skills that many of us can acquire overnight.

Preparation for Success

1. Attendance

- Attend all your lectures and seminars/tutorials. If you are a full-time student, you should study— for approximately 35 hours per week. If you are a part-time or distance-learning student, your time management will be even more crucial to success.

- Fully prepare for the seminars in advance. You will gain much more from them if you have had a go at answering your questions before you attend. Additionally, be prepared to speak up when given an opportunity. There is nothing more depressing for a tutor than to be faced by twenty people who prefer to stay quiet for the whole session. It does not matter if you make a mistake; that is what seminars are for. You will find out where you went wrong and not make the same mistake again.

- Do attend a revision lecture if one is given. Many students fail to realize that their lecturers are usually the ones who set the examination questions.

- Examiners like to examine on new areas of law, so if there have been any Supreme Court decisions or the coming into force of statutes which affect tort law, do not be surprised if your examiner sets you a question, or part of a question, on this. You will not find this information in text books, no matter how recently your book as has been published. If your text book has a link to a website update, make sure that you visit the page.

2. Practice

- If you are given an opportunity to submit a formative assignment for feedback, take up this offer. This is the only way that you will get detailed feedback on how to improve your answers to achieve the mark you want.

- Use previous exam papers to prepare you for the big day. Work out how many minutes you have to answer each question, and then have a go at answering one under timed conditions, with or without your books. The time passes very quickly. The skill is to produce, in the time allowed, an answer that is well written, accurate, and as comprehensive as possible. Ask your tutor for feedback.

- Nowadays, students type rather than taking notes by hand. Examiners can only mark what they can read. Make sure that you practise sufficiently so that your writing is legible, but also that you can write fast enough to include all the law that will get your high mark. If you have large handwriting, your examiner will prefer if you leave a line between each line that you write on.

3. Revision

- Start revising early. Tort law exams require you to discuss case law, and lots of it! It will help you considerably if you start learning the names of the parties and the significance of these cases as soon as you have been introduced to them in the lectures. If you forget a name of a case in the exam, you can write out the key facts, but it is much quicker to write *Donoghue v Stevenson* than to write 'the case where the lady fell ill because she had a snail in her opaque glass bottle'. (Besides if you forget **that** case name your examiner will not be impressed!)

- At this point double check the number of questions on the exam paper, and the number you have to answer. Has there been a change to your exam structure? Are there are any compulsory questions or sections?

- **Make sure that you know the date, time, and venue of the exam.**

- One of the main reasons for students not achieving a high grade is because they have not answered enough questions. Sometimes this is because they have run out of time, but often this is due to 'revision gamble.' In other words they choose to revise the same number of topics as the number of questions they have to answer. These students are risking 'exam panic' when they realize that they cannot identify their chosen areas, either because the examiner has omitted a topic from the exam or because the candidate does not recognize the format that the topic has been set in.

- You should be prepared to answer any topic as both a problem and essay question and cover enough topics to give you the chance to be able to answer the right number of questions convincingly. For example, it is virtually certain that at least one question (and usually more than one) on the tort of negligence will appear on your exam paper; but there are many aspects to the study of negligence—have you mastered them all?

- In tort law, there are some topics that you should revise even if you do not wish to answer a whole question on them; namely defences and remedies. These are topics that can form standalone questions, or they might be examined as part of a question on, for example, private nuisance or negligence. You cannot properly advise your client unless you can offer them a remedy.

4. The Examination

- Arrive in plenty of time, bringing your statute book and your pens. It is surprising how many students ask invigilators for a pen. It is even more surprising how many students request a 'trip to the bathroom' during the exam. If you are after a high grade, you do not have time to leave your desk.

- Do not have any unauthorized material with you, eg typed notes, mobile phones, or smart watches. This can lead to disciplinary procedures. Statute books should be unannotated, that is, **no** writing in them. You might be able to highlight them, but check this before you mark up your book. If in doubt, ask your tutor.

- Sit in your allocated seat and try to remain calm. You will probably be nervous, but think positively. Consider the exam as your opportunity to show how much you have learnt and understood. If you enjoy answering the questions, your examiner will enjoy reading them.

- When you are allowed to, read through the questions and identify the ones that you think you will answer best. Then read these questions again carefully. **You score highly if you answer the specific question set**, rather than just generally discussing the topic. This is particularly the case for **essay**-style questions.

- For **problem** questions, firstly identify who you have been asked to advise. This is normally found either at the start or the end of the question. If you are advising 'X', make sure that you tailor your advice to X's point of view. This does not mean giving a one-sided opinion; but your conclusion should be giving advice as required—the pros and cons of the situation. You will score highly if you identify all the issues in the scenario, **and** have advised on these issues comprehensively. As with all books in this series, the IRAC method of problem-solving technique has been adopted. IRAC stands for identify the issues, explain the rule, apply the law to the facts, and reach a conclusion, and will be demonstrated throughout this book.

- For essay questions, look closely at what has been set. You may be given a long quote at the beginning of the question, which is followed by a specific instruction afterwards. It might be as brief as 'discuss' but it usually seeks your opinion as to whether the statement reflects the law correctly. A common mistake in answering essay questions is to do so in the style of a 'history lesson', or by just stating everything you know about a topic in no particular order. Essay questions are often considered more difficult than problem questions, because you require in-depth research into the relevant cases, academic literature, and contentious areas where reform may be required. The PEA model—point, evidence, analysis—has been adopted by this book.

- Other issues to consider during the exam:
  - start each answer on a new page;
  - write the correct question number in the space provided;
  - please do not write in the margins—that is for your examiner;
  - use headings for problem questions;
  - highlight or underline cases and statutes;
  - write the date of the statute in your answer, but not big chunks of statute law (just a key word and then the section, subsection, etc.)

- Make sure that you answer the correct number of questions. If you are asked to answer FOUR questions, and you only answer THREE, your chances of success will be slim. **If you are running**

out of time, stop the question you are doing and start your last question, even if you can't complete it. Write in bullet points to put your knowledge of relevant law on the paper.

● Afterwards, do not torture yourself by discussing the exam with your colleagues. They will not have the same answers as you. This is law. Unless you go to court you will not know for certain which side is going to win.

● Most of all, enjoy the day! You have worked hard for several months; now prove to everyone, and most of all to yourself, that you have made the most of that time.

Online Resources   www.oup.com/uk/qanda/

Go online for extra essay and problem questions, a glossary of key terms, online versions of all the answer plans and audio commentary on how selected ones were put together, and a range of podcasts which include advice on exam and coursework technique and advice for other assessment methods.

Negligence I: Duty of Care

2

ARE YOU READY?

ARE YOU READY?

In order to answer questions on this topic, you need an understanding of the following:

- A general understanding of the tort of negligence
- The development of duty of care in negligence, in particular the key cases of *Donoghue v Stevenson* [1932] AC 562; *Anns v Merton LBC* [1978] AC 728; *Caparo plc v Dickman* [1990] 2 AC 605
- The development of duty of care in specialized aspects of negligence:
  - economic loss—negligent misstatement
  - economic loss—negligent acts
  - psychiatric damage
- Liability for omissions
- Liability of public authorities

KEY DEBATES

For decades the courts have refused to find that the police owe a duty of care to litigants, unless there are outstanding reasons to do so. In 2015, *Michael v Chief Constable of South Wales* [2015] UKSC 2 again confirmed that the police do not owe a duty of care in negligence to protect victims from the potential harm caused by third parties. In the more recent decision of *Robinson v West Yorkshire Police* [2018] UKSC 4, Lord Reed stated that 'the Police are not normally under a duty of care to protect individuals from a danger of injury which they have not themselves created, including injury caused by the conduct of third parties, in the absence of special circumstances such as an assumption of responsibility'.

How might this ruling effect the work of emergency services from now on?

QUESTION | 1

'Establishing a duty of care in a novel situation is a matter of policy rather than justice.'

With reference to case law, critically analyse this statement.

CAUTION

- This is a broad question which gives you a chance to demonstrate a wide range of knowledge. However, make sure that you select the material where policy implications have been noted by the judges themselves. Remember that psychiatric damage and economic loss are issues of duty of care.

- For some answers in this chapter, there may be cases cited which are not listed on your syllabus, and you should consider this. However, you should be familiar with all those mentioned in this particular answer.

DIAGRAM ANSWER PLAN

Identify the development of duty of care in tort law. Consider the policy aspects of *Donoghue v Stevenson*.

⬇

Identify how the *Donoghue* test has been modified by the courts, and the policy reasons behind such changes.

⬇

What difficulties have occurred as a result of the various changes to the 'neighbour' test?

⬇

Where is the law now? You will need to assess the current test in *Caparo v Dickman*. Have mechanisms been found to circumvent this test?

⬇

Draw all these themes together to form your conclusion.

SUGGESTED ANSWER

To be successful in an action in the tort of negligence, the claimant must prove not only that the defendant's negligent actions caused the claimant damage (whether physical or financial) but also that the defendant owed the claimant a duty of care in the first instance.

This is usually a straightforward issue to consider, with claims in negligence considering mainly whether the defendant had breached his or her duty of care. However, in a small percentage of negligence claims, the court must establish whether the defendant owed a duty of care to the claimant in the first instance. Needless to say, the courts are very careful to ensure that a finding of a duty of care in a novel situation does not establish a precedent that opens the 'floodgates' to litigation.

1. It is important to note that the concept of 'duty of care' occurred prior *to Donoghue v Stevenson*.

Prior to *Donoghue v Stevenson* **[1932] AC 562** [1.]'duty of care' situations were identified by considering specific relationships between the parties and were limited in number (eg occupier/visitor, doctor/patient, employer/employee). Since that time, the tort of negligence has undergone substantial periods of change and in many situations the role of policy has become crucial in identifying when a duty of care is owed.

Donoghue v Stevenson established the principle that a defendant owes a claimant a duty of care if there is a relationship of 'neighbourhood' in the sense that the claimant can be reasonably foreseen as likely to be affected by the defendant's act (or, in limited circumstances, omission). This test identifies the person to whom a duty of care may be owed, but it says little about when or in what circumstances the duty is owed. This is where issues of policy begin to creep in. However, in reference to *Donoghue v Stevenson* itself, it is fair to say that justice was firmly in the forefront of their Lordships' minds when considering the case.

Since *Donoghue v Stevenson*, the courts adapted Lord Atkin's 'neighbour' principle, at first by expanding the tort of negligence, as occurred in *Home Office v Dorset Yacht Co* [1970] AC 1004, and further in [2.]*Anns v Merton London Borough Council [1978] AC 728*, when Lord Wilberforce set out his 'two-stage' test to identify whether a duty of care was owed. This test, which appeared to depart from the *Donoghue* test, specified that the a duty of care will be established if firstly there is a 'relationship of proximity or neighbourhood', such that the defendant's carelessness may be likely to cause damage to the claimant, and that there are no 'considerations which ought to negate or limit the scope of the duty' (ie policy reasons) or limit any damages that might arise.

2. From an academic perspective this is an important case to mention. Why was the test thought suitable at the time, but then moved away from?

3. Make sure you are armed with academic critique to create a good answer; your examiner will expect you to produce evidence from acknowledged scholars to support your arguments.

It can be seen then that, as far as the House of Lords were concerned, they were attempting to find justice for victims of negligence. [3.]However, this test was found to be too expansive. Considering it from this angle, it might be argued that the *Anns* broad approach was unjust to defendants. It was unsurprising that this generous ruling was soon under scrutiny in the House of Lords in [4.]*Caparo plc v Dickman* **[1990] 2 AC 605**.

4. As this is the current test to assess whether a duty of care is owed in a novel situation, you will be expected to discuss it.

Caparo, which is still the test for identifying a duty of care in novel situations, established a tripartite test: reasonable foresight of harm; proximity of relationship; and whether it is fair, just, and reasonable to hold that the defendant owes the claimant a duty of care in the situation at hand. Although these appear to be three distinct features, Lord Oliver in *Caparo* describes them as, 'in most cases, in fact, merely facets of the same thing'. For example, what is foreseeable depends on issues of policy, justice, and proximity. But what a proximate relationship is depends on the other criteria, and so on. It is for this reason that Lord Wilberforce in *Anns v Merton LBC* is now regarded as having oversimplified the process in separating the issues of foresight of harm and policy in his two-stage test.

Crucially, what the court considers fair, just, and reasonable will be influenced by questions of policy, especially any effect on the development of the law and on the wider public interest. The main policy issues are now considered. First, the floodgates argument; would the establishment of a duty situation create a potentially large number of, possibly unwarranted, claims? This was probably at issue in *Alcock v Chief Constable of South Yorkshire Police* [1992] 1 AC 310 and characterizes the development through case law of the legal principles in relation to psychiatric harm negligently inflicted on 'secondary' claimants (ie those who were not themselves at risk of physical injury, but whose claim is based on psychiatric injury caused by negligent injury to a third party).

[5.] Nor is it considered fair or reasonable for a defendant to be burdened with liability in negligence to individuals who cannot be accurately identified. This idea was famously expressed by Cardozo CJ in *Ultramares Corporation v Touche*, 174 N.E. 441 (1932), in which he stated that the law should not admit 'to a liability in an indeterminate amount for an indeterminate time to an indeterminate class'.

Moreover, in appropriate cases, particularly those which fall within the general scope of the rule in *Hedley Byrne & Co Ltd v Heller & Partners Ltd* [1964] AC 465 concerning economic loss resulting from the provision of negligent advice, it has become apparent that an additional consideration is whether the defendant has voluntarily undertaken a responsibility towards the claimant for the accuracy of the advice given (*Spring v Guardian Assurance plc* [1994] 3 All ER 129; *Henderson v Merrett Syndicates Ltd* [1994] 3 All ER 506; *White v Jones* [1995] 1 All ER 691). Reasons of policy would consider it unjust to pin liability onto a person who did not know their words were to be acted on to another's potential detriment.

Whilst trying to establish justice, policy is overtly relevant when the courts consider the practical effect of a decision to impose a duty. [6.] For example, the ruling of *Marc Rich v Bishop Rock Marine Co Ltd* [1995] 3 All ER 307 reflects the House of Lords' concern that risk of civil liability might cause organizations whose primary duty was to work for the collective welfare of the public (in this case marine surveyors) to introduce defensive practices which might cause the imposition of unduly burdensome safety requirements. It might even

[5.] Keep referring back to the question. This specifically asks you to discuss case law, so make sure you do.

[6.] You do not need to approach cases in chronological order; in fact it is often more interesting if you do not.

deter, for example, local authorities from undertaking certain safety inspections altogether.

This concern has now arisen in the context of policing, subsequent to the recent Supreme Court decisions of *Robinson v Chief Constable of West Yorkshire* [2018] UKSC 4 and *Commissioner of Police of the Metropolis v DSD & Anor* [2018] UKSC 11, which both confirm that in certain circumstances the police can be liable not just in tort (*Robinson*) but for breaches of the European Convention of Human Rights (*MPP*).

7. If you are in the initial stages of legal studies, it is sometimes difficult to understand the relationship between Parliament and the courts. Spend some time considering this aspect during your studies.

7. Second, is this an issue for Parliamentary intervention? If Parliament has already acted, the courts may be disinclined to impose a common-law duty which goes further. This seems to have been one motivating factor in **Murphy v Brentwood DC [1991] 1 AC 398** where the **Defective Premises Act 1972** was thought to be the appropriate route, despite the fact that it was so narrow in scope as to be almost useless!

8. Ensure your conclusion pulls through the themes established in the question.

8. In summary, policy considerations feature strongly in determining whether a duty of care is owed, and the simple fact of a particular type of relationship is not conclusive. However, likewise, the courts have justice firmly in mind when considering all aspects of the case. The use of a criterion of reasonable foresight of harm on its own might, in some cases, create a range of problems including the danger of indeterminate liability or an unacceptable depletion of public funds, either by payment of damages to individual claimants or by encouraging expensive defensive practices. While the courts may be disinclined to take on the role of legislators, the passing of the Human Rights Act in 1998 has had some impact here, and the courts can fall back on the will of Parliament, in promoting Human Rights, if applicable. (*Commissioner of Police of the Metropolis v DSD*). Beyond this, they do have to take steps to keep the tort of negligence within reasonable bounds and to uphold justice in the best possible manner. It is the use of policy considerations which allows them to do so.

 ## LOOKING FOR EXTRA MARKS?

- Preparation during your study period will be essential to ensure your essay obtains a good grade. An examiner will require you to discuss 'policy' issues noted by the judges, not just discuss the facts of a case and its ratio.
- Consider changing the structure of the answer to discuss the *Caparo* test first. This might assist in strengthening your analysis of the question.

Foundations Builders plc construct a factory. The flooring work is subcontracted to Golam and the plumbing work to Hilda. The finished building is sold to Ezekiel, who plans to use the factory as a bakery. Shortly after the sale, Foundations Builders plc goes into liquidation.

Ezekiel discovers that the factory floor, laid by Golam, will not take the weight of his mixing machines, despite having been told by Foundations Buildings that the flooring would be adequate. He spends £10,000 having the floors reinforced.

Shortly after production at the factory begins, Ezekiel notices that the floors are often wet. He does not investigate this, but simply arranges to have them mopped on a regular basis. A month later, the tanks installed by Hilda burst due to faulty plumbing. In fact, these tanks had caused the wet floors. The water damage to the ceilings and floors caused by the burst will cost £5,000 to repair, and it will cost a further £3,000 to replace the tanks.

Ezekiel employs Imran to fix the tanks and the water damage. He tells him to subcontract the re-installation of the tanks to Jordan, which Imran does. Jordan installs the tanks so badly that Ezekiel has to employ Katie to redo the work at a further cost of £1,000. Imran is declared bankrupt.

To help with his cash-flow difficulties, Ezekiel accepts a contract with a well-known supermarket to bake 20,000 cakes to celebrate a Royal Wedding. Many cakes have been ordered in advance. Two weeks before the wedding, Lummock negligently severs the electricity cable which serves Ezekiel's factory, causing all Ezekiel's machines to halt. Cake mixture is thrown everywhere and jams all the machines. The cable belongs to Heistprice Electricity.

Ezekiel's machines need at least two weeks to clean and repair. The cakes in production are ruined and Ezekiel is unable to produce any more until after the wedding. He loses this contract, but also the possibility of any future contracts with the supermarket, who had suggested that they might enter into a contract with him again.

Advise Ezekiel in his claims in negligence against Golam, Hilda, Jordan, and Lummock.

CAUTION

- This is a complex question which focuses on issues of duty of care for economic loss for negligent acts. Keep your claimant firmly in your mind as you work through your answer.

- As with all problem questions, make sure that you understand the key judgments in this area of law.

DIAGRAM ANSWER PLAN

Identify	What losses has Ezekiel suffered? Can these be claimed in contract law? Will the losses be considered property damage or consequential economic loss (recoverable) or pure economic loss (not recoverable)?
Relevant law	*Murphy v Brentwood District Council* [1991] 1 AC 398. *Spartan Steel & Alloys Ltd v Martin & Co (Contractors) Ltd.* *D & F Estates Ltd v Church Commissioners.* *junior Books v Veitchi Co Ltd.*
Apply the law	Who is responsible for the various acts? Does the complex structure theory assist Ezekiel's claim against Hilda? Will he be able to claim for all of the losses flowing from the power cut?
Conclude	Ezekiel is unlikely to succeed with an action for flooring. He may have a claim against Hilda and he will be partially successful against Lummock, but he is unlikely to be successful in his claim against Jordan.

SUGGESTED ANSWER

[1.] Some examiners do not like the use of 'we' and would prefer that you write in the third person. Assess whether this writing style will acceptable in your institution.

[1.] We are asked to advise Ezekiel as to his claims in negligence against a variety of other people, regarding economic loss. Unfortunately for Ezekiel, the general principle is that there is no negligence liability in tort for pure economic loss caused by acts, as opposed to negligent misstatements. This is particularly the case where the situation would undermine contractual intentions. Although such a situation was in reality undermined by *Junior Books v Veitchi Co Ltd* [1983] 1 AC 520, it is important to note that this case has never been followed. It has been described as 'uniquely proximate' (*D & F Estates Ltd v Church Commissioners* [1989] AC 117) and is considered to be confined to its particular facts.

'Defective-product economic loss' as seen in *D & F Estates Ltd*, and applied by *Murphy v Brentwood District Council* [1991] 1 AC 398, is usually not recoverable. However, for consequential economic loss, where personal injury or property damage occur, it may be possible to claim (*Spartan Steel & Alloys Ltd v Martin & Co (Contractors) Ltd*

[1973] QB 27). For this to be possible, a claimant will need to show that he or she has a proprietary interest in the damaged property (*Cattle v The Stockton Waterworks Company* (1875) LR 10 QB 453; *Weller v Foot and Mouth Diseases Research Institute* [1966] 1 QB 569).

2. In this answer, it has taken a while to reach the start of the application. If you are short of time, start advising your client at the beginning of your answer.

[2.]With this in mind we shall turn our attention to the individual tortfeasors, and see if it is possible to establish liability for any, if not all, of their actions.

Golam

Golam had a contractual arrangement with Foundations Builders plc, to lay the floor. The finished building is sold to Ezekiel. Although initially it may appear that this has similar facts to *Junior Books v Veitchi Co Ltd*, it is important to note that at no time did Ezekiel have anything to do with the decision to subcontract the floor to Golam.

3. Make sure you familiarize yourself with the facts of important cases. You may be required to 'distinguish' cases as well as follow them.

[3.]This is a similar situation to *Department of the Environment v Thomas Bates & Sons* [1990] 2 All ER 943, where the claimants (who were leasees) could not recover the cost of strengthening the pillars (ie 'defective-product economic loss').

If Foundations plc were still running, Ezekiel would be able to sue them in contract. However, they have become insolvent, so Ezekiel will not be able to pursue this avenue. It is also likely that the courts will decide that [4.]Ezekiel should have had surveys carried out if he was planning to operate a business, and relying on the maxim *caveat emptor* will award him nothing.

4. Note how tort and contract law work together. Do not be afraid to discuss contract law in a tort question—as long as it is relevant.

Hilda

Having spent £10,000 fixing the floors, Ezekiel shortly afterwards has to mop them on a frequent basis. This is due to faulty plumbing, as becomes apparent when the tanks burst. At initial glance it is unlikely that he will be able to recover the cost of tank replacement, as this is pure economic loss. However, he may be able to claim for the subsequent damage.

This is likely to depend on whether the defect was latent (recoverable) or patent. If the defect would have been identified had there been an inspection (ie patent), it is unlikely that Ezekiel will succeed (*Baxall Securities Ltd v Sheard Walshaw Partnership* [2002] Lloyd's Rep PN 231). However, if the defect was latent, Ezekiel will be able to claim for the other property damage, even though he does not have a contract with Hilda. This is due to the ruling in *Murphy v Brentwood District Council* which gave this scope to houses constructed using subcontractors, Lord Jauncey stating that this might operate:

5. If you are looking for extra marks, make sure you incorporate quotes in your answers. However, use them wisely and with purpose.

[5.]'… where one integral component of the structure was built by a separate contractor and where a defect in such a component had caused damage to other parts of the structure …'.

NEGLIGENCE I: DUTY OF CARE   13

Jordan

Ezekiel employs Imran to install the tanks, telling him to subcontract to Jordan. Jordan's installation of the tanks proves to be substandard. This appears to be a parallel situation to that in *Junior Books v Veitchi Co Ltd*. Although it may be possible to pursue a claim in this way, any potential claim under the *Junior Books* precedent is extremely doubtful. [6.] As Mance J stated in *Losinjska Plovidba v Transco Overseas Ltd & ors (The 'Orjula')* [1995] 2 Lloyd's Rep. 395, *Junior Books* has 'joined the slumbers of the uniquely distinguished from which it would be unwise to awaken it without very solid reason.' Not only do courts do their best not to follow it (*Muirhead v Industrial Tank Ltd* [1986] 1 QB 507), but they will do their best to avoid it. However, in this instance it is possible that his claim for repair costs may succeed.

Lummock

Unfortunately for Ezekiel, the electricity cable that is severed is owned by Heistprice Electricity; therefore as *Cattle v Stockton Waterworks Company*, he will find his claim severely curtailed as he will not be able to claim for pure economic loss. His situation is akin to [7.] *Spartan Steel & Alloys Ltd v Martin & Co (Contractors) Ltd*, where it was held that the plaintiffs could claim for the metal in the furnace and its loss of profits, but no more. [8.] *Per* Lord Denning: 'The cutting of the supply of electricity ... is a hazard which we all run .... Such a hazard is regarded by most people as a thing they must put up with—without seeking compensation from anyone.'

This means that he will be able to sue for the cakes on the production line and their profits, but not any future baking that may not now take place.

Following *British Celanese Ltd v Hunt (Capacitors) Ltd*, where the owners were allowed to recover for the damaged machines, it may be possible to recover for the cake machines. Although this ruling suggests the future profits may also be recoverable, this ruling predates that of *Spartan Steel*, and it is more likely than not that courts will adopt the latter approach so that any future profits on the advanced cake sales will not be recoverable. A particularly severe application of *Spartan Steel* can be seen in the judgment of *London Electricity plc v Quattro UK Ltd* [2000] All ER (D) 1410, an indication of the likely outcome of Ezekiel's case. However, Ezekiel may be able to relay on the ruling of *Conarken Group Ltd and another v Network Rail Infrastructure Ltd* [2011] EWCA Civ 644, which specified that, where reasonably foreseeable, economic loss as a result of property damage may be recoverable.

[9.] Consequently, although Ezekiel will be partially successful against the various tortfeasors, he may still face a large economic loss.

[6.] You will read cases with unmemorable names. These are often shipping cases. Under exam conditions the name of the ship is usually sufficient (eg *The Orjula*), but make sure you ask your lecturer's advice on this.

[7.] Be prepared to identify a *Spartan Steel* situation. They frequently appear on examination papers.

[8.] Incorporate quotes in the body of your writing, and use them to argue your points. Just placing a quote on its own in the body of the text does not advance your arguments.

[9.] A brief summary helps to conclude an answer

LOOKING FOR EXTRA MARKS?

- Think beyond your tort law syllabus, and consider incorporating law which you consider to be 'contract law' or 'land law', etc. This demonstrates that you understand how tort law interweaves the other areas of law in order to arrive at justice.
- The *Junior Books* case is an interesting and controversial one. Be sure that you understand the uniqueness of the case, should you wish to discuss it in an answer.

QUESTION | 3

Punter, a partly qualified accountant, has recently been left a substantial sum of money by his late aunt, which he now wishes to invest. He is told by Spiv, a stockbroker client of his employers, that Flybinight plc is currently enjoying considerable success and that since the company's shares are underpriced, Punter should buy now. He offers to undertake the purchase for Punter when given the go-ahead by him. Punter meets Hackett, an old friend of his, for a drink in a pub. Hackett has recently been appointed undermanager at Eastminster Bank and Punter asks him about the wisdom of buying the shares. Hackett says that although he does not have much experience in financial advising as yet, he is interested in business matters and always reads the relevant papers. He says that *Whizz Weekly*, one of the more respected financial papers, predicts that Flybinight is undervalued since the company seems poised to declare record profits. Hackett therefore concludes that on the basis of this report and his general overview of business affairs, Punter should go ahead and buy.

Following the advice he received, Punter invests heavily in the company. After two months the company is put into liquidation by its creditors and Punter loses his investment.

Advise Punter as to whether he has any legal redress to recover his losses against Spiv, Hackett, and *Whizz Weekly*.

CAUTION

- To answer this question you need to focus on the law of negligent misstatement. Do not be tempted to discuss issues of 'duty of care' in a generalized manner.

DIAGRAM ANSWER PLAN

Identify

Why is the advice both prepared and communicated?
Is advice given on a social occasion actionable?
Have any of the advisers voluntarily assumed a responsibility to Punter for the advice they give?

Relevant law

Caparo plc v Dickman.
Choudhry v Prabhakar.
Burgess v Lejonvarn [2017] EWCA Civ 254.
Henderson v Merrett Syndicates Hedley Byrne & Co v Heller & Partners Ltd.
Customs & Excise Commissioners v Barclays Bank plc.

Apply the law

Regarding Spiv, consider the tests identified in *Customs & Excise Commissioners v Barclays Bank plc*
Regarding Hackett, are conversations during social occasions sufficient to establish a duty of care?
Regarding *Whizz Weekly*, consider the issue of 'proximity'

Conclude

Whereas it may be possible to establish a duty of care with regard to Spiv, a successful claim against Hackett and Whizz Weekly appears less likely.

SUGGESTED ANSWER

¹·Discussing the policy issues behind various cases helps to establish why claims for negligent misstatement are limited.

¹·The ***Donoghue v Stevenson*** **[1932] AC 562** 'neighbour principle' alone is not sufficient to address the issue of economic loss caused by a carelessly made statement, with the result that the courts have developed more restrictive tests importing policy reasoning to avoid the possibility of indeterminate liability to an indeterminate class of claimants. Unlike careless acts that result in physical harm where losses tend to rest where they fall, advice can be relied upon by any number of people who come into contact with it. In formulating the rules governing liability, the courts have long been mindful of the so-called floodgates argument, encapsulated in Cardozo CJ's warning against the possibility of 'liability in an indeterminate amount for an indeterminate time to an indeterminate class' (***Ultramares Corp v Touche*** **(1931) 174 NE 441**).

2. If you are planning to answer a question on negligent misstatements, make sure that you understand and learn the different tests.

2. Whether Spiv owes Punter a duty of care in respect of his advice to purchase the shares will depend on one of three different tests identified in *Customs & Excise Commissioners v Barclays Bank plc* **[2006] UKHL 28**. One test asks whether the defendant has voluntarily assumed responsibility for what he said and did. Alternatively, there is a threefold test of reasonable foresight of loss; whether the relationship between the parties is sufficiently proximate; and whether it is fair, just, and reasonable to impose liability (*Caparo Industries v Dickman* **[1990] 2 AC 549**). Thirdly, there is the incremental test (*Sutherland Shire Council v Heyman* **(1985) 157 CLR 424, 481** *per* Brennan J) which indicates that new duty situations should be developed only incrementally and by analogy with existing cases, rather than by massive leaps into new areas.

These alternative tests assist in identifying whether the relationship between the parties can be described as a 'special relationship' under the rule in *Hedley Byrne & Co v Heller & Partners Ltd* **[1964] AC 465**. For these purposes the relationship between representor and representee must be such that the latter reasonably relies on the advice given by the former and that the representor is aware, or ought to be aware, of this. Furthermore, in advice cases where the defendant gives information to X on behalf of Y, it needs to be asked whether the defendant has assumed responsibility to X or whether he was merely discharging his responsibility towards Y (*Williams v Natural Life Health Foods Ltd* **[1998] 2 All ER 577**).

3. Highlight which test is likely to be relied on, and apply it to your situation.

3. The 'assumption of responsibility' test has been noted to be particularly useful in determining whether a defendant owes a duty of care in respect of advice given by him to the claimant (*Customs & Excise Commissioners v Barclays Bank plc* **[2006] UKHL 28** at [35] *per* Lord Hoffmann). Likewise, it is relevant to consider whether the defendant has assumed responsibility for advice given for one purpose, when the claimant relies on that advice for another, different purpose (*Caparo Industries v Dickman* **[1990] 2 AC 605**). In determining whether there is a voluntary assumption of responsibility, it is important to apply the test objectively and it is not to be answered by reference to what the defendant thought or intended (*Henderson v Merrett Syndicates Ltd* **[1994] 2 AC 145**). Thus, as was observed by Lord Griffiths in *Smith v Eric S Bush* **[1990] 1 AC 831, 862**, the phrase 'assumption of responsibility' can only have any real meaning if it is understood as referring to the circumstances in which the law will deem the defendant to have assumed responsibility to the claimant (see also *White v Jones* **[1995] 2 AC 207**).

4. You may find it hard to write out the tests as written in the judgment, so practice drafting a precis of the relevant law during your revision period.

4. Generally, the decision in *Caparo Industries v Dickman* makes four factors relevant to the question of whether a duty of care is owed, namely:

1. Was the representor fully aware of the nature of the transaction which the claimant had in contemplation?

2. Did the representor know that the information would be communicated to the claimant, either directly or indirectly?

3. Did the representor know that it was very likely that the claimant would rely on the information when deciding whether or not to engage in the transaction in question?

4. Was the purpose for which the claimant relied on the information one that is connected with interests which it is proper to expect the representor to protect?

In applying the rules laid down in *Hedley Byrne (as interpreted by the House of Lords in Caparo v Dickman and Customs & Excise Commissioners v Barclays Bank plc)* to Spiv, [5.]it is suggested that there may be a 'special relationship' between Punter and Spiv, as a stockbroker ought to know that the advice, 'buy now', was directly communicated and was likely to be relied upon for investment purposes. As a professional, Spiv obviously has skill and it is reasonable and proper to expect Spiv to have due regard to the interests of those who receive his advice and information. The meaning of 'special skill' has been held to include special knowledge (*Henderson v Merrett Syndicates Ltd* [1995] 2 AC 145, *per* Lord Goff). Further, as a stockbroker, Spiv may be held to be in a fiduciary relationship with Punter, in which case there is no need for the claimant to prove foreseeable reliance if a fiduciary duty is owed (*White v Jones* [1995] 2 AC 207). Lord Browne-Wilkinson observed that in the case of a fiduciary, it was sufficient that the defendant was aware that the claimant's financial welfare was dependent upon the exercise of proper care by him and, that being the case, a 'special relationship' arises.

The advice given by Hackett to Punter requires consideration of the circumstances in which the advice was given and the nature of the relationship between him and Punter. In *Hedley Byrne* Lord Reid observed that opinions expressed on social occasions may be given without the care that would normally be accorded if they had been asked for professionally. Hackett's status as an undermanager may suggest a lack of specific expertise on his part. [6.]Despite all of this, it was held in *Choudhry v Prabhakar* [1988] 3 All ER 718 that a duty of care may still be owed where advice was given in a social context by a friend with no special skill. The more recent decision of *Burgess v Lejonvarn* [2017] EWCA Civ 254 again highlights the difficulties of mixing business with friendship, albeit that the defendant did hold themselves as having some relevant experience.

Since Hackett had informed Punter that he lacked relevant experience and did not profess to be an expert, coupled with the fact that the advice appears to have been tendered on a social occasion, the court may not impose a duty of care in these circumstances. Hackett appears to have been a transmitter of information, rather than taking on a project-management role (as in *Burgess v Lejonvarn*), and is therefore less likely to owe a duty of care.

[5.] Your examiner will not (usually) make it easy to spot, be prepared to find establishing a 'special relationship' difficult in your scenarios.

[6.] *Choudhry v Prabhakar* is a controversial case, and is therefore one worth considering.

The imposition of a duty of care on *Whizz Weekly* is also unlikely, since in **Hedley Byrne** the House of Lords recognized the danger of formulating rules which could result in the maker of a careless statement being liable to a wide, indeterminate class of claimants. For this reason, Lord Bridge in **Caparo** emphasized the need for 'proximity' between the claimant and defendant, and warned against the dangers of holding a defendant liable 'to all and sundry' for any purpose they may choose. The statement that the shares of Flybinight are 'undervalued' does not amount to an unequivocal recommendation that the company's shares should be bought. Moreover, there does not appear to have been any direct or indirect contact between *Whizz Weekly* and the claimant such as to give rise to an inference that there has been a voluntary assumption of responsibility for the advice contained in the paper (**Williams v Natural Life Health Foods** [1998] 2 All ER 577).

LOOKING FOR EXTRA MARKS?

- Make sure you are familiar with the policy issues that have shaped numerous decisions regarding negligent misstatement.
- Consider the issue of *Hedley Byrne* and the overlap with exclusion clauses. How has recent law changed its approach in this respect?

QUESTION | 4

Ali, the driver of a stock car, negligently fails to maintain his vehicle. During a race, which is being televised, Ali's brakes fail and his car crashes into a crowd of spectators. The car narrowly misses Dwaine but strikes and kills Brad. Brad's daughter, Claire, is very badly injured, but survives and is taken to hospital.

Dwaine, a person of unusually nervous disposition, develops an anxiety neurosis.

Sharma, a friend of Brad, is present at the scene of the accident. At first, she attempts to help, but realizing that Brad is dead and that Claire is being dealt with by professionals, Sharma rushes back to tell Brad's wife, Glenda, what has happened. Sometime later, Glenda, who is also Claire's stepmother of six months' standing, drives to the hospital and asks to see Brad and Claire. Glenda is shown Brad's body, and sees Claire on a hospital trolley, awaiting treatment, crying in pain and in a badly disfigured state.

Harriet, Brad's mother, sees a live television broadcast of the events, recognizes her son in the crowd, and realizes that Ali's car has crashed into the area where her son is standing.

Sharma, Glenda, and Harriet are all horrified by what has happened. Sharma suffers from post-traumatic stress disorder, whilst Harriet, who is helping to look after Glenda and Claire following the accident, gradually becomes depressed. Meanwhile, Glenda has become a recluse because of her inability to come to terms with Brad's death and the physical injuries suffered by Claire.

Advise Dwaine, Sharma, Glenda, and Harriet regarding their claims in negligence. You do not need to consider issues of breach of duty or causation.

CAUTION

- You are asked to advise several clients. Be careful that you do so. You can start off with general advice, but then identify the unique issues with each claimant.
- You should point out the tensions in the law, but as this is a problem question do not get sidetracked into identifying areas for reform.

DIAGRAM ANSWER PLAN

Identify	The question focuses on claims for psychiatric damage. Identify whether the claimants can meet the test of 'primary victim' or 'secondary victim'. Have they suffered from psychiatric damage; is it as a result of the sudden horror of the event?
Relevant law	Primary victims: *Page v Smith; White*—are there any claimants in the 'zone of danger'? Secondary victims: Specify the three-point 'control test' in *Alcock*.
Apply the law	Can Dwaine and Sharma meet the requirements of primary victim? Was Dwaine in the 'zone of danger'? Can Sharma be considered 'a rescuer'? If not, might they be a secondary victim? Glenda and Harriet will be secondary victims if they meet the requirements, but do they?
Conclude	If Dwaine is a primary victim he may succeed. If not, his claim will fail. Sharma may succeed as a 'rescuer'. Glenda, as secondary victim, may have difficulty proving she was 'proximate' to the event. Harriet's claim will fail—she was not proximate, and her psychiatric illness appears to be gradual rather than sudden.

SUGGESTED ANSWER

The claimants should be advised that their action lies in the tort of negligence, and specifically the issue as to whether they are owed a duty of care for the psychiatric damage they have suffered.

When considering a claim for psychiatric damage, it is important to note that not every form of mental suffering will be sufficient to establish a duty situation. As specified by Lord Denning in ***Hinz v Berry***

[1970] 2 QB 40, **1.** 'In English law no damages are given for grief or sorrow ... but for any recognized psychiatric illness caused by the breach of duty by the defendant.' Therefore, it is important to assess which, if any, of the claimants have suffered recognizable psychiatric illness.

2. On this basis, the fact that Sharma, Glenda, and Harriet are 'horrified' will not be sufficient to establish a claim. By contrast, the reactive depression suffered by Sharma and Harriet, as a recognizable psychiatric illness, will be sufficient, as will Dwaine's anxiety neurosis. Glenda's personality change and inability to cope with everyday life may indicate a qualifying condition.

For each claimant, the next question to be asked is whether they will be considered a primary or secondary claimant. Primary claimants are those described by Lord Lloyd in *Page v Smith* **[1996] AC 155** as being within the class of persons who, without the benefit of hindsight, might foreseeably have suffered physical injury. In *Page*, the test applied in the House of Lords was to ask whether it was foreseeable to the defendant that her conduct would expose the claimant to a risk of personal injury, whether physical or psychiatric. If the answer to that question was yes, it was irrelevant that the claimant did not suffer physical injury or that the claimant's actual injury was due to his being of an unusually nervous disposition, since the defendant was required to take the claimant as he found him. **3.** From the facts in front of us, Glenda and Harriet will not be considered primary victims, whereas it is possible that Dwaine and Sharma will.

Dwaine

If Dwaine, having been 'narrowly missed', can show that he falls within a class who could foreseeably have been physically injured, his claim will succeed, even though he is a person of unusually nervous disposition. He may also seek to rely on cases in which the claimant suffered psychiatric harm after fearing for his/her own safety because of the defendant's actions (*Dulieu v White* **[1901] 2 KB 609**). If **4.** Dwaine cannot show that he is a primary claimant, he must satisfy the requirements for a secondary claimant.

Secondary claimants are those whose psychiatric harm stems from their reaction to physical harm caused to someone else by the defendant's negligence. Due to concern about the potential for a great number of claims arising from one incident, *Alcock v Chief Constable of South Yorkshire Police* **[1992] 1 AC 310** established 'control mechanisms'; a series of tests to identify who should be allowed to claim as secondary victims in such situations.

To be considered a secondary victim, the claimant must be a 'loved' one of the immediate victim and must be proximate to the accident. Further, the psychiatric harm must have been caused by the sudden horror at the event. Further, the claimant must prove that such an illness would have occurred in a 'reasonable' person.

Regarding the first requirement, it is presumed that spouses/civil partners, and parents and children, would have a 'close tie of love and affection' with the primary victim, although it is open to anyone to attempt to prove this.

Considering Dwaine, if his claim as a primary claimant is rejected, he will not be able to establish a close tie of love and affection with the victims; he will be a 'bystander'. Under *Alcock*, it appeared that a bystander might be able to claim if something sufficiently gruesome happened close to him. However, this line of reasoning was rejected in *McFarlane v EE Caledonia* **[1994] 2 All ER 1**. This latter approach to bystanders was endorsed by the House of Lords in *White v Chief Constable of South Yorkshire Police* **[1999] 1 All ER 1**.

Therefore, if assessed as a secondary claimant, Dwaine's claim will fail. Sharma's claim may also fail for the same reason, but there may be another way for her to succeed. [5.]We will address this later.

5. Keep your reader informed of what you are planning to do.

Glenda

Glenda, as Brad's wife, would meet the first criterion for being considered a secondary victim; that of being a 'loved one'. The second hurdle for Glenda to overcome is that she must have been proximate in time and space to the incident (ie actually there). The facts tell us that she was not present, and this may be problematic. However, in this respect there is some leeway, as their Lordships approved an extension established in *McLoughlin v O'Brian* **[1983] 1 AC 410** to a claimant who comes upon the 'immediate aftermath', albeit some two hours after a road traffic accident involving her husband and children. The impact of the scenes to which she was exposed, and within such a short timescale, was held to be equivalent to her having been present at the accident.

Therefore, Glenda's experience at the hospital may suffice, provided it can be categorized as occurring the immediate aftermath. She arrived 'some time later', and it is not clear what length of delay may still qualify as immediate— [6.]a time lapse of eight hours in *Alcock* was considered too great, while two hours was accepted in *McLoughlin*. Further, in *Galli-Atkinson v Seghal* **[2003] Lloyd's Rep Med 285**, a mother's claim was successful after seeing her daughter in the mortuary, albeit this was more than two hours after her daughter's death. Provided Glenda arrived at the hospital very soon after the incident at the race track, and was confronted by a sufficiently shocking scene, she might be able to recover damages. She would, of course, have to prove that her personality change is considered psychiatric damage.

6. Use cases to illustrate tensions in the law. You should assess the situation from both sides of the argument.

Harriet

The last Alcock requirement specifies that the 'shock' must have been caused by the sudden horror of the incident. Applying this to our situation, Harriet's claim will fail as her depression was not caused by shock—a sudden assault on the senses—but by the long-term effects of caring for the other victims. [7.]This was a scenario specifically excluded by Lord Keith in *Alcock*.

Her claim also faces another difficulty. Although, as Brad's mother, there will be a presumption of love and affection, Harriet was not present at the scene of the accident; she observed the events on a live television broadcast. In *Alcock* it was emphasized that it is also necessary to look at how the shock is caused. In that case, it was considered relevant that the police were aware that the football match was being televised (thus eliminating any argument that broadcast by a third party was a *novus actus interveniens*), but the police were also aware of a code of ethics which forbade the showing of pictures of the suffering of identifiable individuals. Although she had seen Brad in the crowd, his death was not shown as such. This would suggest that Harriet would not have a claim.

Sharma

Although Sharma was present at the scene of the accident, there is no suggestion that she was close enough to be a primary claimant. As a secondary claimant, she must first establish that she has a close tie of love and affection with the victims. Merely being a friend of Brad will not be enough, unless she can prove that their friendship was equivalent to a close familial tie. If she can do so, she will satisfy the other requirements having been proximate in time and space to the shocking event and having experienced it with her own unaided senses.

If she cannot establish the requisite tie, she may have another route to compensation. Under *Alcock*, a person who performed the role of rescuer was seen, based on *Chadwick v British Transport Commission* [1967] 1 WLR 912, as an exception to the bystander class in the same way as rescuers enjoy a special position in relation to the rules of negligence in other cases. However, it is difficult for courts to identify what an individual must do to claim this special status. [8.]In *McFarlane* the claimant had assisted by handing out blankets. This was not held to be sufficient to make him a 'rescuer'. The result of *White v Chief Constable of South Yorkshire Police* [1999] 1 All ER 1 is that any claimant lacking a close tie with the victims must either be objectively at risk of physical injury or reasonably believe himself to be so (ie be a primary claimant). The facts do not suggest that Sharma was, or felt herself to be, in danger. If this is the case, her claim will also fail.

---

7. You have ruled out Harriet's claim, so you could stop at this point. However, to obtain extra marks, see if there are other aspects of the claim that need addressing.

8. In a question on psychiatric damage, it is likely that you will have to address the issue of a rescuer—Sharma is your chance.

LOOKING FOR EXTRA MARKS?

■ Read through your answer carefully—have you addressed every aspect of the question? In this question, you might choose to discuss just one aspect of Harriet's claim, but a better answer will tackle it from every angle.

■ Read around the subject, so that you can add in little extras such as the issue of the ethics of television broadcasting.

QUESTION | 5

'In an ideal world all those who have suffered as a result of the negligence ought to be compensated. But we do not live in Utopia: we live in a practical world where the tort system imposes limits to the classes of claims that rank for consideration as well as to the heads of recoverable damages. This results, of course, in imperfect justice but it is by and large the best that the common law can do.'

White v Chief Constable of South Yorkshire Police [1998] 3 WLR 1509, per Lord Steyn.

With reference to Lord Steyn's judgment, evaluate the current of law of psychiatric damage.

CAUTION

■ This question tests your ability to analyse the current law of psychiatric damage, therefore the examiner is not looking for you to address each case as it was decided.

■ There are three seminal judgments to include in this answer; make sure you have read them thoroughly and can identify the policy reasons and the legal tensions that each produce.

DIAGRAM ANSWER PLAN

Introduce your essay, identify what is meant by the term 'psychiatric damage', and specify this is an issue of a restricted duty of care.

Identify problematic aspects with claims of psychiatric damage. Firstly, what is meant by the term 'psychiatric damage'?

Consider the categories of primary victim and secondary victim. Are these categories fair? Your examiner will expect to see you mention the key authorities of *Alcock*, *White*, and *Page v Smith* in this discussion.

This is an area of law which has been subject to much academic criticism, so include academic views. Also refer to the works of the Law Commission.

Conclusion—what is your opinion on the law in this area; can it be improved or is it satisfactory as it stands?

1. The question asks for an evaluation of current law, so try to evaluate as you progress through your essay.

When claimants suffer any physical injury due to another's negligence, they may also claim for any psychiatric illness (formerly known as 'nervous shock') resulting from the incident. [1.]Further, *Dulieu v White* (1901) 2 KB 669 established that negligent acts or omissions that lead to a victim suffering from psychiatric damage alone may be actionable. This appears to be fair. However, as this is an issue of duty of care, with the possibility of extensive litigation should a number of claimants be involved, the courts have set 'control mechanisms' in place to assess claims of 'pure' psychiatric damage. These mechanisms limit the scope of such actions, [2.]despite the courts acknowledging that 'psychiatric harm may be more serious than physical harm' (*White v Chief Constable of South Yorkshire Police* [1998] 3 WLR 1509, *per* Lord Steyn). However, far from being the 'best that common law can do', according to Professor Jane Stapleton in her work, 'In Restraint of Tort', liability for psychiatric illness is not just 'imperfect' as Lord Steyn acknowledged, but 'the area where the silliest rules now exist and where criticism is almost universal.' Therefore this question will evaluate the current law of psychiatric damage, and assess whether it is 'the best that the common law can do' or whether it deserves the criticism that Stapleton reports.

2. The question focuses on a quote in *White*, so if you can incorporate other quotes from the same case, it will demonstrate to the examiner that you are fully engaging with the question.

To be successful in a claim for psychiatric damage, the claimant must first prove that s/he has been caused to suffer from a recognized psychiatric illness, not just grief or anxiety (*Hinz v Berry* [1970] 2 QB 40). [3.]Here lies the first difficulty with any such claim. As noted by Lord Steyn in *White*, extreme grief can be debilitating but it may not amount to a recognized psychiatric injury, unless it constitutes pathological grief disorder (*Vernon v Bosley* [1997] 1 All ER 577). Currently, the lack of clear medical distinction appears unfortunate, but more difficulties follow in this respect.

3. As you proceed, identify difficulties with claims of psychiatric damage. Use opposing case law to highlight the difficulties.

In the seminal judgment of *Alcock v Chief Constable of South Yorkshire Police* [1991] 3 WLR 1057, which considered the significant number of claims following the Hillsborough Stadium disaster in 1989, the House of Lords held that, in addition to usual negligence requirements, claimants in claims of psychiatric harm must prove that they are either primary or secondary victims. Lord Oliver distinguished between the two. [4.]He asserted that primary victims were defined as those 'mediately or immediately' involved as participants (those who suffered psychiatric harm as a result of fear for their own safety, be they rescuers or involuntary participants). By contrast, secondary

4. When answering a problem on the law on psychiatric damage, your focus should be on the three seminal House of Lords judgments. Make sure that you know them in depth.

victims are those who witness incidents and suffer psychiatric harm

5. Do not discuss the 'eggshell-skull rule' in detail, but you may consider using the rule in *Brice v Brown* [1984] 1 All ER 54 as a comparator.

because of their fear for the safety of others. [5.] Whereas, the 'eggshell-skull rule' is applicable to primary victims (the 'eggshell-skull rule' specifies that even if the extent of the damage was not foreseen, the claimant can claim for the full damage, provided it is foreseeable that they would suffer some harm), since *Page v Smith* [1995] 2 WLR 644, it appears that a secondary victim will have to be a person of 'ordinary phlegm' to be able to claim at all **Bourhill v Young [1943] AC 92**. This, it is submitted, is an unreasonable burden to place on claimants. It is even more so as secondary claimants must also pass a three-point 'control' test.

The first test facing a secondary victim is to show a 'close tie of love and affection' with the primary victim. Secondly, they must be in 'close proximity' to the incident in time and space. Thirdly, a secondary victim must prove that the harm was induced by the sudden shock of the event.

6. This is the third limb of the *Caparo v Dickman* test.

At first glance, the *Alcock* test can be promoted as [6.] 'fair, just, and reasonable' on the grounds that it controls the 'floodgates' of litigation, especially in cases involving a potentially high number of claimants, and assisting in the management of striking out unreliable and potentially fraudulent claims for psychiatric harm. It does so by allowing claims from those who are most directly affected by the incident, but not those who hear the 'mere recital' of the facts. However, as will be discussed, there are issues of unfairness regarding all of the 'control mechanisms'.

Regarding 'close tie of love and affection', the law presumes that such relationships occur between 'husband and wife or parent and child'. As Lord Keith explained, this does not rule out other relationships, but must be proved by the claimant. In *Alcock*, a brother's claim failed, despite witnessing the death of his two brothers, because he failed to produce sufficient evidence of close ties. This aspect of the 'control mechanisms' has been noted by many academics, and indeed

7. Make sure you are familiar with Law Commission reports— especially if your module coordinator has specified that you should read these.

the Law Commission itself, as being unfair. [7.] In its report 'Liability for Psychiatric Illness' LC 249, the Law Commission proposed a statutory 'fixed list of relationships' which would include siblings, and civil partners who have lived together for two years or more. Currently the law remains unaltered in this respect.

Further criticisms surround the issue of 'proximity'. Prior to the *Alcock* ruling, in *McLoughlin v O'Brian* [1983] 1 AC 410 a mother's claim succeeded whilst not being 'proximate in time and space'. In this instance, her claim was upheld because, despite there having been a two-hour gap between the accident and her arrival at the hospital, her family had still to be cleaned up after the accident, and she saw them (and her deceased daughter), as she would have done had she been at the scene. Her shock was deemed to have been in the 'immediate aftermath' of the accident.

8. Make your points and back them up with case law examples.

8. One might have supposed that *Alcock* would draw an end to such claims in the future. However this has proved not to be so, as shown in the case of *Galli-Atkinson v Seghal* [2003] Lloyd's Rep Med 285, where a visit to the mortuary was considered the 'immediate aftermath' part of an 'uninterrupted sequence of events' (Latham LJ). It appears that the 'aftermath' requirement is ineffective as current law stands. Professor Stapleton, in **9.** 'In Restraint of Tort', poses the question 'how dry does a child's blood have to be before a parent's claim will be struck out?'. It is not an unreasonable question, but it is one to which the law currently has no answer.

9. Jane Stapleton, 'In Restraint of Tort', in P B H Birks (ed), *The Frontiers of Liability*, vol 2 (1994) 83 at 95.

Finally, how sudden does the 'shock' have to be for a victim to be awarded damages? In *Sion v Hampstead Health Authority* [1994] 5 Med LR 170, a father was unable to claim as the death of his son occurred some fourteen days after the injuries were caused, whereas in *North Glamorgan NHS Trust v Walters* [2003] PIQR P16, incidents over 36 hours were said to be a single event.

A further tightening of restrictions was to come. *Alcock* was criticized by some for not being clear on where the distinction between 'primary' victims and 'secondary' victims lies. This desire for clarity led to the distinction being developed in *Page v Smith*, where Lord Lloyd defined a primary victim as one who is 'directly involved in the accident, and well within the range of foreseeable physical injury'. By comparison, a secondary victim is 'a spectator or bystander'.

Firstly, the distinction does not allow a general claim for rescuers if they are not directly in the zone of danger or do not have a 'close tie of love and affection'. This was the difficulty established in *White*, where the police were unable to claim as they failed to meet the criteria for either category.

10. Specify the name of the author and the title of the article, as a minimum (this refers to Stephen Todd, 'Psychiatric Injury and Rescuers' (1999) 115 LQR 345).

Some might argue that this is effective, as it allows no claim based purely on rescuer status, and consequently it allows the law to treat everyone equally (Lord Hoffman). Whilst **10.** Stephen Todd has concluded that *White* has removed uncertainty in the definition of primary victim, **11.** many have argued that it merely adds to the confusion. Indeed, since *White* some cases have found a claimant to be a 'primary victim' even if they do not meet the *White* criteria (*Salter v UB Frozen and Chilled Foods Ltd* 2003 SLT (News) 261, where a claimant who was able to claim despite being in physical danger himself).

11. Who are these many?

It is apparent, therefore, that there are indeed some imperfections in the common law approach to claims in psychiatric damage. The most significant areas for reform are the category of 'close tie of love and affection' and the difficulties surrounding current case law specifying that the 'eggshell-skull rule' is not applicable to secondary victims. In this respect, it can be argued that our current law on psychiatric damage is not 'the best that the common law can do'. However, despite several prompts by the Law Commission, statute has yet to be passed in this area. Until Parliament is prepared to take on responsibility for this, the common law, as imperfect as it may be, will have to suffice.

LOOKING FOR EXTRA MARKS?

- In an essay of this nature, refer to academic argument such as the debate between Stephen Todd and others. There are plenty of writers to choose from. Research and read recent literature; is this still an area for academic argument?
- Quotes from the Law Commission will raise the bar of your answer, and will show that you can appreciate the reasons for the proposed difficulties with the law.

QUESTION | 6

Hayley lives on the ground floor of a block of flats owned by Ontown City Council and the Council has recently served an eviction notice on Reggie, Hayley's neighbour, alleging that he has engaged in antisocial behaviour towards Hayley and other residents in the block of flats. Ontown City Council has not warned Hayley of these events.

David, a painter and decorator who lives opposite the block of flats, knows that Hayley is keen to have her flat decorated and he offers to do the job for her at the weekend saying that if he ever needed a return favour he would know where to come.

On the Saturday when David paints the flat, Hayley spends the afternoon sunbathing in the communal area and listening to music on her headphones. As it is sunny, David keeps the lounge window wide open to let out the smell of paint fumes.

While David is painting the kitchen window, Reggie, who believes Hayley to be responsible for reporting him to the City Council, enters the flat through the lounge window, steals Hayley's valuable antique ornaments, and causes serious criminal damage to the living room by throwing acid across the room. In addition, Reggie takes the opportunity of letting himself out of Hayley's flat, and into the shared hallway. He breaks into the flat opposite as he knows that the flat's owner Pam is away on holiday.

Reggie ran off and has not been caught.

Advise David, Hayley, Pam, and Ontown City Council as to their respective rights and duties.

CAUTION

- This question requires consideration of the general rule that tortious liability is not ordinarily imposed for the failure to act to prevent harm (nonfeasance), in the absence of any voluntary assumption of responsibility on the part of the defendant. You will also need to discuss how third parties can interact in a scenario to effect the initial tortfeasor's liability.

DIAGRAM ANSWER PLAN

Identify	Consider the nature of David's undertaking to Hayley. Does a public authority owe a duty of care to protect a person against the possible actions of a third party? Consider when occupiers of property may be placed under a duty to take reasonable precautions against the wrongdoing of third parties. Does Hayley owe a duty of care to Pam?
Relevant law	*Smith v Littlewoods Organisation Ltd.* *Home Office v Dorset Yacht Co Ltd.* *P Perl (Exporters) Ltd v Camden LBC.*
Apply the law	Consider if, by keeping the door open, David has voluntarily assumed responsibility for Hayley's property. Is Hayley still in control of her property? Should she be accountable for a third party's actions? Is the City Council likely to be held accountable for Reggie's actions?
Conclude	David is unlikely to owe a duty of care to Hayley. Likewise, Hayley is unlikely to owe a duty to Pam. The council is also unlikely to be found to owe a duty of care.

SUGGESTED ANSWER

The central issue is whether either David or Hayley can be held responsible for failing to prevent the infliction of damage by the act of a third party. It is also necessary to consider whether the City Council owes a duty of care to Hayley when it fails to warn her that it intends to serve an eviction notice on Reggie.

[1.] The general rule is that there is no duty, at common law, to prevent persons harming others by their deliberate wrongdoing, however foreseeable such harm may be, since the law of torts does not generally impose liability for pure omissions. Thus in ***Smith v Littlewoods Organisation Ltd* [1987] AC 241**, the House of Lords held that [2.] the defendants, who were unaware that vandalism was a problem, were not liable for damage caused to neighbouring property by vandals who had broken into the defendant's premises. Of primary concern to their Lordships was that if a duty of care were to be imposed

[1.] Start by considering the general rules then focus in on the scenario.

[2.] Choose an example of case law which confirms the general rule.

3. Consider the implications or future actions, if too wide a duty were to be established in such a case. Here the defendant was a borough council.

on occupiers of property in such circumstances, **3.** it could not be discharged short of placing an intolerable burden on the occupiers to mount a 24-hour guard on empty premises. In *Stovin v Wise* **[1996] AC 923** Lord Hoffmann justified the restrictive approach to liability for omissions on political, moral, and economic grounds. Politically, it would be an invasion of a person's freedom to impose liability for doing nothing.

In examining David's duty to Hayley, it is important to determine the nature of the undertaking he makes since a positive duty to prevent harm may arise depending on what was said and understood by both parties. **4.** If there is a contractual relationship between them, liability for the theft of the antiques may arise out of an implied term in the contract for services, by virtue of the **Supply of Goods and Services Act 1982, s. 13, as amended by the Consumer Rights Act 2015**. Similarly, a decorator will owe a duty of care in respect of property stolen by a thief, if he has been given specific instructions to lock the front door of the apartment block in which he is decorating if he should decide to go out: *Stansbie v Troman* **[1948] 2 KB 48**.

4. You may feel it important to cite the statute here, but it merely states: 'In a relevant contract for the supply of a service where the supplier is acting in the course of a business, there is an implied term that the supplier will carry out the service with reasonable care and skill.' Remember that although the examiner will want to see you refer to statute, you will not be awarded marks for writing it out.

There may be other circumstances in which a defendant is liable for an omission if he is in control of the person or thing that causes harm to a third party: see *Home Office v Dorset Yacht Co Ltd* **[1970] AC 1004**. As Lord Diplock observed, control imports responsibility but that responsibility was restricted to the harm caused in the course of an escape from a correction centre to those in close physical proximity.

5. You have discussed the law; now apply it to the facts. Do not be tempted to discuss the law in detail and condense application into the very last line of you answer, as some candidates do.

5. Applying these authorities to our facts, it seems unlikely that David will be considered to owe a duty of care to Hayley. Carrying out the job on the loose understanding that if he 'ever needed a return favour he would know where to come' does not of itself suggest a contract between them from which a term can be implied to keep the door locked. Moreover, as Hayley is sunbathing in the garden, it is likely that she will still be in control of the premises rather than David.

Pam is in an analogous position to the neighbouring property owners in *Smith v Littlewoods Organisation Ltd*. In considering the situation where a thief gains access to property through the failure of an adjacent neighbour to keep his property lockfast, Lord Goff opined that liability cannot be imposed on the neighbour for the burglary since every occupier must take such steps as he thinks fit for the protection of his own property. His Lordship stated that when considering what precautions should be taken, an occupier should take into account the fact that, from time to time, his neighbours may leave their properties unlocked. Such a proposition follows from the rule that there is no general duty to prevent third parties causing damage to others. Lord Goff went on to explain that, exceptionally, liability for the activities of others may arise in two situations. First, where a landowner has knowledge, or the means of possessing knowledge, that trespassers have created a risk of fire on his property, and then fails to abate that risk. It is clear that the given facts do not fall within this exception. Secondly, where a landowner creates, or allows to be created, an unusual source of danger on his land and it is reasonably foreseeable that a third party may interfere with it thereby causing damage to another (*Haynes v Harwood* **[1935] 1 KB 146**). Lord Goff stressed that liability under this principle should only be imposed where a defendant has negligently caused or permitted a source of danger and it is foreseeable that a third party may 'spark it off'.

[6.] If the act of the third party is deliberate or reckless, it will normally sever the chain of causation if that act is no more than a mere possibility. To render the defendant liable, the third-party action must be more probable than a 'mere possibility': *Chubb Fire Ltd v Vicar of Spalding* **[2010] EWCA Civ 981**. Hayley's failure to ensure that her decorator keeps the apartment block locked is not of itself likely to result in theft from a resident, and therefore cannot be described as creating a source of danger which was foreseeably 'sparked off' by Reggie.

In *P Perl (Exporters) Ltd v Camden LBC* **[1984] QB 342** a local authority was not liable for a burglary in the claimant's flat when it failed to secure an unoccupied basement flat in the same block of flats. The relationship of neighbouring property owners was not sufficient to impose on one owner the duty to guard the other against the foreseeable risk of burglary through unsecured property. In *Smith v Littlewoods* [7.] Lord Goff thought that *Perl* was correctly decided and pointed out that the law has to accommodate 'the untidy complexity of life' and therefore there are situations where considerations of practical justice will preempt the imposition of a duty of care. See also *Topp v London Country Bus Ltd* **[1993] 1 WLR 976**. Applying the language of *Caparo Industries plc v Dickman* **[1990] 2 AC 605**, it would not be 'fair, just, and reasonable' to recognize a duty of care on the facts since any affirmative duty to prevent deliberate wrongdoing by third parties, if recognized by English law, is likely to be strictly limited. Accordingly, it is submitted that Pam is not owed a duty of care by Hayley to prevent Reggie gaining access to the building by her failure to ensure that her decorator kept the building lockfast during the repainting. Given that this factual situation does not fall within the exceptional circumstances outlined by Lord Goff, [8.] it would not be just and reasonable to subject Hayley to such a duty. Therefore, the facts fall squarely within the principle formulated by Lord Sumner in *Weld-Blundell v Stephens* **[1920] AC 956** that, in general, 'even though A is in fault, he is not responsible for injury to C which B, a stranger to him, deliberately chooses to do'.

[6.] Although the answer touches on causation, do not spend too much time on this issue; it is not the main focus of the question.

[7.] Note that the law is not 'clear-cut'.

[8.] Incorporate extracts of judgments into your arguments.

Hayley may try to argue that Ontown City Council should have warned her of its intention to serve an eviction notice on Reggie; however, this too raises the issue of liability for an omission. A similar issue arose in ***Mitchell v Glasgow City Council* [2009] UKHL 11** when the Council served notice on one of its tenants that he would be evicted. The tenant became verbally abusive, returned to the flats in which he lived, and killed his neighbour with an iron bar. The family of the deceased argued that the Council should have warned the deceased as soon as the meeting with the violent neighbour was over. However, the House of Lords held that fore-seeability of harm alone is insufficient to establish the existence of a duty of care. Liability will only arise if the Council had assumed responsibility to advise the deceased of the steps it was about to take. On the facts, there was nothing to suggest to the Council that the violent neighbour might kill the deceased. Accordingly, no duty of care was owed. On similar lines of reasoning, [9.] it seems unlikely that Ontown City Council will be liable for the actions of Reggie in stealing Hayley's antiques and causing criminal damage to her flat.

[9.] Try to find the time to proofread your work. Under exam conditions, it is easy to write 'likely' rather than 'unlikely', but this completely changes your advice.

LOOKING FOR EXTRA MARKS?

- Balance out your discussion of the law with its application. The examiner is interested to see how you use your knowledge of law in the situations that they have set.

TAKING THINGS FURTHER

- Law Commission Report No. 249 'Liability for Psychiatric Illness'.
- Gilliker, P., 'Revisiting Pure Economic Loss' (2005) 25 LS 49.
- Mulheron, R., 'Rewriting the Requirement for a "Recognized Psychiatric Injury" in Negligence Claims' (2012) OJLS vol. 32 (1) 77–112.
- Norris, W., 'The Duty of Care to Prevent Personal Injury' (2009) 2 JPIL 114.
  Considers the relationship between the assumption of responsibility by the tortfeasor and the reliance of the victim on that.
- Stapleton, J., 'In Restraint of Tort' in P. B. H. Birks (ed), *The Frontiers of Liability* Oxford University Press, 1994 vol 2 , pp 94–6.
  This considers the law of psychiatric damage.
- Todd, S., 'Psychiatric Injury and Rescuers' (1999) 115 LQR 345.
- Witting, C., 'Justifying Liability to Third Parties for Negligent Misstatements' (2000) 20 OJLS 615.

Negligence II: Breach of Duty

3

KEY DEBATES

The Supreme Court decision of *Montgomery v Lanarkshire Health Board* [2015] UKSC 11 reconsidered the law on disclosure of risk for medical care. The unanimous verdict of seven judges acknowledged that the previous test, set out in *Sidaway v Bethlem Royal Hospital Governors* [1985] AC 871, was no longer satisfactory law. At the time *Montgomery* caused alarm among some healthcare practitioners—there were concerns as to how medical practice might alter as a result. Rob Heywood and José Miola investigate the potential effect of *Montgomery* on healthcare in the future, and consider how radical the *Montgomery* decision really was.

For the last thirty years, Captain George Murray has held an annual charity fete in his grounds at Victory Mansions in Portsmouth. The most popular attraction has always been the shooting competition, in which members of the public are given expert tuition by him in how to load and fire an eighteenth-century musket. The best three participants are then selected take part in a 'Shot Frenzy' in which contestants have one minute to load and then fire as many shots as possible at a target.

Although the spectators are placed in seating behind the competitors, they are not kept behind any glass safety barriers, due to the cost of such panels—although panels are usually installed in such competitions. Additionally, it is possible for spectators to stray beyond the competitors and into the firing line. Despite this, there has only been one accident since the start of the competition, when a drunken spectator ran in front of the marksmen and was killed instantaneously.

Horatio Nelson and his secretary, John Scott, decide to have a go. Eventually, John was selected to join the 'Shot Frenzy', and Horatio took his place in the spectators' stand to watch. All the competitors were warned not to shoot at an angle, and to stop shooting immediately if a spectator ran in front of them.

The contest was going well for John until his musket jammed. When John tried to investigate what was wrong, the musket exploded in his hand, killing him outright. A stray piece of the shot flew into the crowd, hitting Horatio in his right eye.

Horatio was taken to Solent hospital where he was seen by Thomas Hardy, an overworked junior doctor on his first day in the Accident and Emergency Department. Dr Hardy investigated Horatio's eye, and informed him that he would need surgery immediately to prevent loss of sight in that eye. He did not inform Horatio of the 2 per cent risk of arm paralysis that occurs with the proposed operation, but he asked his senior colleague William Beatty to check over Horatio and explain the operation and the side effects to him, as he was unsure of all the details. Beatty was in a hurry to go and play golf, so he did not bother explaining any potential risks; he just informed Horatio that the operation may not work. Horatio agreed to go ahead with the operation. Unfortunately, not only did Horatio lose the sight in his right eye, but through no fault of the duty surgeon Henry Chevalier, who performed the operation, Horatio's right arm became paralysed, and he can no longer use it.

Horatio wishes to make claim in negligence against Captain George Murray, Thomas Hardy, William Beatty, and Henry Chevalier. Advise him as to whether any of these parties have breached their duty of care towards him.

DIAGRAM ANSWER PLAN

Identify	This question raises issue of possible breach of standard duty of care regarding the injury to the eye. It also requires consideration of breach of professional duty of care in not informing of the risks of the procedure.
Relevant law	The objective standard of care—the 'reasonable person': *Blyth v Birmingham Waterworks Co* (1856) 11 Ex 781. Factors relevant to the standard of care. Variations of the objective standard. Sporting events: *Hall v Brooklands Auto Racing Club* [1933] 1 KB 205 (CA) and utility of defendant's conduct; s. 1 Compensation Act 2006. Skilled persons 'professing to have a special skill'—disclosure of risk: *Montgomery v Lanarkshire Health Board* [2015] UKSC 11.
Apply the law	The objective test—would the reasonable person have acted in a similar manner bearing in mind the 'magnitude of mischief' and/or the frequency of potential breach *Bolton v Stone* [1951] AC 850 (HL)? What of the costs to eliminate risks? Have the doctors breached their duty by lack of skill during the procedure and not informing of the risks?
Conclude	The eye injury—possible breach of duty. Paralysis—breach of duty by doctors for not warning of the risks of the procedure.

CAUTION

- You have been asked in this question to **advise on breach of duty**, therefore do not spend time discussing general issues in negligence. However, if such a question purely states **'advise'**, the examiners will want you to discuss all the essential elements of a negligence claim, even if they are non-contentious.

- When discussing breach of duty, be prepared to tackle both the objective standard of care and variations of the objective standard.

[1.] If you have been asked specifically to address breach of duty, do not spend a long time discussing other aspects of negligence.

[2.] For every legal term you introduce, you need a definition. It is not enough to say 'reasonable man/person'; you need to explain who he or she is.

[3.] You have discussed general principles, now apply them to the scenario that you have been given.

[4.] Try to back up any statement you make with a legal authority, particularly where the basic principle of law is more complex.

[1.] When advising Horatio in the tort of negligence, it is essential to establish that a breach of duty of care has occurred, which has caused the damage. To establish breach of duty of care, it must be shown that, on an objective test, the defendants' conduct fell below what was required in that situation. The objective test is that of the [2.] 'reasonable man' (*Blyth v Birmingham Waterworks Co* (1856) 11 Ex 781), a person 'independent of the idiosyncrasies of the particular person whose conduct is in question' (*Glasgow Corporation v Muir* [1943] AC 448). There are several people who may have breached their duty of care towards Horatio, and each requires further investigation.

Captain Murray

[3.] The facts specify that Murray has arranged for spectators to sit unprotected from flying debris. This is in contrast with the usual arrangements for such a competition, and consequently an indication that Murray's behaviour has not been 'reasonable'. On previous occasions, the court has found that ignoring a rule or common practice is evidence of a person's breach of duty. [4.] Such an example can be found in the case of *Bolito v Arriva London* [2008] EWHC 48, when a bus driver moved off with a passenger trapped in the bus door. It was held that ignoring a rule in the driver's rule book was clear evidence of the driver's negligence. However, Horatio should be advised that departing from common practice is not conclusive of a breach of duty (*Brown v Rolls Royce Ltd* [1960] 1 WLR 210 (HL)).

However, as a general rule, the greater the risk of injury occurring as a result of the defendant's act or omission, the less acceptable it will be to do it, especially if the 'magnitude of the mischief' (*Paris v Stepney BC* [1951] AC 367) is potentially high. Conversely, if the activity carried little risk of injury to spectators, it may be considered reasonable to take that risk, particularly if the circumstances are of social value. Such was the case of *Bolton v Stone* [1951] AC 850 (HL), where the claimant was hit by a rogue cricket ball whilst outside of the cricket ground. Further, a defendant will not be required to go to great expense to eliminate every possible risk occurring, but will be required to have acted as a reasonable person would do in the circumstances (*Latimer v AEC Ltd* [1950] AC 643 (HL)). In this case, it would be important to assess what the 'reasonable person' would have done in Murray's position.

There are numerous cases involving spectators receiving injuries whilst watching sport, and these frequently support the defendant. Such an example can be found in *Hall v Brooklands Auto Racing Club* [1933] 1 KB 205 (CA). In this case, spectators at a racing track were injured when one car shot into the air, hitting the railing where they were sitting. The racing club was not deemed liable as they had done all that was 'reasonable' in the circumstances. Further, the cases of *Murray v Harringay Arena* (1951) 2 KB 529 and the more recent *Browning v Odyssey* [2014] NIQB 39 considered situations where a spectator was hit by a flying object— in both cases hockey pucks. Despite the absence of safety barriers, neither claimant was successful. [5.] Horatio needs to be aware of this if he is considering pursuing a claim.

Additionally, until Horatio's accident, there had never been any accidents to spectators who were seated in the stands. Therefore, bearing in mind that this was a charity event, the courts may not find that Murray had breached his duty by not installing safety barriers. Further, the Compensation Act 2006 was designed to assist those who wished to undertake socially worthwhile activities. The Act requires a court to consider the steps the defendant would have had to have taken to prevent the injury when dealing with a negligence claim, and whether this would have affected the way the sport was played. In this regard, Jackson LJ in *Scout Association v Barnes* [2010] EWCA Civ 1476 informs that it is [6.] 'not the function of the law of tort to eliminate every iota of risk or stamp out socially desirable activities', whilst also noting that social utility does not provide a defence where an activity is inherently dangerous.

[7.] Murray might raise the defences of *volenti non fit injuria* (as was raised successfully in *Murray v Harringay Arena* (1951) 2 KB 529), as Horatio is a voluntary spectator at the event. If this defence is made out, it will absolve Murray of all liability and Horatio will be unsuccessful in his claim. However, this defence will only be successful if Murray is deemed not to have been negligent. Whereas an ice puck flying into the crowd may be an inherent risk of watching an ice hockey match, considering all the facts of the incident, a musket shot injury should not have been foreseeable to a spectator. Hence Horatio is unlikely to be deemed to have accepted such a risk, and his claim is likely to be successful.

Claims against Medical Practitioners

When considering a breach of duty by doctors, during their employment, the 'reasonable man' test is modified. The general test for breach of duty is that devised in *Bolam v Friern Hospital Management Committee* [1957] 1 WLR 582—that of the [8.] 'standard of the ordinary skilled man exercising and professing to have that special skill'.

Thomas Hardy

Although Dr Hardy is a junior doctor, his actions will be compared to that of a 'reasonably competent doctor' performing the same role (*Wilsher v Essex AHA* [1988] AC 1074; [1987] QB 730; *FB v Princess Alexandra Hospital NHS Trust* [2017] EWCA Civ 334). If a doctor has

---

[5.] It is always good to advise your client on the worst-case scenario.

[6.] Looking for extra marks? You can achieve a high mark without direct quotes in problem questions, but it is an extremely satisfying feeling to incorporate one. This shows your depth of knowledge

[7.] You have been asked to advise on breach of duty, so it is not necessary to go into details on defences for this question.

[8.] Looking for extra marks? To show that you have mastered your subject, ensure that you can quote the essential ratios from cases.

been asked to carry out a procedure beyond his or her skills, the hospital trust or health authority will be liable. However, to mitigate the apparent harshness of the *Wilsher* decision, Glidwell J further added that one skill is knowing when to ask for help. In this respect, a defendant's duty of care can be discharged by asking for advice from a senior. This appears to match the scenario here. Hardy asked his senior colleague to explain any side effects to Horatio, as he was unsure of the details. This would suggest that Dr Hardy has not breached his duty of care towards Horatio.

Dr Beatty

By contrast, Beatty, an experienced doctor, has failed to pay due care and attention to Horatio, by not warning him of a significant risk associated with the treatment.[9] At one time, if a patient did not specifically ask about potential side effects, doctors were not obliged to inform them (*Sidaway v Board of Governors of the Bethlem Royal Hospital Governors* [1985] AC 871). However, the recent case of *Montgomery v Lanarkshire Health Board* [2015] UKSC 11; [2015] 2 AC 1450 has changed the legal approach here, and a doctor will be held liable in negligence if he or she fails to warn a patient of a [10] material risk occurring.

In Horatio's situation, there was a substantial risk of paralysis, and it is hard to believe that a 'prudent patient' would not have wanted to know of this risk before proceeding with the operation. In this respect it can be said that Dr Beatty breached his duty of care towards Horatio. However, as this was an emergency operation, Horatio may not be able to argue that he would have put off the operation for another day had he been warned of the risks, unlike the claimant in *Chester v Afshar* [2004] UKHL 41.

[11] Henry Chevalier

The facts clearly state that Horatio's injuries had not resulted on the part of the duty surgeon Chevalier. Though Horatio lost his sight, it appears that this was a direct consequence of the accident with the shot, earlier in the day. In regard to the subsequent paralysis, that appears to have been an unfortunate side effect of the operation, as occurred in the recent case of *Thefaut v Johnston* [2017] EWHC 497 QB. Chevalier appears to have completed the procedure adequately.

[12] In conclusion, Murray may have breached his duty of care to Horatio and if so will be held accountable for the loss of sight in the latter's right eye. In regard to Horatio's paralysis, it appears that Dr Hardy has discharged his duty of care by seeking help from his superior, whereas Dr Beatty (and possibly Mr Chevalier) has breached his duty of care for failure to warn Horatio of the risk of paralysis. Ultimately it is possible that all the damages will be borne by Captain Murray, as, but for his breach of duty, neither injury would have occurred.

---

[9] In a problem question it is usual to advise solely on current law, and not discuss previous cases. If you advise using out-of-date law, be prepared to have your marks reduced.

[10] Delve deeper and analyse why, with reference to *Montgomery*, a 2 per cent risk of limb paralysis would amount to a 'material risk'.

[11] Sometimes you will be asked to discuss a potential defendant, where there is no real detail. Do not invent the facts in this situation; advise on both sides of the argument.

[12] Students often worry, unnecessarily, that they have not reached the 'right conclusion'. Just draw your own conclusion from the law that you have applied to the problem.

LOOKING FOR EXTRA MARKS?

- In problem questions, structure is key. It is important to deal with each defendant separately. The examiner requires you to address different legal issues for each defendant.

- Ensure that you know all the legal principles and authorities to be able to master a question. This includes being able to quote from key cases. But use your knowledge wisely. In this question there is no mention of children, so do not discuss how the law is altered if the defendant is a child.

- Consider incorporating academic literature into your work, particularly if you are taking tort at Level 5 or above.

QUESTION | 2

Consider the issues of breach of duty of care in negligence raised by the following facts. Do not consider issues of vicarious liability.

Calvin, who was walking along the street, was hit by a milk bottle which fell from one of the upper windows of the local primary school. The local education authority claims that there were no children in the school at the time because lessons had ended 45 minutes earlier and all the children had gone home. Calvin wishes to sue the local education authority in negligence.

Omolade's hand was cut when, on hearing an explosion in the street outside, her manicurist, Liz, momentarily took her eyes off Omolade's hand, and looked out the window. Liz was a 15-year-old, on her first day at work. Liz gave her a sticking plaster for the cut, but the cut has left a temporary scar. Omolade seeks your advice regarding suing Liz in negligence.

Penny was injured when she was rescued by the air-sea rescue team after bad weather capsized her boat. The rescue team used only a rope, instead of the padded harness usually employed by rescue teams, to hoist her into a helicopter. Penny received several cracked ribs in the process. She seeks your advice in relation to a potential negligence action against her rescuers.

DIAGRAM ANSWER PLAN

Identify

This question raises issues of possible *res ipsa loquitur* regarding the injury to Calvin in the absence of other evidence.

Identify variations of the standard of breach of duty of care, the rules of novices and children when advising Omolade, and the duty owed by professionals/rescuers to Penny.

Relevant law

The three-part test for *res ipsa loquitur* as specified in *Scott v London and St Katherine Docks Co* (1865) 33 H & C 596.

The objective standard of care—the 'reasonable person'. *Blyth v Birmingham Waterworks Co* (1856) 11 Ex 781.

Factors relevant to the standard of care: novices, *Nettleship v Weston* [1971] 3 WLR 370; children, *Mullin v Richards* [1998] 1 All ER 920.

Variations of the objective standard: the *Bolam* test.

Apply the law

Can Calvin meet the three requirements of *res ipsa locquitur*?

In the objective test, would the reasonable person have acted in a similar manner as Liz in firstly causing an injury, then applying first aid unsatisfactorily? How, if at all, is the test modified for a novice/child?

Have the rescuers breached their duty of care towards Penny by using incorrect equipment? Apply the *Bolam* test.

Conclude

Calvin is likely to be successful in raising the issue of *res ipsa locquitur*.

Omolade is unlikely to be successful in proving Liz has breached her duty of care.

Further information would be required to establish whether Penny's claim will be successful. It will require experts witnesses.

CAUTION

You are required to advise three separate claimants. When writing answers to questions which require you to address two or more independent issues, the examiner will prefer you to advise the claimants in the order that they appear on the paper, as it will assist them with marking. Whatever you do, make sure that you do not discuss them all together.

1. Start advising straight away.

2. Your examiner will frequently write scenarios that are loosely based on actual cases. Here, the falling milk bottles mirror falling bags of sugar, as in *Scott v London and St Katherine Docks Co* (1865) 33 H & C 596.

3. Take each requirement in turn, analyse, and apply to your question.

4. This would be a good place to quote from the relevant cases and academic articles on the subject.

5. Remember *res ipsa loqitur* is a rule of evidence regarding a breach of duty, not a separate action in negligence.

6. Start with general principles, then address variations in the standard of care.

Calvin faces a problem of proving negligence on the part of the [1.]local education authority. However, as the accident is of a kind that does not normally occur in everyday life, [2.]Calvin may invoke the doctrine of *res ipsa loquitur* (let the thing speak for itself), as, in the absence of direct evidence on how any defendant behaved, or how the injury occurred, the elements of duty of care, breach, and causation are inferred from an injury that does not ordinarily occur without negligence.

In order to invoke the doctrine, Calvin must [3.]satisfy three requirements, as specified in *Scott v London and St Katherine Docks Co* **(1865) 33 H & C 596**. He must show first that the accident was of a kind that does not normally occur without negligence. [4.]In *George v Eagle Air Services Ltd* **[2009] UKPC 21,** the Privy Council held that aeroplanes do not normally crash without negligence. Calvin may argue that milk bottles do not fall without negligence.

Secondly, he must show that the defendant had exclusive control over the thing which has caused him harm. The facts specify that the bottles fell from the defendants' premises and were thus under their exclusive control since the school had closed some 45 minutes earlier.

Finally, Calvin [5.]must show that the defendant has no other plausible explanation of how the accident might have occurred. On the facts given, there is no evidence of an alternative explanation of how the bottles fell, unlike in the case of *Ng Chun Pui v Lee Chuen Tat* **[1988] RTR 298,** in which a bus had crossed the central reservation. Here, the defendant was able to defeat the doctrine by stating he had to swerve to avoid another vehicle. On balance, Calvin has a realistic chance of being successful in his claim.

Regarding Omolade's injury, the law requires that the defendant should have behaved in a manner consistent with the [6.]actions of a reasonable person (*Blyth v Birmingham Waterworks Co* **(1856) 11 Exch 781;** *Glasgow Corp v Muir* **[1943] AC 448**), that is doing what a reasonable person would have done or omitting to do what a reasonable person would not have done. This is an objective standard, related chiefly to the nature of the activity undertaken. In *Blyth v Birmingham* it was the standard of the reasonable operator of waterworks and pipes, and in *Glasgow Corp v Muir* it was the standard of the reasonable café manager who, as Lord Macmillan noted, should be neither too fearful of something happening nor over-confident that accidents will not occur. Even though Liz is a 'novice', she will be deemed to owe Omolade the same standard of care as a professional manicurist performing the same duty, *Nettleship v Weston* **[1971] 3 WLR 370.** Following from this, Liz should be assessed as the reasonable manicurist.

At first glance it appears that, by cutting Omolade during her work, Liz has indeed breached her duty of care. However, in **Marshall v Osmond [1983] QB 1034,** [7] it was held, in the context of a road traffic accident during a police chase, that errors of judgement in the heat of the moment should be regarded as errors that 'a reasonable person' might make and, therefore, not actionable. This would appear to apply even more compellingly to Liz, whose reaction to the explosion seems entirely involuntary.

[7] Do not spend too long discussing cases, but the bare facts are sometimes helpful to you and your examiner.

Additionally, Liz's age may be taken into consideration. In **McHale v Watson (1965) 111 CLR 384,** for example, [8] a decision of the High Court of Australia, the fact of the defendant's age (he was a 12-year-old boy) was held relevant to the standard-of-care issue. This approach was adopted in England by the Court of Appeal in **Mullin v Richards [1998] 1 All ER 920**. It seems highly likely that a teenager will be distracted if hearing the noise of an explosion.

[8] Although you should advise using English cases, the Supreme Court and Court of Appeal often utilize international jurisprudence to assist them in deciding a case in a novel situation. Therefore, you may do so too.

Regarding the plaster, Liz assumed responsibility (**Barrett v Ministry of Defence [1995] 3 All ER 87**), therefore it is relevant to ask whether her 'treatment' of Omolade was negligent. Here, Liz will rely on the authority of **Philips v William Whitely [1938] 1 All ER 566**. In the **Philips** case, a jeweller was held not liable in respect of an infection in the claimant's neck caused (allegedly) by the jeweller's ear-piercing. The court in that case held that the standard required in respect of hygiene, etc. was that of a jeweller doing such work, not that of a doctor. If this authority is followed, Liz will be judged by the standard of someone offering basic first aid. [9] Arguably, she has met this standard in supplying her client with a sticking plaster. A temporary scar is a likely result from any cut, regardless of how proficient the actual treatment was.

[9] For this question you were instructed not to 'consider issues of vicarious liability', so do not be tempted to do so.

So far as Penny is concerned, the standard of care demanded of the rescue team is that of any organization offering such a service and possessed of the skills required to do the same job, namely 'the standard of an ordinary skilled man exercising and professing to have that special skill' (**Bolam v Friern Hospital [1957] 1 WLR 582**, *per* McNair J). The fact that other air-sea rescue teams use different, safer equipment begs the question of whether this team was negligent in merely using a rope. The answer to this lies in two stages. First, it could be argued that if a 'significant body of professional opinion', from other rescue teams, supports the use of a rope alone, that may prove that the rescue team has not breached its duty of care. However, if the decision to use a rope alone could be shown to be so unreasonable a choice that no reasonable rescue team could have made it, an action for negligence might still lie (**Bolitho v City and Hackney Health Authority [1997] 4 All ER 771**). As regards the reasonableness of using a cheap rope rather than an expensive harness, the court would be entitled to consider whether the cost of preventing an injury outweighed the risk of the injury (both in terms of the magnitude and likelihood of that injury occurring: *Bolton v Stone* **[1951] AC 850**; *Latimer v AEC Ltd* **[1953] AC 643**).

The rescue team might argue that, since this was a life-and-death situation, they were forced to act swiftly with whatever (non-ideal) tools they had to hand, such as in *Watt v Hertfordshire CC* **[1954] 1 All ER 835** where the emergency services used an inappropriate lorry to transport a jack desperately needed to rescue a casualty and a fireman was injured when steadying the jack on the lorry. The employer was held not liable because the risk inherent in the decision to proceed using this lorry was not unreasonable in light of the importance of the objective to be achieved—the genuine need to save a life. However, there have been cases where emergency vehicles going to an emergency have been driven carelessly, causing harm, and liability has been found, for example [10.]*Ward v London County Council* **[1938] 2 All ER 341**. It is clear that all the circumstances must be weighed in the balance, so on the facts of the scenario there may be no liability if the risk to the claimant in not doing anything to rescue him was apparent and this outweighed the risk in using the rope.

[10.] Many of your cases on negligence are 70–80 years old. Keep checking for recent cases as you go through your studies.

LOOKING FOR EXTRA MARKS?

- In an exam situation, do not invent facts—answer the question set, without discussing irrelevant issues.

- However, to test your knowledge prior to the exam, use past papers to ensure you practise the full range of potential scenarios coming your way.

- For example, in this question you were instructed not to 'consider issues of vicarious liability'. However, what if the question had asked you to advise on that as well? Likewise, you may wish to consider the question, 'How, if at all, would your advice differ if Omolade was a hand-model, and lost a modelling job worth £2,000?' Would your advice be different?

QUESTION | 3

In *Montgomery v Lanarkshire Health Board* [2015] UKSC 11 at paragraphs 87 to 90 it was said that a doctor is 'under a duty to take reasonable care to ensure that the patient is aware of any material risks involved in any recommended treatment, and of any reasonable alternative or variant treatment'.

In what respect, and why, has the case of *Montgomery v Lanarkshire* changed the standard of care in negligence for claims against professional persons?

DIAGRAM ANSWER PLAN

> Brief explanation of what you are going to cover in your answer.

> The law before *Montgomery*—the *Bolam* test, *Sidaway*, and how courts have modified Bolam over the years; the decline of medical paternalism in general.

> The judgment of *Montgomery* itself and its effect on the law regarding disclosure of risk.

> How the courts have applied *Montgomery* in recent cases, both medical and non-medical.

> Conclusion.

! CAUTION

- To answer a question like this, it is essential that you have read not just the case but also the literature referred to in the case itself.

- Examiners are known to set 'specialized' questions such as this, which often come as a disappointment to the student who has not revised sufficiently. This is an example of why it is essential to revise more topics than you are required to answer during your exam, in case you have learnt material for a question that does not come up as you hoped it would.

 ## SUGGESTED ANSWER

For over seventy years, the *Bolam* test has been applied to all aspects of professional negligence, including the failure to warn patients of the inherent risks of an operation. This was confirmed by *Sidaway v Bethlem Royal Hospital Governors* [1985] AC 871. However, in 2015, the Supreme Court's unanimous judgment of *Montgomery v Lanarkshire Health Board* [2015] UKSC 11 changed the law on disclosure of the risks of medical treatment, by stating that the previous approach in *Sidaway* could no longer be considered appropriate.

[1.] It is always helpful to an examiner to indicate what they are going to be reading in the next few minutes. It also helps you keep your structure in the forefront of your mind.

[1.] This question investigates why the change in law was considered necessary and the extent to which the standard of care in medical negligence claims has been altered by this ruling, and examines whether *Montgomery* has affected the law on breach of duty of care in situations beyond medical law.

The standard test for breach of duty of care for professional persons, the test devised in *Bolam v Friern Hospital Management Committee* [1957] 1 WLR 583, states that a doctor is not guilty of negligence 'if he has acted in accordance with a practice accepted as proper by a responsible body of (professional persons) skilled in that particular art.'

At the time of this judgment, medical treatment was paternalistic in nature. The later case of *Sidaway*, in which the claimant alleged negligence by a surgeon for the failure to disclose the inherent risks of the procedure, confirmed the application of the *Bolam* test in such situations. The House of Lords agreed that a doctor could be held liable in negligence if they did not answer questions when specifically asked by a patient, but, by a majority decision, decided that a doctor would not be held liable, if the patient did not specifically ask for information, unless such risks were substantial. In this case, the risk of 1–2 per cent occurrence was not deemed to be substantial. Lord Scarman, dissenting, stated that 'English law must recognize a duty of the doctor to warn his patient of risk inherent in the treatment which he is proposing', unless such a warning would be detrimental to a patient's health. His Lordship further noted that this 'duty is confined to material risk'.

Over the years, the *Bolam* test has gradually been modified. In *Bolitho v City & Hackney Health Authority* [1997] 3 WLR 1151, which considered the case of a child who suffered brain damage, Lord Browne-Wilkinson specified that [2] if 'professional opinion is not capable of withstanding logical analysis, the judge is entitled to hold that the body of opinion is not reasonable or responsible'. Such a situation occurred in *Marriott v West Midlands Regional Health Authority* [1999] Lloyd's Rep Med 23, when a GP failed to send the claimant for a brain scan after a severe head injury.

Meanwhile, in *Pearce v United Bristol Healthcare NHS Trust* [1999] PIQR P53, Lord Woolf took up Lord Scarman's approach in *Sidaway*, in supporting the rights of patients to be warned of adverse consequences, though he did use the term 'significant risk' as opposed to 'material risk'. Further, according to Professor McLean in her book *Autonomy, Consent and the Law*, *Chester v Afshar* [2004] 41 UKHL [3] 'reinforced the basic concept that doctors' duties flow from patients' rights, not the other way around.' In this case a clear breach of duty was established for failure to answer a patient's direct question effectively, their Lordships being asked to consider the issue of causation for non-negligent side effects.

[4] In the light of such decisions, and in consultation with their own research, the General Medical Council (GMC) and the British Medical Association (BMA) initiated moves towards improving practice in obtaining informed consent—both an ethical and a legal responsibility for doctors. To obtain informed consent means that the patient must be alerted to all available information regarding a proposed

[2] It is difficult to remember direct quotes from cases and/or literature under exam conditions, but if you can, you will impress your examiner.

[3] This is evidence. By incorporating academic literature you have indicated that you have broadened your research.

[4] This is your answer to the 'why' part of the question. It was not that the judges changed medical practice; they changed the law to tie in with existing changes in medical practice.

treatment, including both the benefits and the risks. As specified by the **5.**GMC in 'Consent: Patients and Doctors Making Decisions Together' (2008), doctors must be satisfied that they have valid consent before carrying out a procedure and that 'serious or persistent failure to do so will put their registration at risk.' It is therefore clear that a paternalistic approach to medical treatment had been losing support for many years. **6.**Consequently, prior to its overruling by *Montgomery*, support for the *Sidaway/Bolam* test had also diminished. Taking all this into account, the judgment in *Montgomery* should have come as no surprise.

Mrs Montgomery, an insulin-dependent diabetic, was under consultant care during her pregnancy. Diabetic women are known to have large babies which cause problems during delivery. Her consultant neither informed her of the 9–10 per cent risk of shoulder dystocia (which was a known risk that the court considered to be substantial) or of the possibility of delivery by caesarean section. Additionally, it was known that these babies were at risk of cerebral palsy occurring, and, although the risk was as low as 0.1 per cent, this unfortunately occurred. Had the baby been delivered by caesarean section, this risk would have been avoided.

Despite the fact that other medical specialists supported the defendant's actions (ie the consultant had passed the *Bolam* test), the court found in the claimant's favour. Referring to Lord Scarman's judgment in *Sidaway*, their Lordships specified that doctors must take reasonable care to ensure that the patient is aware of any 'material risks' involved in any treatment. The court specified that a 'material risk' is one in which **7.** 'a reasonable person in the patient's position would be likely to attach significance to the risk, or the doctor is or should reasonably be aware that the particular patient would be likely to attach significance to it.' In Mrs Montgomery's case, the Court found that the risk of shoulder dystocia, and the risk of the harm to the child, were relevant to her decision-making. She should have been informed of these risks and given an opportunity to elect to undergo a caesarean section. This decision therefore appears to be a resolute move away from 'reasonable doctor', towards a patient-centred perspective, **8.**but in realistic terms it merely enshrines in law the principles already specified by the GMC.

Since its ruling, several medical negligence cases have relied on *Montgomery* in the hearings. The facts of *Webster v Burton Hospital NHS Foundation Trust* [2017] EWCA Civ 62 mirrored those of Montgomery. It was therefore unsurprising that the court found in the claimant's favour. In *Hassell v Hillingdon Hospitals NHS Foundation Trust* [2018] EWHC 164, *Montgomery* also supported the claimant's argument, when she suffered tetraplegia as a result of an operation. The court found that the claimant would not have proceeded with the operation had she been informed of this potential risk beforehand.

9. This is a broader question than just medical negligence. Be guided by your lecturer on the cases you may need to study.

[9.] In other areas of negligence, *Montgomery* has been cited by parties regarding inheritance tax (*Barker v Baxendale Walker Solicitors (A Firm)* [2017] EWCA Civ 2056), banking and finance (*Marz Ltd v Bank of Scotland plc* [2017] EWHC 3618 (Ch)), and successfully in regard to a client's claim against a solicitor (*Baird v Hastings (t/a Hastings and Co Solicitors)* [2015] NICA 22). In this latter case, Mrs Baird claimed damages against her solicitor for negligence and breach of contract in relation conveyancing transactions in 2007. More poignantly, in *O'Hare and anor v Coutts & Co* [2016] EWHC 2224 (QB) Mr Justice Kerr held that the *Bolam* test was inappropriate to establish whether a private banker had breached their duty of care to their client when providing investment advice, instead noting that *Montgomery* was to be preferred to the *Bolam* test because: 'a duty to explain in terms not dissimilar to the *Montgomery* formulation is found in the [FCA's Conduct of Business Sourcebook] rules.'

10. It is crucial to write a conclusion, though many candidates fail to do so. Your conclusion should sum up what you have discussed in your answer.

[10.] In conclusion, despite recent modifications to the *Bolam* test, rather than rewriting the law on breach of duty of care, *Montgomery* has merely endorsed current medical ethics and practice, in line with that promoted by professional organizations. Further, a perusal of recent cases has established that although *Montgomery* is likely to be relied upon by claimants in medical negligence claims, it has not created a wide-scale change to the 'standard of care' test in general negligence, its effects being confined to issues of professional negligence. Perhaps the most successful aspect of *Montgomery* is the warning it sends out to professionals to ensure they pay adequate attention to the advice they give to their clients. However, unless there are issues concerning 'disclosure of risks' in a professional context, *Montgomery* is unlikely to be of assistance to further claimants.

 LOOKING FOR EXTRA MARKS?

- In a selective essay such as this, it is essential to mention the key aspects of the case, and wherever possible incorporate direct quotes to indicate your detailed knowledge and understanding.

- In any seminal judgment, judges will refer to previous case law and also academic and/or practitioner sources. Therefore, if you are preparing for a question on a specific case, also make sure that you are familiar with the supporting literature, so that you weave this into your answer too.

- Always write a conclusion—it is surprising how many students fail to do this.

TAKING THINGS FURTHER

- Bagshaw, R., 'Modernising the Doctor's Duty to Disclose Risks of Treatment' (2016) 132 LQR 182.
- Heywood, R. and Miola, J., 'The Changing Face of Pre-operative Medical Disclosure: Placing the Patient at the Heart of the Matter' (2017) 133 LQR (Apr) 296.
- McGrath, C. P., '"Trust Me, I'm a Patient": Disclosure Standards and the Patient's Right to Decide' (2015) 74 CLJ 211.

  The above are three articles to read on the Montgomery no *case and its effect.*

- McLean, S. A. M., *Autonomy, Consent and the Law* (Routledge-Cavendish 2010).
- Mulheron, R., 'Legislating Dangerously: Bad Samaritans, Good Society, and the Heroism Act 2015' (2017) 80 MLR 88.

  This analyses the **Social Action, Responsibility and Heroism Act** *2015* **(SARAH)**.

- Williams, K., '*Res Ipsa Loquitur* Still Speaks' (2009) 125 LQR 567.

Online Resources

www.oup.com/uk/qanda/

Go online for extra essay and problem questions, a glossary of key terms, online versions of all the answer plans and audio commentary on how selected ones were put together, and a range of podcasts which include advice on exam and coursework technique and advice for other assessment methods.

Negligence III: Causation and Remoteness of Damage

4

ARE YOU READY?

To answer questions on this topic, you need an understanding of the following:

- The concept of causation in negligence
- Causation in fact: The standard 'but-for' test
- Variations of the 'but-for' test:
  - unknown causes
  - consecutive causes
  - cumulative causes
- Causation in law: the test for 'remoteness of damage'
- The 'eggshell-skull' rule
- *Novus actus interveniens* (new intervening acts):
  - the act of the claimant
  - the act of third parties
  - natural events

KEY DEBATES

The traditional 'but-for' test has come under scrutiny many times in the court, particularly in situations where there has been a 'material contribution' to harm or where there has been a 'loss of the chance'. As a result, claimants and defendants are put in the position where they might find themselves contesting cases to which the outcome is in doubt. Do variations to the 'but-for' test help or hinder the process of law?

Dan, an industrial cleaner, was spending his holiday riding his new bicycle. He was cycling east, approaching a green traffic light in his favour at a crossroads, when it turned red. He did not stop, as he did not see any cars waiting at the lights. However, Scott, who was travelling south on his motorbike, was approaching the traffic lights, which had now turned green in Scott's favour. He did not pay attention to Dan's actions, and although not going fast, he could not stop his motorbike in time, when Dan rode in front of him. Consequently, the impact knocked Dan off his bicycle. Dan fell on the road, which caused damage to Dan's right ankle and lower leg. Out of nowhere, Kevin, driving at a speed of 90 mph in his Jaguar, drove over Dan's right leg and severed it below the knee. Scott and Kevin remained uninjured during these events.

At the hospital, doctors diagnosed that Dan had a rare blood disorder, which meant they had to remove his leg from the hip. There was evidence that the leg would have had to be removed within five years anyway because of this medical condition.

They also discovered that Dan was suffering from bubblitis—a serious lung disease caused by frequent use of industrial detergent. Dan's last three employers—Ahmed, Bebe, and Crystal—all asked him to use this type of cleaner.

Dan was eventually discharged from hospital with a temporary artificial limb, but because of this he had difficulty walking, and he fell down his stairs at home, breaking his arm.

Advise Dan as to the issues on *causation* that may arise in his claims for negligence against other parties. Do not discuss defences.

DIAGRAM ANSWER PLAN

Identify	Who owes Dan a duty? Have they breached this? Show where the application of the but-for test is appropriate, and anywhere deviations from the standard but-for test may be required.
Relevant law	But for: *Cork v Kirby Maclean, Barnett v Chelsea & Kensington*. Deviations: *Baker v Willoughby, Jobling v Associated Dairies*. Material contributions: *Fairchild v Glenhaven*. *Novus actus interveniens: Wieland v Cyril Lord, McKew v Holland, Wright v Lodge*.
Apply the law	Who is the 'but-for' of Dan's injuries? Have Kevin's actions eradicated Scott's liability? The 'eggshell-skull' rule will apply. Can one employer be found responsible for bubblitis? Consider the material increase approach.
Conclude	It is likely that Kevin will be found responsible for Dan's injury to leg and arm. Damages awarded for the leg will be limited to five years, and a reduction for Dan's contributory negligence. The employers may be found jointly and severally liable, or responsible on a length-of-time basis.

CAUTION

You have been asked in this question to 'advise Dan'. Although the law should be the same which-ever side you are considering, try to focus on your claimant; this means indicating to them both the strengths and weaknesses of their case.

When discussing causation, do not forget to consider the issue of remoteness of damage.

SUGGESTED ANSWER

[1] The question does not require you to deal with duty or breach, so deal with these briefly.

[1] The 'neighbour principle' established in the seminal judgment of *Donoghue v Stevenson* [1932] AC 562, and later developed by the House of Lords in *Caparo Industries plc v Dickman* [1990] 2 AC 605, can be used to identify that all road users owe a duty of care to each other. Further, the standard of care owed is that of a reasonable driver, namely a competent and experienced driver, whether the driver is

qualified or still a learner, as described in the case of *Nettleship v Weston* [1971] 2 QB 691.

Applying this to the facts in the question, as fellow road users, Scott and Kevin owed Dan a duty of care, and both have breached that duty, as the 'reasonable road user' does not collide with another road user.

However, to pursue a successful claim in negligence, a claimant must show that not only did the defendant owe him or her a duty of care and breach that duty, but they must also prove that the breach was the direct cause of the claimant's injury, and further that the injury received was one that was not too remote [2.]*Overseas Tankship (UK) Ltd v Morts Dock & Engineering Co Ltd (The Wagon Mound No 1)* [1961] AC 388.

2. Under exam conditions it is usually sufficient to refer to the case by its short name, but you should specify *The Wagon Mound No 1* for actions in negligence.

The general starting point in determining causation is factual causation, known as the 'but-for' test (*causa sine qua non*), as explained by Denning LJ in *Cork v Kirby Maclean Ltd* [1952] 2 All ER 402, 'if you can say that the damage would not have happened but for a particular fault, then that fault is in fact a cause of the damage.'

This does not settle the question of liability, as there may be a *novus actus interveniens* (new intervening act) which breaks the causal chain; however, the but-for test does rule out some cases initially. It is traditional for the test to be proved on a balance of probabilities. An example of this can be seen in *Barnett v Chelsea and Kensington Hospital Management Committee* [1969] 1 QB 428, where, despite the hospital's negligence, it was found that the night watchman would have died of arsenic poisoning even if he had received proper care. If factual causation is proved, then legal causation must be addressed.

3. If you are answering a problem question, it is important to apply the law that you have discussed as soon as possible.

[3.]Turning our attention to Dan, he is hit by one vehicle after another. On a strict application of the but-for test, it could be argued that Dan is the author of his own misfortunes as, but for Dan going through a red light, he would not have been injured at all. A similar situation can be found in *Fitzgerald v Lane* **[1989] AC 328**, where ultimately all three parties were found liable. [4.]If this was the situation here, Dan would be held to be contributorily negligent and his damages award would be reduced as a result. Is it possible, then, to apportion the full blame to either Scott or Kevin?

4. You may like to consider the case of *Eagle v Chambers* [2004] 1 WLR 3081 in relation to contributory negligence.

Scott and Kevin

Regarding Scott, he appears to be the direct cause of the injury to Dan's lower leg and ankle. (It is not stated how severe this injury is at this point.) Kevin then severs the same leg below the knee. If factual causation can be proved against Scott, then legal causation must be addressed. Following the ruling in *Baker v Willoughby* [1970] AC 467, Scott would be found liable for the total loss, as his actions placed Dan in the path of Kevin, especially if Kevin can prove that the leg would have needed amputation anyway.

However, the facts indicate that there were issues of dangerous driving, as in *Wright v Lodge* **[1994] 4 All ER 299**. This would suggest that Kevin's actions were a *novus actus interveniens*, which would break the chain of causation. In such an instance, it is likely that Kevin's criminal action will eradicate Scott's liability, and Kevin would be found solely liable. Further, to strengthen Dan's claim, under the **Civil Evidence Act 1968, s 11**, if Kevin is convicted of a criminal offence relating to driving, the conviction will be admissible evidence in any relevant civil proceedings brought by Dan.

The Injuries

In this situation, the initial injuries sustained by Dan (an injured leg) are typical of road traffic accidents. However, that fact suggests that Kevin did not injure Dan's upper leg. [5.]Can Dan claim for the whole of this injury? Despite the ruling in *The Wagon Mound (No 1)* that a defendant must foresee the kind of damage that results, following the eggshell-skull rule, formulated in *Dulieu v White* **[1901] 2 KB 669** and confirmed in ***Smith v Leech Brain & Co Ltd*** **[1961] 3 All ER 1159**, a tortfeasor will be liable for the whole of the injury, even if the injury is more significant than initially appeared. Therefore, Dan will be able to claim for the loss of his leg. However, unfortunately for Dan, it is shown that his loss would occur in five years' time anyway. Therefore, following the ruling in *Jobling v Associated Dairies Ltd* [1982] AC 794, his damages award would be limited to five years only, the time that his loss would have occurred in any event.

[6.]Before moving on to consider the liability of other tortfeasors, it is important to note that Dan's accident on his return home, caused by the artificial limb, is a direct result of his original accident involving Kevin and Scott. If it can be found that his actions in descending his stairs are reasonable, as was found in *Wieland v Cyril Lord Carpets Ltd* [1969] 3 All ER 1006, and not unnecessary as the claimant's actions were found to be in *McKew v Holland* [1969] 3 All ER 1621 which was considered to be a *novus actus interveniens* caused by the claimant himself, then Dan will be able to claim further damages from the tortfeasor/s. In this scenario, especially if Dan lives alone and has no one to help him, it is more likely than not that the court will be sympathetic towards him, and his damages award will be increased in line with current compensation rules.

Regarding bubblitis, it is not stated how this disease developed. It appears to be completely independent from the road traffic accident, and found by chance at the hospital. Bubblitis could be a disease of accumulation; the longer the exposure to an injurious chemical, the worse the illness. Such are the cases of *Allen v British Rail Engineering Ltd* [2001] ICR 942, where the claimant suffered from vibratory white finger, and *Holtby v Brigham & Cowan (Hull) Ltd* [2000] 3 ALL ER 421,

[5.] Try to avoid writing too many questions in your response—even if you are just about to answer them! Some examiners do not like this style.

[6.] You may find it more logical to answer the question in a different order than the facts state. If you do so make sure you signpost this to your examiner.

where the claimant contracted asbestosis. In this case it is likely that Ahmed, Bebe, and Crystal, will all be found liable in a proportion to the length of the employment with each.

[7.] Make sure you discuss an issue from every angle.

[7.]On the other hand, should it be decided that bubblitis develops in a similar way to mesothelioma, causation will be very difficult to establish, as it will be impossible to identify who was responsible for the disease. Several years ago, Dan may have found that he could not claim from any of his previous employers at all. However, the rules of causation were modified by *McGhee v National Coal Board* [1973] 1 WLR 1, where despite an 'evidential gap', the House of Lords found in the claimant's favour. This decision was used as a basis for the policy decision found in *Fairchild v Glenhaven Funeral Services* [2002] 3 All ER. The claimants had been unsuccessful in the Court of Appeal, as they had failed the but-for test. However, their Lordships treated each defendant as 'a material increase in risk', and found that the defendants had been jointly and severally liable. A later decision (with similar facts to *Fairchild*), *Barker v Corus (UK) plc* [2006] UKHL 20, apportioned the damages according to the length of time of each employment, but by virtue the Compensation Act 2006 s 3, such damages will now be calculated jointly and severally. However, this Act specifies 'damages for mesothelioma', and is therefore unlikely to assist Dan.

Nevertheless, the more recent case of *Bailey v Ministry of Defence* [2008] EWCA Civ 883, in which a claimant ultimately suffered brain damage, saw the Court of Appeal departing from the traditional but-for test,

[8.] If you have sufficient time, go into policy reasonings as part of your answer. Ultimately, it helps in establishing how the outcome might be decided.

[8.]preferring instead to apply the approach that the defendants had 'materially contributed' (*Bonnington Casting v Wardlaw* [1956] AC 613) to the claimant's damage.

In Dan's case, there can be no doubt of the cause of the injury; it is the industrial detergent. Therefore, in the absence of proof as to which potential tortfeasor is responsible, it seems reasonable that the

[9.] Try to avoid the phrase 'it is up to the courts to decide'. We know that, but we want **your** opinion on the issues.

Fairchild principle is applied in his favour, [9.]and that he be allowed to claim damages from his former employers, jointly and severally. Or, if this does not receive the approval of the court, that he is compensated by apportioning the damages according to the length of time of each employment as in *Barker v Corus*.

➕ LOOKING FOR EXTRA MARKS?

- Consider ways in which you can incorporate academic literature into the answer. This is more difficult to achieve in problem questions than in essays, but there is always scope. Identify the most challenging aspect of this scenario to introduce this.
- If you read through the other questions, you will see that policy-driven deviations from the but-for test are controversial, and therefore worth investigating. Read academic literature which considers this area, and then see if you can find a way to rewrite the answer including it.

QUESTION | **2**

Wilma, a student, invited a couple of friends from university, Chi and Astan, to stay at her family's farmhouse during the vacation. One evening, after drinking a bottle of wine, Wilma suggested taking shotguns up into the fields to see what they could shoot. Neither Chi nor Astan had ever handled a shotgun before, but Wilma announced that there were enough guns for all of them and that she would show them what to do. When Wilma opened the gun cabinet she noticed that her shotgun licence had expired the week before, but as she did not want to disappoint her friends she gave each of them a gun and some pellets.

Although they had been intending to shoot in a field across the road from the farmhouse, the sight of a road sign proved too much temptation for them and all three fired at it at once. Jatinder, a social worker, who had just cycled into range, was struck in the eye by a single pellet, while Wilma suffered several injuries from pellets ricocheting off the sign. Both casualties were rushed to hospital, where the shotgun pellets were removed but there was nothing to indicate from whose gun any of the pellets had been fired.

Consider the potential liability of the parties in negligence. You may assume that issues relating to duty of care and breach have already been resolved.

CAUTION

- This is a narrow question, and as a result requires a narrow answer. General discussions regarding causation will not be sufficient to obtain a good grade.

DIAGRAM ANSWER PLAN

Identify	Is the standard test for causation (but-for) applicable? Consider situations in which for policy reasons the standard test might be adapted. Are there any defences that need to be addressed?
Relevant law	But for: *Cork v Kirby Maclean*, *Barnett v Chelsea*. Deviations: *Wilsher v Essex AHA*, *Bonnington Castings v Wardlaw*, *McGhee v NCB*, *Fairchild v Glenhaven Funeral Parlours*, *Cook v Lewis*. Defences: contributory negligence, *volenti*, *ex turpi causa*.
Apply the law	The but-for test will not establish a tortfeasor. The facts suggest that *Cook v Lewis/Fairchild* would yield a positive result for the claimants. Consider issues of policy that differentiate the claimants.
Conclude	Jatinder is likely to be successful with her claim. Wilma's claim is likely to fail due to the application of defences.

 SUGGESTED ANSWER

This is a complex situation, in which the two claimants are Jatinder, the injured social worker, and Wilma, who is also a potential defendant along with her two friends, Chi and Astan. Since the facts state that the issues of duty and breach have been resolved, the starting point is with causation. [1.] Each claimant will be considered in turn.

Jatinder

The traditional approach to identifying causation is to apply the but-for test (***Barnett v Chelsea and Kensington Hospital Management Committee* [1969] 1 QB 428** [2.] in which a doctor's negligence in failing to see a patient was eliminated as a factual cause because the victim was already beyond saving prior to the time of the negligence), and ask whether, but for the negligence of the defendant(s), he would not have been injured. This is problematic because claimants must prove their case against defendants as individuals. In the right circumstances, it is possible to establish that more than one defendant contributed to the overall damage. Such a situation occurred in ***Fitzgerald v Lane* [1989] AC 328**, where a careless pedestrian

[1.] Some candidates try to discuss both claimants at the same time. It is clearer to read if you separate them. Notice that this answer is structured in a different way to the first answer.

[2.] Consider whether the facts of this case are actually needed here (see note 3).

suffered multiple injuries from being struck by two negligently driven vehicles.

On the facts given, Jatinder has been injured by a single pellet so only one of the defendants is responsible, and the burden of proof lies on Jatinder to show, on the balance of probabilities, who is responsible. This will not be possible in the absence of any further evidence. There are three potential tortfeasors; each has only a one-in-three, or 33 per cent, chance of being the person responsible. In such a situation Jatinder's claim looks likely to fail [3.] (***Wilsher v Essex AHA [1988] AC 1074***).

However, in certain circumstances, the House of Lords has adopted a modified approach to the test for causation, to reach the perceived justice of the case. [4.] The majority of these cases involve employees who have suffered injury or illness through exposure to a single substance; but in circumstances where they cannot prove as a fact that it was negligent exposure by their employer that caused the harm, or that it was a specific employer out of a number of equally negligent candidates who bore the responsibility. So, in ***Bonnington Castings v Wardlaw [1956] 1 All ER 615*** and ***McGhee v National Coal Board [1972] 3 All ER 1008***, the claimants suffered, respectively, from pneumoconiosis and dermatitis from exposure to dust. In ***Wardlaw***, the claimant worked in an environment in which negligent dust was mixed with dust that could not reasonably have been avoided and which was therefore classed as 'innocent'. McGhee worked in a hot, sweaty environment where brick dust became (unavoidably) stuck to his body, but the negligent failure of his employer to provide showers prolonged the contact since he was obliged to travel home in the same condition. Neither claimant was able to prove scientifically that it was the 'negligent' dust that had caused the damage.

In ***Wardlaw***, the House of Lords concluded that it was sufficient for the claimant in circumstances such as these to prove on the balance of probabilities that the negligent dust had 'materially contributed to the disease' (*per* Lord Reid). A similar approach was applied in ***McGhee***, and although it was noted that while it could be shown that pieces of brick dust had contributed to McGhee's condition (by contrast with Wardlaw's case in which every particle of dust could be shown to have played its part in causing the disease), Lord Reid observed that: 'I can see no substantial difference between saying that what the respondents did materially increased the risk of injury to the appellant and saying that what the respondents did made a material contribution to his injury.'

Further, in ***Fairchild v Glenhaven Funeral Services Ltd [2002] UKHL 22***, the appeals concerned sufferers from mesothelioma, a cancer which may be triggered by inhalation of a single fibre, rather than by an accumulation of asbestos. Consequently, any individual who

[3.] Sometimes, examiners require more than just a case name after a point of law. Why does applying **this** case suggest Jatinder's claim will fail?

[4.] This would be an opportunity to incorporate academic literature to show wider reading.

had been negligently exposed to asbestos during periods of work for different employers could never prove scientifically that any individual employer had caused the disease, nor could s/he prove that any individual had materially contributed to it. [5.]This was a situation in which the law was left with a hard choice between two potential injustices: (i) apply a strict test for causation—proof of causation of the *damage* or, at least, of material contribution to it—and the rights of the gravely injured employees must go unprotected; or (ii) apply a modified approach—material contribution to the *risk* of damage—and a defendant might have to shoulder liability without being responsible. The House of Lords was unanimous in adopting the modified approach, building upon, amongst other things, the reasoning in *McGhee* that to allow the current shortcomings of medical science to inhibit the claims of injured employees would be to empty the employer's duty of any legal content.

Lord Hoffmann, in *Fairchild*, observed that the law must reflect the fact that 'the just solution to different kinds of case may require different causal requirement rules'.

[6.]Lord Bingham, in *Fairchild*, considered cases from a range of jurisdictions, each involving negligent shootings (***Litzinger v Kintzler* Cass civ 2e, 5 June 1957, D 1957 Jur 493**; ***Summers v Tice* (1948) 199 P 2d 1**; *Oliver v Miles* **(1926) 50 ALR 357**; *Cook v Lewis* **[1951] SCR 830**) and which involved findings of joint and several liability on the part of each defendant who had fired the bullet which had caused the injury to the claimant. In each case, this outcome had been held preferable to the prospect of leaving a negligently injured claimant uncompensated.

Turning back to the problem, this line of reasoning could undoubtedly assist Jatinder, since it would relieve her of the burden of proving causation on the but for test. Each of the three defendants has, by discharging their gun, materially contributed to the risk of Jatinder's injury, so causation is made out. Remoteness of damage is readily established, and there are no applicable defences.

No doubt Wilma would be pleased to adopt the same argument regarding causation. Although she has suffered a number of injuries, there is still nothing to indicate from whose gun the pellets were fired, and it is even possible they all came from her own weapon. Her position (being also one of the defendants in the case) is, on the face of it, analogous to one of the mesothelioma victims in *Barker v Corus* **[2006] UKHL 20**, who had also been exposed to asbestos during a period of self-employment. [7.]The House of Lords, in *Barker*, adopted a new approach, quantifying the liability of each tortfeasor according to the contribution to the overall exposure, although this approach was rapidly nullified by Parliament (at least in asbestos cases) by the passing of the **Compensation Act 2006**.

---

5. Although you are answering a problem question, it is perfectly acceptable to discuss issues of policy, if you have time to ensure that you cover all the essential elements of the claims.

6. Some students are reluctant to incorporate jurisprudence from outside the UK; however, where there is a good example from another common law jurisdiction it is sensible to use it—after all, the House of Lords did! However, remember that law from other jurisdictions has persuasive authority only.

7. Consider if this paragraph is strictly relevant to answering the question. How are you hoping to use this in your advice?

More recently, in *Sienkiewicz v Greif (UK) Ltd* [2011] **UKSC 10** the Supreme Court again confirmed this approach in mesothelioma cases, at least until such a time as medical science can identify more clearly a connection between a specific exposure and the onset of the disease, the Court holding that any negligent exposure that was more than negligible should, given the present state of ignorance, attract full liability. Therefore, Wilma may be able to establish causation.

8. An important aspect of this question is explaining why these two claimants are likely to be treated differently by the courts.

[8.]However, what might seem to fair in respect of Jatinder appears less acceptable in respect of Wilma.

A court wishing to avoid compensating Wilma would have two options open to it: (i) revisit the test for causation in her case; or (ii) use other principles to deny her a remedy. Option (i) would be problematic as it risks bringing the employment-based *Fairchild* principle into disrepute. However, other principles may well offer a 'just' solution.

9. Regardless of how many topics in negligence you are preparing for the exam, it is crucial that you revise defences. You will find that you need to discuss them in most questions. In this answer it is crucial for advising one of the clients.

[9.]It could be argued that the principle of *volenti* applies, since Wilma understood the nature of the risk involved and yet went ahead, thereby voluntarily assuming the risk that materialized. Alternatively, it could be argued that the principle *ex turpi causa non oritur actio* (also known as the illegality defence) would act as a bar to an action (*Ashton v Turner* [1980] 3 All ER 870; *Pitts v Hunt* [1990] 3 All ER 344). *Ex turpi* considers if the claimant's action at the time of the negligent injury was not only unlawful but so wrong as to make it morally unacceptable for the court to assist her in seeking compensation. It is submitted that the expiry of a shotgun licence is not enough to trigger the defence, but encouraging and participating in the discharge of shotguns on the highway, especially in light of Jatinder's injury, might well suffice. Wilma is therefore unlikely to succeed in her claim.

LOOKING FOR EXTRA MARKS?

■ Although written in the form of a problem question, a good answer will discuss policy issues throughout. Make sure you are prepared by looking at how the defences operate in the tort of negligence, and how similar facts can yield different results depending on the 'blameworthiness' of the claimant.

QUESTION | 3

'Although the but-for test is a useful rule of thumb, it leads to absurd results where there is more than one sufficient cause of C's damage.'

(Winfield & Jolowicz)

Discuss.

DIAGRAM ANSWER PLAN

Before starting, write down key cases that you think will help you answer the question.

▼

Introduce your essay, indicating what you are planning to discuss. One paragraph is often sufficient.

▼

An explanation of the but-for test, and how it is used to rule out liability.

▼

Discuss cases involving multiple causes of damage and the modifications applied to the but-for test.

▼

Conclusion—do you agree with the quote or not?

 CAUTION

- You should notice that the law required to answer this essay question is the same as to answer problem question 2. This has been done to show that that you must be prepared to answer your chosen topic as both an essay and a problem question.

- Make sure that your revision incorporates knowledge of policy reasons and/or academic debate in this area. Although you may not have an opportunity to demonstrate this during a problem question, you should attempt to incorporate this in an essay question.

 SUGGESTED ANSWER

To be successful in a claim in negligence, the claimant must (usually) prove on a balance of probabilities that not only did the defendant breach his or her duty of care, but that this breach caused the injuries the claimant received. At times, the court struggles to decide whether a breach has both factually and legally caused the resulting damage. If there is no causal link, there is no claim.

[1] Inform your examiner that you are answering the question that they have set. The focus is the but-for test.

[2] You can use evidence from experts in the field to develop your themes and/or to back your argument.

[1] The usual starting point to establish causal connection is to assess whether the defendant is the *causa sine qua non*—the 'but-for' of the damage. As explained by Denning LJ in *Cork v Kirby Maclean Ltd* [1952] 2 All ER 402 (CA): 'If you can say that the damage would not have happened but for a particular fault, then that fault is in fact a cause of the damage.' [2] This initially looks a straightforward test, but proving causation is not always straightforward in practice, and the but-for test 'is no more than an aid, for the choice of cause rests ultimately on common sense evaluation' (Dias and Markenesis).

However, far from common-sense evaluation, at times the but-for test does lead to 'absurd results'. Before addressing situations where the courts have departed from the standard but-for test, it is important to assess the efficacy of the test itself. For this, the case of *Barnett v Chelsea and Kensington Hospital Management Committee* [1969] 1 QB 428 will be considered. Although this case only dealt with the aspect of medical negligence, as the facts reveal, another agent was at play.

[3.] In *Barnett*, the claimant's husband and two colleagues went to the casualty department complaining of severe stomach ache and episodes of vomiting. [4.] The duty doctor refused to come to the hospital to examine them, and told them to 'call in their own doctors'. The claimant's husband died of arsenic poisoning some five hours later. The claimant sued the hospital for negligence, but it was held that although the doctor had breached his duty of care, this did not cause her husband's death—he would have died even if he had been correctly diagnosed and treated on arrival at the hospital. As the widow was unable to prove the but-for test, her claim failed, despite the poor service given by the doctor.

It might be said that it was 'absurd' that the widow's claim failed in the face of extremely poor medical treatment, however the ultimate 'but-for' of Barnett's death, was, of course, the person who administered the arsenic. [5.] When one considers it from this angle, it is patent that the decision was not 'absurd', merely unfortunate for the widow.

However, there have been subsequent cases when, in the absence of the claimant proving the but-for test due to 'cumulative causes', the courts have found tortfeasors responsible on the grounds of being a 'material contribution' to the claimant's damage. Such a situation occurred in *Bonnington Castings Ltd v Wardlaw* [1956] AC 613, where a steelworker contracted pneumoconiosis after being exposed to silica dust created by the pneumatic hammer and swing grinders that he worked with. The company had not breached its statutory duty in respect of the hammer, but they had breached their duty in respect of the grinders. Therefore, to establish liability the court had to decide whether the dust that had caused the damage came from the grinders or the hammer. Although it was not possible to prove the 'but-for' of the illness, the courts held that, on the balance of probabilities, dust from the grinders had materially contributed to the injury. The claimant was said to have proved that 'at least that on a balance of probabilities the breach of duty caused or materially contributed to his injury' (*per* Lord Reid).

This case was followed by *Bailey v Ministry of Defence & Anor* [2008] EWCA Civ 883, in which several cumulative causes were the potential 'but-for' of the claimant's injuries. The claimant received negligent care after a gallstones procedure under the defendant's control, before suffering from a cardiac arrest and brain damage. The court decided that 'but for' the defendant's initial negligence causing the claimant to be in a weakened state, the ultimate damage might not have occurred. Their negligence had been a material contribution. [6.]It could be argued that, in both of these cases, it was 'absurd' to prove a claim where no conclusive evidence was offered.

This approach has also been used where there is one unidentifiable cause. In *McGhee v National Coal Board* [1973] 1 WLR 1, the claimant alleged that his dermatitis was caused by inadequate washing facilities at the workplace. Although it was likely that the claimant's employment, working in a brick kiln, was the main cause of the dermatitis, it was held that the (negligent) failure of the board to provide washing facilities on site had 'materially increased the risk' of his injury, and hence the claim was established. As (again) this decision was found despite their being an 'evidential gap', it might be said that in moving away from the but-for test, this ruling in itself was absurd and that the but-for test should have been applied.

[7.]The situation changed in *Hotson v East Berkshire Area Health Authority* [1987] 1 AC 750, when a claimant's injury took five days to be correctly diagnosed and treated and the claimant was left with a permanent disability. The hospital admitted negligence, but there was a conflict of expert evidence regarding causation. The Lords held that the evidence indicated that the injury, not the delay, was the 'but for' of the ultimate damage.

The but-for test was also applied in *Wilsher v Essex Area Health Authority* [1988] 1 AC 1074, in which a premature baby became blind. He had negligently received too much oxygen, but this was only one possible cause of blindness, none of others being the fault of the defendants. The Court of Appeal, basing its decision on *McGhee*, held that the claimant was entitled to succeed because the defendants had 'materially increased' the risk of damage to the claimant. However, this decision was reversed by the House of Lords. [8.]Their Lordships affirmed that in all cases the claimant must establish the causal connection on a balance of probabilities, stating the law required proof of fault, and that it was the work of Parliament to change the law, not the courts.

Whereas it might be argued that the decision in *Wilsher* (where the negligence was only 20 per cent of the overall potential cause) was not 'absurd', this case failed to safeguard situations where a claimant could prove up to 50 per cent liability, but not a fraction more. Such a situation had faced the Canadian courts in *Cook v Lewis*, where two grouse hunters allegedly fired at the claimant simultaneously by mistake. [9.]As neither owned up to being the party responsible for the claimant's injury, on an initial hearing the court found for the defendants—a judgment that was not only 'absurd' but, in the words of Rand J, 'perverse'.

---

6. Keep referring to the question. Offer evidence. Your examiner will wish to see you identify arguments both for and against the quotation.

7. A good essay question will evaluate all the pertinent House of Lords/Supreme Court cases in the answer; but remember, the examiner is not wanting to mark a casebook.

8. Investigate policy implications for decisions. Examiners will be delighted to see that you have read Hansard and Law Commission Reports.

9. If you can identify words in judgments to back up your arguments, you will impress your examiner.

It was this spectre that faced the Court in *Fairchild v Glenhaven Funeral Services & Ors* [2003] 1 AC 32. In this case, employees had developed mesothelioma from exposure to asbestos dust at work. It was not known which employer was responsible for the specific exposure causing the disease. The Court of Appeal had held that for this reason the but-for test could not be proved. However, the Lords overturned the decision, and held that, where the precise causative point could not be identified, it was sufficient to find that the wrongdoing of each employer had 'materially increased' the risk of contracting the disease. Their Lordships noted that there are certain circumstances where justice requires a relaxation of the but-for test to cater for claimants who are otherwise prevented in proving their case, simply because the deficiencies of medical science. However, although visited in subsequent cases, notably **Barker v Corus plc [2006] UKHL 20** and **Sienkiewicz v Greif (UK) Ltd [2011] UKSC 10**, this proves to be a narrow doctrine, as the following case of **Gregg v Scott [2005] UKHL 2** shows.

In *Gregg*, the court was invited to consider damages for a claimant whose prospects of a positive medical outcome had been reduced from 42 per cent to 25 per cent by his doctor's negligent delay in diagnosis. While acknowledging that 'lost chance' claims were available in some areas of negligence, the majority were emphatic that in medical negligence cases the claimant must meet the 'balance of probabilities' standard or lose his case. Here the claimant was unsuccessful; as the but for test could not be satisfied, the claimant could not prove that the delay in diagnosis was the cause of his likely premature death.

[10.] Make sure you conclude. Your examiner will be interested to see what you have decided. Tie it back to the quotation that you have been asked to discuss.

[10.] Overall, it can be seen, that the but-for test has, at times, appeared to give rise to absurd results. However, for reasons of policy, the courts have tried their utmost to find justice, without opening the floodgates to litigation. There can be no absurdity about this approach.

LOOKING FOR EXTRA MARKS?

- Although this essay refers to policy, it does not directly quote from policy documents, nor does it incorporate much academic literature. Reading around a policy-driven area in law will help you to master the information that you need to use.

- Make sure you incorporate it in your answers, particularly essay questions. Essay questions are devised to give you the scope to demonstrate your wider reading.

- The aim of pursuing a claim in negligence is to be awarded a remedy; therefore, in your answers, always consider what remedies might be available to claimants. Ensure you consult your tort law syllabus, to see how much coverage on damages you are required to learn. Some modules require quite detailed knowledge on this aspect.

TAKING THINGS FURTHER

- Bailey, S. H., 'Causation in Negligence: What Is a Material Contribution?' (2010) 30 LS 167.
  This paper investigates the principle of material contribution to harm.

- Burrows, A., 'Uncertainty about Uncertainty: Damages for Loss of a Chance' [2008] JPIL 31.
  This considers the issue of loss of a chance, and its effect.

- Hamer, D., 'Factual Causation and Scope of Liability: What's the Difference?' (2014) 77(2) MLR 155–88.
  The author argues that factual causation may require value judgement, whereas scope of liability often involves an assessment of the causal connection between breach and harm.

- Khoury, L., 'Causation and Risk in the Highest Courts of Canada, England and France' (2008) 124 LQR 103.

- Stapleton, J., 'Cause in Fact and the Scope of Liability for Consequences' (2003) 119 LQR 388.

- Steel, S., 'Justifying Exceptions to Proof of Causation in Tort Law' (2015) 78(5) MLR 729–58
  This article defends a number of exceptions to the but-for test of causation in tort law.

Online Resources   www.oup.com/uk/qanda/

Go online for extra essay and problem questions, a glossary of key terms, online versions of all the answer plans and audio commentary on how selected ones were put together, and a range of podcasts which include advice on exam and coursework technique and advice for other assessment methods.

Employers' Liability and Vicarious Liability

5

ARE YOU READY?

To answer questions on this topic, you need an understanding of the following:

- Tort of negligence
- Statutory duties, and the effect of breach of statutory duty
- The Employers' Liability (Defective Equipment) Act 1969, and the meaning 'PPE'
- Vicarious liability, and specifically *The Catholic Child Welfare Society and others v Various Claimants and The Institute of the Brothers of the Christian Schools* [2012] UKSC 56
- Defences to negligence

KEY DEBATES

At one time, an employer could rebut any action in negligence if it could be proved that an employee was on a 'frolic of his own'. However, over time the test has become more stringent. *The Catholic Child Welfare Society and others v Various Claimants and The Institute of the Brothers of the Christian Schools* [2012] UKSC 56 saw an employer's shield dented yet further. Has the test become too pro-claimant, or do you think that employers should always be held accountable for their employees, no matter how outrageous an employee's act might have been?

QUESTION | 1

Statutory regulations impose an obligation for all employers in the petrochemical industry to supply their employees with protective boots and gloves to wear during working hours. Sloth Ltd, who specialize in buying in products and rebranding them, provide their employees with gloves, but do not issue boots. Instead they instruct their employees to buy their own footwear, and on production of the receipt employees will be refunded for the cost. Employees are told that boots must be made of leather, and must not have any canvas material on the outside. Jim, who works in the warehouse, orders a pair of boots online, but when they arrive he finds that they have a canvas strip on the outside. He decides to wear them anyway. Later that morning he is helping Adeniran to load a trolley with tins containing a highly corrosive chemical. Jim is so concerned about his boots that he does not realize that Adeniran has taken off his gloves temporarily. Jim accidently gives a damaged tin to Adeniran, who takes it before realizing that the chemical has started to leak out of the tin. The chemical burns Adeniran's hand. In his shock, Adeniran drops the tin on Jim's right foot. The chemical seeps through the canvas on Jim's boot, burning his foot.

Advise.

CAUTION

The question does not specify which party/parties you are required to advise, so consider the overall effect of the scenario, and advise with all parties in mind.

You may find yourself doubling up on some of the advice, so you are entitled to say 'as discussed' to prevent repetition.

DIAGRAM ANSWER PLAN

Identify	How have the parties been injured and who might be responsible? Where might a breach of duty have occurred?
Relevant law	Employers' Liability (Defective Equipment) Act 1969 Section 1(1). *Wilsons and Clyde Coal Ltd v English* [1937] UKHL 2. *The Catholic Child Welfare Society and others v Various Claimants and The Institute of the Brothers of the Christian Schools* [2012] UKSC 56.
Apply the law	In what way and how have Sloth Ltd breached their duty? Does the defence of contributory negligence assist them?
Conclude	It is likely that Sloth Ltd will be held liable for supplying faulty equipment, but any award of damages will be reduced for both claimants under the principle of contributory negligence.

Sloth Ltd, as an employer, owes a duty of care towards Jim and Adeniran. Therefore Jim and Adeniran's actions will fall under employer's liability. [1.]In order to be successful in their claims, Jim and Adeniran will have to argue that their employer has breached its statutory duty and/or was negligent. An employer owes various duties to its employees. Those duties can arise from both statute and common law. Regarding common law, there are four headings which must be considered to assess whether Sloth has breached its duty, namely that Sloth must ensure competent staff (unlike the employer in *Hudson v Ridge Manufacturing Co* [1957] 2 QB 348), a safe place of work, proper plant and equipment, and a safe system of work (***Wilsons and Clyde Coal Ltd v English*** [1937] UKHL 2).

Assuming that Jim and Adeniran are considered competent staff (and there is no suggestion that on a day-to-day operation this is not the case), this aspect can be ignored for the moment. Neither is there any suggestion that Sloth have failed to supply a safe place of work. The facts suggest the prima facie cause of the injuries was in a failure to provide proper plant and equipment, and possibly a failure to ensure a safe system of work. It is submitted that the best cause of action will focus on the leaking tin.

Jim and Adeniran have handled a tin which is clearly faulty. Regardless of who has manufactured the tin, Sloth may be liable for the supply of defective 'equipment', by virtue of Employers' Liability (Defective Equipment) Act 1969 section 1(1) which states that:

[2.]**(1)** Where ...

    (a) an employee suffers personal injury in the course of his employment in consequence of a defect in equipment provided by his employer for the purposes of the employer's business; and

    (b) the defect is attributable wholly or partly to the fault of a third party (whether identified or not),

    the injury shall be deemed to be also attributable to negligence on the part of the employer ...

The tin will clearly be considered 'equipment' within the meaning of the Act, as section 1(3) specifies that equipment 'includes any plant and machinery, vehicle, aircraft and clothing'. [3.]Therefore, as far as Jim and Adeniran's claims are concerned, it does not matter who manufactured the tin; Sloth will be liable for the defective equipment supplied to them for the purposes of their employment.

Sloth will argue that in providing gloves they have discharged their duty in this respect, and that none of the injuries would have occurred if Jim and Adeniran had worn their protective equipment as instructed.

---

1. Consider the order of this introduction. Could you rearrange this to make it flow better? Remember you are assessed on your command of English, not just your knowledge of law.

2. This section has been inserted for your convenience, but do not write all this out in an examination answer.

3. You have considered the issue and you have concluded. Try to conclude every point you make as you work your way through the answer.

Considering Adeniran first, one cause of action might be to argue that Jim was negligent in not checking to see whether Adeniran was wearing gloves before handing up the tin. In this case, any negligence on Jim's part would fall onto the employer under the principle of vicarious liability for the primary negligence of the employer's failure to provide a safe system of work (*General Cleaning Contractors v Christmas* [1953] AC 180). It is clear from the facts that although Jim was not paying full attention to Adeniran, he was not on a 'frolic of his own'.

4. Be inventive with your use of cases. Several cases use this phrase.

[4.]*N v Chief Constable of Merseyside Police* [2006] EWHC 3041. Further, the case of *The Catholic Child Welfare Society and others v Various Claimants and The Institute of the Brothers of the Christian Schools* [2012] UKSC 56 had made it more difficult for employers to not be held accountable for the actions of employees. Clearly the facts lead us to the conclusion that should Jim be negligent, then Sloth will be vicariously liable.

Regarding Adeniran, it is clear that 'but for' the handling of the faulty tin, he would not have been injured (*Barnett v Chelsea and Kensington Hospital Management Committee* [1968] 3 All ER 1068).

5. You may want to consider whether this is useful in answering your question, or whether to go straight to any defences.

[5.]Sloth may argue a *novus actus inteveniens*, in the form of the claimant himself. Had Adeniran not removed his glove, he may not have been injured. It would have to be assessed whether Adeniran would have received any type of injury had his gloves remained on his person, as it is possible that even if Adeniran had worn his gloves, by the time he took hold of the tin, the contents might have caused some burning. [6.]However, it might well be the case that Sloth have not instructed their employees to wear gloves at all times, and therefore Sloth's argument might fail on this ground. Not only that; Sloth cannot argue that the ultimate cause of the injury was not the faulty tin they have been deemed to supply.

6. Where the facts are non-specific you can spend a lot of time discussing various scenarios. Try to focus your train of thought and reach firm conclusions.

Having had a case made against them, Sloth will look to assess whether any damages award can be reduced by the application of a defence. *Volenti* is not a defence to breach of an employer's statutory duty. However, there is a specific defence—that the employer did all s/he could reasonably and practically do—which is often provided in regulations. Here we are not informed of the details of the regulations.

It is important to consider contributory negligence. The Law Reform (Contributory Negligence) Act 1945 section 1 provides[7.]:

7. As before, you will get little credit for writing in a huge chunk of statute law.

'Where any person suffers damage as the result partly of his own fault and partly of the fault of any other person or persons, a claim in respect of that damage shall not be defeated by reason of the fault of the person suffering the damage, but the damages recoverable in respect thereof shall be reduced to such extent as the court thinks just and equitable having regard to the Claimant's share in the responsibility for the damage.'

Therefore if either claimant is deemed to be partially at fault for their injuries, their damages award will be adjusted accordingly. While, as a general rule, the courts are reluctant to find employees responsible for their own injuries whilst at work, they will do so if the situation warrants it. In *Bux v Slough Metals Ltd* [1974] 1 All ER 262 an employee who refused to wear his goggles was deemed contributorily negligent. We are not informed of the reason behind Adeniran's removal of gloves, but the less reasonable the removal, the more difficult it will be for Adeniran to specify that he was not contributorily negligent. If it can be proved that Sloth have issued employees with instructions on wearing the gloves, and what to do if the gloves have to be removed, then this argument will fail, and it is likely that Adeniran will be considered to be contributorily negligent, to a percentage a decided by a court.

Jim may also be considered contributorily negligent for failure to wear the correct footwear. Although Sloth have not provided his footwear, they have been specific as to the footwear to be bought. By a failure to conform to the standards issues Jim can be considered contributorily negligent. Sloth may argue that Adeniran is the sole cause of Jim's injuries,[8] but, as discussed previously, Adeniran was working for Sloth, and his actions cannot be considered a frolic of his own, so Sloth will be considered vicariously liable for Adeniran's actions.

[8.] You may cross-refer in a question, but not cross-refer to another answer.

LOOKING FOR EXTRA MARKS?

■ Be more systematic with your answer so that you are clear as to when you are looking at negligence and when you are looking at breach of statutory duty.

QUESTION 2

The (fictional) Safety at Work (Miscellaneous Provisions) Regulations 2018 state:

(i) Employers shall ensure, so far as is reasonably practicable, that all abrasive wheels are safe to use.

(ii) It shall be the responsibility of both employer and employee to ensure that safety harnesses are worn when work is carried out more than six metres from ground level.

(iii) Where inflammable materials are stored in the workplace, it shall be the responsibility of the employer to ensure that for the protection of employees and the community at large all fire appliances are adequately maintained.

The regulations state that breach of the provisions is a criminal offence punishable by the payment of a fine. No provision is made for civil law remedies.

Eric and Roland are employed to clean the windows in a factory operated by Plasticraft Ltd. Neither is wearing a safety harness. Roland is working five metres from ground level and Eric is working seven metres from ground level. Eric slips and falls onto Roland. Both are injured. The noise causes Norman to look away while he is sharpening a chisel on an abrasive wheel. Norman's finger is badly injured when it touches the rotating wheel. Evidence shows that a device could have been fitted to the wheel which would cause it to stop as soon as a chisel ceases to make contact. Plasticraft Ltd claim not to have the resources to be able to fit such a device. During the incident, a spark created by moving parts ignites some rags on the floor. Because fire extinguishers have not been properly maintained, the fire spreads and damages a car owned by Percy, a visitor to the factory.

Advise Plasticraft Ltd of their tortious liability for breach of the Regulations.

CAUTION

- To answer this question you should describe the nature of the tort and the general principles underpinning it, backing up your arguments with a wide range of cases to apply to the facts.
- You do not need any detailed knowledge of specialist legislation, although relevant cases may strengthen your answer.

DIAGRAM ANSWER PLAN

Identify	What is the statutory duty? Does Parliament intend this to confer a private law action for damages? Is the claimant part of an identified class protected by the statutory duty?
Relevant law	*Larner v British Steel plc* [1993] 4 All ER 102. *Fytche v Wincanton Logistics plc* [2004] UKHL 31.
Apply the law	Is the harm suffered within the language of the statutory provision? If the statutory duty is owed does it impose strict or fault-based liability? Is there a breach and has it caused the harm complained of?
Conclude	Plasticraft Ltd may be deemed responsible for their failure to ensure that a safety harness is used by Eric.

1. Start with a convincing opening paragraph which confirms that you understand what the question entails.

1. When deciding whether a breach of a statutory regulation gives rise to an action for damages, two principal issues must be considered. First, it must be asked whether the regulation confers an action in tort, and for this we must assess Parliament's intentions. Second, it must be asked whether there actually is an actionable tort.

Whether or not a statutory provision creates a civil cause of action turns on an interpretation of the intention of Parliament (*Hague v Deputy Governor of Parkhurst Prison* [1991] 3 All ER 733). Lord Denning thought (in *Ex parte Island Records* [1978] Ch 122) that you might as well toss a coin to decide the point. There is a primary assumption that where a statute creates an obligation and provides for its enforcement in a particular manner, it does not confer a civil cause of action unless it is intended to protect an identified class of persons (*Lonrho Ltd v Shell Petroleum Ltd* [1981] 2 All ER 456).

2. Note how a few facts have been given, to put the case in context.

2. The penalty for breach of these regulations might suggest that this is the only intended consequence of breach, as in *Atkinson v Newcastle Waterworks Co* (1877) 2 Ex D 441, where a water authority owed no private law duty to individual customers. Indeed, if the statutory provision does provide an adequate remedy, there is a presumption that there will be no civil action for damages (*Wentworth v Wiltshire County Council* [1993] 2 WLR 175 where it was decided that the **Highways (Miscellaneous Provisions) Act 1961** offered only a limited cause of action for a breach of duty). However, it is important to assess the adequacy of the statutory remedy. Thus, there may be cases in which a remedy is provided which a civil court may not regard as adequate recompense for an injured claimant (*Read v Croydon Corp* [1938] 4 All ER 631). Furthermore, the existence of the statutory duty does not prevent a claimant from pursuing an alternative cause of action, such as one for negligence, if the evidence supports this. Even if the presumption against a civil cause of action were not to apply, it would also have to be established by the various potential claimants that they formed part of an identifiable class of persons Parliament intended to protect. Importantly, employees are, generally, treated as a sufficiently identifiable class to warrant protection (*Groves v Lord Wimborne* [1898] 2 QB 402).

3. Consider whether this sentence is really needed to answer the question. You do not have time under examination conditions to incorporate material that is not strictly relevant.

3. Moreover, a visitor to unsafe premises may sue for breach of fire safety regulations: *Solomons v Gertzenstein Ltd* [1954] 2 QB 243. However, persons forming part of a very wide class such as highway users (*Phillips v Britannia Laundry Ltd* [1923] 2 KB 832) or water consumers (*Atkinson v Newcastle Waterworks Co*) are unlikely to be owed a duty.

4. Conclude your arguments for each section before moving on to the next issue.

4. These rules might be taken to indicate that regulations (i) and (ii) which are intended for the benefit of employees will confer an action in tort, but that regulation (iii) may be construed so as not to give rise to an action in tort.

Even if the claimant falls within a protected class, the wording of the duty must be such that the harm suffered is of a type intended to be protected against by the statute. For example, a statutory provision requiring an employer to keep protective boots in good repair has been interpreted to extend only to protecting an employee's feet from heavy falling objects rather than from frostbite in cold weather: *Fytche v Wincanton Logistics plc* **[2004] UKHL 31**. Along similar lines, fire safety regulations are likely to be aimed at the protection of individuals rather than their property. This would seem to suggest that Percy may have no cause of action under the 1994 Regulations in respect of the damage to his car.

Norman is likely to bring an action for damages based on the breach of regulation (i) which clearly places a duty on employers to ensure, so far as is practicable, that all abrasive wheels are safe to use. The phrase 'so far as is practicable' might suggest a standard of reasonable care on the part of the employer, although it has been held to impose a stricter standard (*Edwards v National Coal Board* **[1949] 1 All ER 743**) and its presence in a statutory provision may place the burden of proving the practicability of precautions on the employer: *Larner v British Steel plc* **[1993] 4 All ER 102**. The employee would still have to prove that the lack of safety was the cause of his injury. (See also *Nimmo v Alexander Cowan & Sons Ltd* **[1968] AC 107**.) Moreover, it is for the defendant to plead and prove that it was not reasonably practicable to keep the workplace safe, which will involve an assessment of the degree of risk and the time and cost involved in averting the risk (*Mains v Uniroyal Engelbert Tyres Ltd* **(1995) The Times, 29 September**).

Assuming the safety device that could have been fitted is not exorbitantly expensive, Plasticraft may not have taken reasonably practicable precautions, in which case they may be liable for Norman's injury.

Regulation (ii) places joint responsibility on the employer and his employees to ensure that safety harnesses are used when work is carried out at a height greater than six metres from ground level. The wording of regulation (ii) is so specific that it seems unlikely that anyone working at a height lower than six metres will be owed a duty (*Chipchase v British Titan Products Ltd* **[1956] 1 QB 545**). On this basis, Rowland will have no remedy under regulation (ii) since he is working only five metres from ground level; but Eric's position is different. It must be considered whether Plasticraft's alleged breach of the duty is the cause of the harm suffered by Eric, but the problem is that Eric is also in breach of the duty which rests on him to ensure

5. See how the argument is developed on both sides. Remember we are looking for you to discuss both sides of a potential action and then inform us what you think the courts will find.

that a safety harness is used. 5. The answer to this problem may turn on whether there were further precautions which could have been taken by the employer to ensure compliance with the safety regulation, as in *Ginty v Belmont Building Supplies Ltd* **[1959] 1 All ER 414**, where the employer could not have done more than he had to explain to employees the importance of using crawling boards when working on an unsafe roof, so that the employee's actions were the cause of the harm suffered (see also *Brumder v Motornet Services Ltd* **[2013] EWCA Civ 195**). However, in *Boyle v Kodak Ltd* **[1969] 2 All ER 439** the employer could have better explained how to use a ladder, with the result that his breach of duty was the cause of injury. It follows that if Plasticraft Ltd could have done more, their failure to ensure that a safety harness was used by Eric is the cause of the injury.

LOOKING FOR EXTRA MARKS?

■ Keep a clear dialogue going between you and the examiner. The main focus of the marking will be on evidence of knowledge and the ability to reason and reach a conclusion. The extra marks come from in-depth knowledge of academic sources combined with a flair for English. This requires work.

TAKING THINGS FURTHER

■ Giliker, P., 'The Ongoing March of Vicarious Liability' (2006) 65 CLJ 489.
  This article argues that, as far as non-delegable duties in the law of tort are concerned, a new approach is needed for dealing with claims for vicarious liability.
■ Levinson, J., 'Vicarious Liability for Intentional Torts' [2005] JPIL 304.
■ McBride, N. J., 'Vicarious Liability in England and Australia' (2003) 62 CLJ 255.
■ McKendrick, E., 'Vicarious Liability and Independent Contractors—A Re-examination' (1980) 53 MLR 770.
■ Morgan, P., 'Vicarious Liability on the Move' (2013) 129 LQR 139.
  This paper argues that the Supreme Court decision of The Catholic Child Welfare Society and others v Various Claimants, although coming to the right decision, requires further clarification.
■ Stanton, K. M., 'New Forms of the Tort of Breach of Statutory Duty' (2004) 120 LQR 324.

Online Resources   www.oup.com/uk/qanda/

Go online for extra essay and problem questions, a glossary of key terms, online versions of all the answer plans and audio commentary on how selected ones were put together, and a range of podcasts which include advice on exam and coursework technique and advice for other assessment methods.

6 Product Liability

ARE YOU READY?

To answer questions on this topic, you need an understanding of the following:

- The general principles of negligence
- The meaning of strict liability
- The Consumer Protection Act 1987, and its relationship with the common law regarding consumer protection

KEY DEBATES

The Consumer Protection Act 1987 includes a 'development risks' defence. How significant might this defence be in relation to the rapid advance of technology? Should this defence be reconsidered?

QUESTION | 1

Ajay is a fruit and vegetable farmer who grows apples, some of which he processes into cider; others he supplies to local retailers. Jatinder purchases five bottles of Ajay's cider and 10 kilos of Ajay's apples from Gaston, a local retailer who has since gone out of business. Jatinder eats one of the apples, but becomes ill due to the presence of insecticide traces on the skin.

The bottles of cider all bear the warning that it has a very high alcohol content and that no more than two litres should be consumed in any period of 24 hours. Ajay is also aware that he has used an additive in the cider which possesses hallucinogenic qualities.

Jatinder arrives home for her evening meal. After the meal, a curry, Jatinder opens a bottle of cider, but as she does so, a plastic plug flies off the bottle top and part of the contents of the bottle splashes into the face of Suki, Jatinder's sister. Suki licks the cider and suffers from a delusion that she can walk on water. She then jumps into Jatinder's swimming pool and drowns. Jatinder consumes three litres of the cider as a means of coping with Suki's death. Subsequently she feels sick. It transpires that her sickness is due partly to a chemical reaction between the contents of the cider and traces of curry she had recently eaten, and partly due to excessive alcohol consumption. An article in the little-heard-of *Journal of Apple Science* has recently identified the possibility of a chemical reaction between certain varieties of curry and strong cider.

Advise Ajay of his potential liability, under the Consumer Protection Act 1987.

CAUTION

- You will need a good knowledge and understanding of the statute before attempting such a question in the exam. Make sure that you refer your examiner to the relevant sections and subsections of the Act to maximize your marks for this answer.

DIAGRAM ANSWER PLAN

Identify

Who is the producer for the purposes of the Consumer Protection Act 1987 (CPA 1987)?
How is fault established?
- Is the manufacturer the cause of the harm suffered?
- What is a defective product under the CPA 1987?
- What defences to liability are available?

Relevant law

Consumer Protection Act 1987, ss. [ss.] 1–6.
A v National Blood Authority [2001] 3 All ER 289.
Tesco Stores Ltd v Pollard [2006] EWCA Civ 393.
EC Commission v United Kingdom (Re the Product Liability Directive) (Case C-300/951) [1997] 3 CMLR 923.

Apply the law

CPA 1987, s. 1(2)(a). Ajay is the producer.
Is there a defect (s. 3 CPA 1987)?
Have the claimants been contributorily negligent (CPA 1987, s. 6(4) and Law Reform (Contributory Negligence) Act 1945)?

Conclude

Regarding the Apple, Ajay is likely to be held liable for Jatinder's illness.
Regarding the cider, Ajay may have a defence under s. 4(1)(e) CPA 1987.

Ajay should be advised that Jatinder and Suki's estate may have an action under **Part I of the Consumer Protection Act 1987 (CPA 1987)** which purports [1.] to create strict liability in respect of defective products that cause physical harm to the person or to property (**CPA 1987, s. 2(1)**). [2.] As a producer of a processed product (the cider) Ajay will be subject to the Act (**CPA 1987, s. 1(2)(a)**) and as the grower of the apples, he will also be a producer.

The **CPA 1987, s. 3(1)** provides that a product is defective if it is not as safe as persons generally are entitled to expect. In determining what persons generally are entitled to expect **s. 3(2)** requires the court to consider (a) the manner in which and the purposes for which the product has been marketed, (b) what might reasonably be expected to be done with the product, and (c) the time of supply. In [3.] *A v National Blood Authority* [2001] 3 All ER 289, Burton J drew a distinction between standard and non-standard products and held that the hepatitis-infected blood supplied by the defendants was non-standard as it differed from the norm that the producer intended for use by the public. In concluding that the blood was defective, Burton J dismissed the defendant's argument that the presence of the defect was unavoidable as this raised issues concerning the conduct of the producer. This might suggest that products containing an abnormal defect will always be regarded as non-standard and therefore defective. However, in *Tesco Stores Ltd v Pollard* [2006] **EWCA Civ 393** the defendants were not liable for injury suffered by a child who opened a 'child-proof' safety cap on a dishwasher detergent container as all the public could expect was that the cap would make it more difficult for a child to open the container, which purpose it did serve.

Here, the apple eaten by Jatinder is a natural product that is contaminated by traces of insecticide and is likely to be a non-standard product that is abnormally dangerous. Although Ajay probably intended such contamination to be eliminated before his apples were put into circulation, the public are likely to expect better, unlike the apparently low expectations of the safety cap in [4.] *Tesco v Pollard*, so it seems likely that Ajay will be liable for Jatinder's illness.

The bottles of cider would appear to raise different considerations, due to their intended target market. As it was an alcoholic drink prepared for human consumption, persons generally would expect it to be consumed only by those over the age of 18. Although Jatinder's age is not stated, it would be reasonable to assume that she is an adult as she appears to own her own house. However, the question remains whether the cider put into circulation by Ajay

[1.] If you are looking for extra marks, consider whether you have time to define strict liability when answering this question.

[2.] Remember that you are required to advise Ajay under the Consumer Protection Act 1987, therefore identify the issues by reference to the statute as you progress with your answer.

[3.] There are not many cases to use in this area, so make sure you incorporate the ones that are available.

[4.] Use the cases to assist your advice.

achieves the desired level of safety in the light of its alleged defects. [5.] The **CPA 1987, s. 3(2)(b)** allows the court to consider what can reasonably be expected to be done with the product, which may raise the issue of consumer misuse in light of the warning printed on the bottles of cider. A danger that is adequately warned against may cease to be a danger at all. In the present case, Jatinder has consumed three litres of the cider in a 24-hour period when the printed warning advises against consumption of more than two litres. This might make it difficult for Jatinder to establish the causal link between the alleged defect in the cider and the harm she has suffered. A court might be persuaded that Jatinder's failure to heed the warning is the cause of the harm she has suffered. Alternatively, it is also clear from the [6.] **CPA 1987, s. 6(4)** that the defence of contributory negligence provided for in the **Law Reform (Contributory Negligence) Act 1945** will apply to an action in respect of a defective product, so that the claimant's damages may be reduced in accordance with her degree of blameworthiness.

The death of Suki raises different considerations if it can be assumed that the cider is a standard product since Ajay is aware of the hallucinogenic qualities of the additive he has used. There is no warning about this danger and Suki has not deliberately consumed the cider with a view to experiencing its hallucinogenic effects, so the question is, what would persons generally expect in terms of safety of a cider possessing these qualities? The cider has been marketed as a product intended for human consumption and if such a small amount as a splash on the lips is capable of producing such extreme consequences as the delusion from which Suki suffers, this might suggest that the cider has fallen below the standard of safety that might generally be expected. [7.] However, Jatinder has also consumed a much larger quantity of cider than did Suki without suffering the same consequences, which may suggest something unusual about Suki. In this last event, a court might be able to conclude that the cider is not unsafe in the light of general expectations. Conversely, if the effect upon Suki is one that is likely to be repeated in other consumers, it would seem to follow that the cider is not as safe as persons generally are entitled to expect. In this case, perhaps the only means of rendering the product safe will be to have it withdrawn from the market altogether.

Jatinder suffers as a result of a chemical reaction between strong cider and curry but this phenomenon is little known to the scientific world. The **CPA 1987** provides for a development risks defence under **s. 4(1)(e)** so that a producer can avoid liability where the state of scientific and technological knowledge was not such that a producer of products of the same description as the product in question might be expected to have discovered if the defect had existed in his products

---

5. Keep referring back to the statute and ensure you cover every salient point.

6. As with all areas of tort law ensure that you consider the availability of defences.

7. You may wish to address the issue of the eggshell-skull rule at this point and how that operates alongside the CPA.

[8.] A sophisticated answer will consider how the Consumer Protection Act 1987 differs in its wording from the European Product Liability Directive (Dir. 85/374/EEC), and whether this has any effect of consumers.

while they were under his control. [8.] This complex wording differs from that used in the **European Product Liability Directive (Dir. 85/374/EEC)**, which asks simply: What was the state of scientific and technical knowledge at the time the product was put into circulation? **Section 4(1)(e)** appears to import a subjective test based on factors relevant to the producer, whereas the **Product Liability Directive** sets an objective test of knowledge. The alleged difference was considered by the European Court of Justice in *EC Commission v United Kingdom (Re the Product Liability Directive)* (Case C-300/951) [1997] 3 CMLR 923 but it was held that s. 4(1)(e) did not set a subjective standard, as at the time there was no evidence that UK courts were misinterpreting the defence. In *A v National Blood Authority* [2001] 3 All ER 289, Burton J considered the position under **Art. 7(e)** of the **Directive (CPA 1987, s. 4(1)(e))** to be that the state of scientific knowledge is the most advanced available to anyone, although this does require an enquiry into what is discoverable evidence. **Article 7** is not concerned with the conduct of the individual producer, but is concerned with the expected conduct of producers, generally, in the light of what was objectively discoverable, but this does not require consideration of standard industry practice. The relevant question, therefore, appears to be whether Ajay should have taken account of the article published in the *Journal of Apple Science*. If the article was published after the cider was put into circulation by Ajay, this will raise an issue of defectiveness, since the **CPA 1987, s. 3(2)(c)** directs the court to consider the time when a product was put into circulation in determining whether it is defective and if that was before the date on which the article was published there is a presumption that the product is not defective, unless the claimant can prove otherwise: *Piper v JRI Manufacturing Ltd* [2007] EWCA Civ 1344.

If the relevant copy of the *Journal of Apple Science* was in existence before the cider was put into circulation the question is whether this is information Ajay should have had regard to before marketing his cider.

[9.] As the Consumer Protection Act 1987 has its base in EU law, it is appropriate to consider EU cases if they assist you answering the question.

[9.] In *EC Commission v United Kingdom (Re the Product Liability Directive)*, Tessauro A-G gave the example of a piece of scientific evidence published in Chinese in a Manchurian scientific journal, compared with an article published in a major scientific publication widely available to the English-speaking world. While the latter would normally be objectively discoverable by a UK producer, the former might not. In the present case, it would be necessary to have regard to the obscurity of the relevant journal and whether other cider producers, generally, might have taken account of it, especially in light of the fact that there is only a possibility of the identified chemical reaction and that the reaction only occurs with some, but not all, varieties of curry.

LOOKING FOR EXTRA MARKS?

- A good answer will include the technical issues of the variations between the European Product Liability Directive (Dir. 85/374/EEC) and the wording of the CPA 1987. It is worthwhile consolidating your knowledge is this respect.

- This would also be a good place to explore academic commentary and incorporate this in your answer.

QUESTION | 2

Koffman Latrash plc manufacture a pharmaceutical product called 'Offenden' which is marketed as a cure for morning sickness suffered by pregnant women, subject to a warning that the drug should not be used by people who suffer from high blood pressure. Extensive trials have failed to reveal any other defect in the drug despite the fact that an article published in a New Zealand medical journal has established that the principal ingredient in 'Offenden' may be capable of causing severe foetal limb abnormalities in rats in 1 per cent of cases in which the drug is used.

Neelam, who knows herself to be pregnant, attends the surgery of Dr Vijay who recommends the use of 'Offenden'. Neelam has high blood pressure, a fact of which she is aware but which is not known to Dr Vijay since he failed to make appropriate enquiries.

Neelam suffers a heart attack in the course of giving birth to her son, Sanjay, but she survives. The heart attack is shown to have been caused by high blood pressure exacerbated by ingredients in 'Offenden'. Sanjay is born with shortened arms and severe sight defects. Two months after the birth of Sanjay, a major scientific journal establishes incontrovertibly that one of the ingredients in 'Offenden' is likely, in more than 50 per cent of cases of use, to cause sight defects in newborn children.

Advise Neelam and Sanjay under the laws of consumer protection.

CAUTION

- This question requires consideration of the liability of a pharmaceuticals manufacturer for injuries caused to the immediate consumer of a drug and the effect of such consumption on an unborn child. However, it also requires the candidate to incorporate other aspects of tort law. In order to master the question, you will need to display a wide knowledge of tort law.

DIAGRAM ANSWER PLAN

Identify	The use of common law: Is there a breach of duty to exercise reasonable care? Does the issue of a warning affect liability? Is the doctor in breach of a duty of care? Components required for successful litigations under the CPA 1987.

Relevant law	*Donoghue v Stevenson* [1932] AC 562. The Consumer Protection Act 1987. *A v National Blood Authority* [2001] 3 All ER 289. Congenital Disabilities (Civil Liability) Act 1976.

Apply the law	How might common law assist the claimants? If this does not work, consider the CPA 1987. Who is to be sued under the CPA? Does the CPA apply to the drug and, if so, is it defective? What defences are available? Consider the doctor's actions.

Conclude	The drug company may not be liable for Neelam's high blood pressure. In this respect, the doctor may have breached his duty of care. However, Koffman Latrash plc may be liable for the foetal abnormality suffered by Sanjay.

 ## SUGGESTED ANSWER

The Common Law Situation

As a consumer of the drug 'Offenden' Neelam is owed a duty of care by the manufacturer, Koffman Latrash plc, [1] under the narrow rule in ***Donoghue v Stevenson* [1932] AC 562**. This states that a manufacturer of products which he sells in such a form as to show that he intends them to reach the ultimate consumer in the form in which they left him, owes a duty to the consumer to take reasonable care.

On these facts, the drug suffers from a design defect, in which case the burden of proof on the claimant is difficult, but not impossible, to discharge.

[1] In this question you have been asked to advise in consumer protection law. This includes common law as well as the CPA 1987.

2. If you are advising in common law liability, use common law defences at this stage.

2. Koffman Latrash plc have warned that the drug should not be used by persons with high blood pressure. Warnings are an effective way of discharging the duty of care owed by a manufacturer: **Kubach v Hollands [1937] 3 All ER 907**. A warning may also raise a reasonable expectation that someone else, such as a doctor, will check that the instructions are complied with. For example, in **Holmes v Ashford [1950] 2 All ER 76** it was decided that a hairdresser is expected to patch test hair dye. Neelam is unlikely to succeed in an action against Koffman Latrash plc, since there is a specific warning against the use of 'Offenden' by patients with high blood pressure; but Dr Vijay may have failed to act as would a reasonable medical practitioner in making appropriate enquiries, having regard to the warning supplied with the product: 3. **Bolam v Friern Hospital Management Committee [1957] 2 All ER 118**, or on advising on any potential risks of the medication, and alternatives to it (**Montgomery v Lanarkshire Health Board [2015] UKSC 11**).

3. You may wish to spend longer discussing these important cases, but beware of spending too long on a specific area when there are a number of issues to consider in your answer.

Despite being unborn at the time damage was caused, Sanjay is owed a duty of care (**Burton v Islington Health Authority [1992] 3 All ER 833**).

Under **s. 1(1)** of the **Congenital Disabilities (Civil Liability) Act 1976**, if a child is born disabled as a result of an occurrence before its birth, and a person other than the child's mother is answerable for those disabilities, then the child may sue for the wrongful damage, but only if he or she is or would have been liable in tort to the parents had actionable damage been sustained (**1976 Act, s. 1(3)**). This may be problematic as the risk of sight defects using 'Offenden' is only discovered after the drug is put into circulation, so that there may not be a breach of duty (**Roe v Minister of Health [1954] QB 66**). A defendant can only be judged by information available at the time of the alleged negligent act, so Koffman Latrash may not be liable in this respect. 4. However, there is evidence to show that the drug has caused foetal abnormalities in rats. If this converts into a similar percentage risk in relation to human beings it may be evidence of negligence on the part of Koffman Latrash plc, if the information is reasonably available to the manufacturer. Since the relevant research is contained in an obscure journal, it may not amount to a failure to exercise reasonable care not to have been aware of it.

4. Proving a defect is not enough on its own; you need to highlight a causal link between the defect and the damage the product caused.

Consumer Protection Act 1987 (CPA 1987)

5. You may prefer to start your answer by reference to the CPA 1987.

5. Both Neelam and Sanjay may sue under the **CPA 1987**. The **CPA 1987** implements the **European Product Liability Directive**, the wording and interpretation of which prevails over the Act: **A v National Blood Authority [2001] 3 All ER 289**.

Koffman Latrash plc are producers of the drug by virtue of the **CPA 1987, s. 1(2)(a)**. Drugs, being substances which are not otherwise excluded from the scope of the Act, are products (**CPA 1987, s. 45(1)**), but the central issues are whether the drug is defective within the meaning of the **CPA 1987, s. 3** and if defectiveness is the cause of the harm suffered by the claimant, which must be proved by the claimant (*Foster v Biosil* **(2001) 59 BMLR 178**). It should be noted that in *O'Byrne v Aventis Pasteur SA* [2010] 1WLR 1412, it was held that the correct defendant to pursue was the distributor of the drug. However, on the facts before us, we are not informed of a separate distributor.

A product is 'defective' if it is not as safe as persons generally are entitled to expect (**CPA 1987, s. 3(1)**). In *A v National Blood Authority*, Burton J considered it relevant whether or not the harmful characteristic in the product caused the injury complained of, and whether the product was a standard or non-standard product.

6. It is important to consider this point in your answer.

6. A standard product is one that has been produced as intended by the producer, whereas a non-standard product is one that fails to reach the normal standard set by the producer. The drug 'Offenden' was produced as designed. This would classify it as a standard product. However, the nature of the design defect will need to be considered as it may cause the product to be unsafe, unless a defence can be pleaded.

What persons generally expect by way of safety must be considered according to how a product is marketed and any instructions or warnings as to its use. As children's bodies respond to medicines in different ways to adults, a product may be defective if supplied to children, regardless as to whether it would not be harmful to an adult (*A v National Blood Authority* **[2001] 3 All ER 289, at [22]**). 'Offenden' is targeted at pregnant women, but it will also be relevant that the drug is likely to be available only on prescription and under the supervision of a qualified medical practitioner, which is relevant as the **CPA 1987, s. 3(2)(b)** allows the court to consider what can reasonably be expected to be done with the product. If the producer can expect supervision by a medical practitioner, taken in conjunction with the warning that the drug should not be used by those suffering from high blood pressure, it may be argued that the drug is not defective, insofar as it has resulted in Neelam suffering a heart attack. Under the **CPA 1987, s. 3(2)(c)** regard should be had to the time at which the product was put into circulation, but the facts tell us that the defects in 'Offenden' existed at the time the product was put into circulation. However, this is not the case for Sanjay, as the only evidence that 'Offenden' may cause foetal abnormality is to be found in an 'obscure' scientific journal article. If the defect did not exist in the product at the time of supply then the manufacturers have a defence (*Piper v JRI (Manufacturing) Ltd* [2006] EWCA Civ 1344).

7. Keep referring back to the facts of the scenario throughout your answer.

7. Although there is incontrovertible scientific evidence regarding sight defects, this comes to light two months after 'Offenden' is first put into circulation, so that the drug will not be defective in relation to Sanjay's vision. However, Koffman Latrash plc may be liable for the foetal abnormality which results in Sanjay's shortened arms, as the facts suggest that the producer may have been aware at the time of supply of the potential for the drug to cause this type of harm.

Although the **CPA 1987** is said to impose strict liability, it also provides a development risks defence in **s. 4(1)(e)**, which gives a defence where the state of scientific and technical knowledge was not such that a producer of products of the same description as the product in question might be expected to have discovered if the defect had existed in his products while they were under his control. The wording of **s. 4(1)(e)** appears to import subjective factors relevant to the individual producer and differs from the purely objective wording of the **Product Liability Directive, Art. 7(e)**. However, the European Court of Justice has ruled in *EC Commission v United Kingdom (Re the Product Liability Directive)* **(Case C-300/951) [1997] 3 CMLR 923** that there is nothing wrong in the wording used in the **CPA 1987**. In *A v National Blood Authority* **[2001] 3 All ER 289**, Burton J thought that the relevant state of knowledge is the most advanced available to anyone, not just the defendants, although this does require an enquiry into what is discoverable evidence. In determining what is objectively discoverable, Burton J considered that standard industry practice could be discounted. [8.] The relevant question, therefore, appears to be whether Koffman Latrash plc have failed to take the necessary precautions to guard against the defectiveness of their product by not considering the article published in the New Zealand medical journal. It would therefore be necessary to consider the obscurity of the relevant journal and whether other drug producers, generally, might have taken account of it, especially in light of the fact that the article is less than conclusive on the matter of foetal limb abnormalities in human beings. [9.] Possibly, it might be a piece of evidence that, objectively, Koffman Latrash plc could have chosen not to consider.

[8.] If you are looking for extra marks, consider every aspect of the question. Have you read through the facts carefully and have you addressed them all?

[9.] You may wish to consider whether you could write a more dynamic conclusion to this answer.

LOOKING FOR EXTRA MARKS?

- A good answer will show diversity by tackling both common law as well as the statute law in this scenario. Make sure that you are prepared to answer a question using all the law in this area.

- If you have time, you may wish to explore the issue of medical negligence in a little more detail, but do not lose focus on what the central requirements of the question are.

TAKING THINGS FURTHER

- Howells, G. et al., *Product Liability*, 3rd edn (Butterworths, 2011).
- Howells, G., and Mildred, M., 'Infected Blood: Defect and Discoverability: A First Exposition of the EC Product Liability Directive' (2002) 65 MLR 95.
  This looks at the effect of **A v National Blood Authority [2001] 3 All ER 289**.
- Newdick, C., 'The Development Risks Defence and the Consumer Protection Act 1987' (1988) 47 CLJ 455.
- Newdick, C., 'The Future of the Development Risks Defence—The Role of Negligence in Product Liability Actions' (1987) 103 LQR 288.
- Tettenborn, A., 'Components and Product Liability: Damage to "Other Property"' [2000] LMCLQ 338.
  This considers the overlap of product liability with the law on economic loss where tort liability for damage to property is excluded if property merely damages part of itself.

Online Resources   www.oup.com/uk/qanda/

Go online for extra essay and problem questions, a glossary of key terms, online versions of all the answer plans and audio commentary on how selected ones were put together, and a range of podcasts which include advice on exam and coursework technique and advice for other assessment methods.

Occupiers' Liability

7

ARE YOU READY?

In order to answer questions on this topic, you need an understanding of the following:

- Occupiers' Liability Act 1957 (OLA 19 [1957] 57)
- Occupiers' Liability Act 1984 (OLA 19 [1984] 84)
- The 'control test'—how 'occupiers' have been identified by the courts
- The difference between a 'visitor' and a 'non-visitor', and the legal differences that arise
- How the courts have interpreted 'reasonable care'
- The concept of 'breach of duty' and 'causation' in negligence
- Excluding or restricting negligence liability under s. 65 Consumer Rights Act 2015
- General defences in tort law

 ## KEY DEBATES

The 2018 'You vs. Train' campaign by the British Transport Police was put into action as a response to the increasing number of deaths occurring as a result of children taking 'selfies' whilst trespassing on railway lines. The research behind this campaign highlights the lack of awareness of the obvious danger involved in this activity.

Current law provides greater protection for 'visitors' as opposed to 'trespassers'. Sometimes a child trespasser will be treated as a visitor, even though they have clearly trespassed. Should occupiers be responsible for every danger that might occur to children on their land? How much should an occupier do to discharge their duty of care? Should an occupier be held liable, even if the risks of an activity appear obvious?

Pleasureland Ltd own and operate Thrill Towers, an entertainment park. At the entrance to the park there is a prominent notice that 'Pleasureland Ltd and Kidikicks Ltd can accept no liability for any injury suffered'. One of the attractions, the 'Serpent', has been leased from Pleasureland Ltd by Kidikicks Ltd; the lease provides for Kidikicks to maintain the ride. The Serpent is a frightening car ride which for part of its route travels underground. At the entrance to the Serpent ride there is a notice which states:

> All possible precautions are taken in the interests of safety. This tunnel for this ride has a low ceiling.
>
> People taller than 6 feet 3 inches are not permitted on this ride.

Adam, aged 21, is 6 feet 4 inches tall but decides that this cannot matter and bends his knees as he passes under the height-checking device provided by Kidikicks Ltd. During the ride, the Serpent dips sharply into an underground cavern and Adam, who is sitting high up in his seat, suffers a blow to the head from a low light used in emergencies which has come free from its support. Sitting behind Adam is Bronwen who is also struck by the light; she is 5 feet 3 inches tall. The light has recently been maintained by Sparky, an independent contractor. Both Adam and Bronwen are seriously injured.

Advise on the potential liability of Pleasureland Ltd and Kidikicks Ltd under the Occupiers' Liability Acts.

CAUTION

- This question clearly states, 'advise under the Occupiers' Liability Acts'; therefore you should not discuss the tort of negligence when answering this question.
- It is usual for an examiner to test you on both the Occupiers' Liability Act 1957 and the Occupiers' Liability Act 1984. It is important to consider this when planning your answer.

DIAGRAM ANSWER PLAN

Identify	Who is the occupier? (There is often more than one.) Has the accident happened on 'premises'? Is the claimant a 'visitor' or 'trespasser'?
Relevant law	Occupiers' Liability Acts 1957 and 1984. Consumer Rights Act 2015. *Wheat v Lacon Ltd* [1966] AC 552. *Tomlinson v Congleton Borough Council* [2003] UKHL 47.
Apply the law	Use OLA 1957 for the claimants and consider the common duty of care. Additionally use OLA 1984 for Adam. Can he prove that the three-point test is satisfied? Consider whether the occupier has taken 'reasonable care'. What is the effect of the Consumer Rights Act 2015 on the exclusion notice?
Conclude	Pleasureland Ltd and Kidikicks Ltd are likely to be occupiers. Kidikicks may have discharged its duty if the company has selected a qualified independent contractor to undertake the maintenance.

SUGGESTED ANSWER

[1.] The first time you mention a statute, write out its name in full. Then you can abbreviate it, but make sure that you specify the year of the Act.

[2.] A good answer focuses on advising the relevant parties rather than just discussing the law in this area.

[3.] Always refer your answer back to the facts of the question. This shows that you are reading the question that has been set, rather than writing out a memorized script.

The duty under the [1.]**Occupiers' Liability Act 1957** (OLA 1957) **and the Occupiers' Liability Act 1984** (OLA 1984) is placed on the 'occupier' of the 'premises' where the injuries happened. Therefore [2.]when assessing potential liability of Pleasureland Ltd and Kidikicks Ltd in occupiers' liability, it is important to establish which company is the 'occupier' of the 'premises' concerned.

There is no definition of 'premises' contained in the statute, although s. 1(3)(a) OLA 1957 refers to any 'fixed or moveable structure'. Consequently, the common law has a broad approach to this. Premises have included a lift (*Haseldine v Daw*), a ladder (*Wheeler v Copas*), and a bowling alley (*D v AMF Bowling*). Therefore, it will easy to establish that the scene of the accidents, namely [3.]the Serpent, will be considered 'premises' for the purpose of the Act.

Having identified that the injuries occurred on the 'Serpent', it is now possible to establish which company is the 'occupier' and therefore bears the potential liability for the accidents.

Section 1(2) OLA 1957 does not define who an occupier is, but states that it is someone 'who would at common law be treated as an occupier'. According to *Wheat v Lacon Ltd* **[1966] AC 552** an occupier is someone with a 'sufficient degree of control' of that part of the premises on which the accident occurs. A person does not have to be in actual occupation of the premises to be considered an occupier (*Harris v Birkenhead Corporation*). There may also be more than one occupier (*Stone v Taffe*).

Here, there appear to be have two occupiers, Kidikicks and Pleasureland, as both have a 'sufficient degree of control' over the premises. However, any liability for the light would depend on who had overall responsibility for it. As the facts state that the [4.]'lease provides for Kidikicks to maintain the ride', liability might fall on Kidikicks.

[4.] Select important facts mentioned, and address them. Remember that you are being assessed on your application of the law to the facts.

For the purposes of the **OLA 1957**, the common duty of care is owed to any person who would have been treated as an invitee or a licensee at common law (**s. 1(2)**). This includes contractual visitors such as Adam and Bronwen, assuming they have paid to enter Thrill Towers.

As regards Adam and Kidikicks, the position is more complex, since, as he is taller than the specified height limit, Adam may be a trespasser. If this is the case the only duty owed to him will arise under the **OLA 1984**.

In *Tomlinson v Congleton Borough Council* **[2003] UKHL 47** the claimant was treated as a trespasser from the time he ran into the water with a view to diving. In *Keown v Coventry Healthcare NHS Trust* **[2006] EWCA Civ 39** an 11-year-old who climbed a fire escape on the underside was a trespasser on the basis of the dictum of Scrutton LJ in *The Carlgarth* **[1927] P 93, 110** that: 'When you invite a person into your house to use the staircase, you do not invite him to slide down the banisters.' (See also *Geary v JD Wetherspoon Plc* **[2011] EWHC 1506**, decided on facts remarkably similar to Scrutton LJ's example.)

If either Act is to apply, the danger complained of must arise from some type of a defect in the premises. Further, the state of the premises must present a foreseeable risk, *W Sussex CC v Pierce* **[2013] EWHC 2030**. In *Tomlinson* a muddy lake with shallow water and variable depth was not defective as it was typical of other lakes, but in *Rhind v Astbury Water Park* **[2004] EWCA Civ 756** a lake with a hard object buried in the silt was unusual and so defective.

[5.] The law in the area is fascinating, but remember you are discussing it to advise your client.

[5.] Applying this to our situation, the light fitting hanging down is clearly a defect in the state of the premises and gives rise to a danger, since it hits both both Bronwen and Adam.

Assuming Bronwen and Adam are visitors, the **OLA 1957** will apply and the duty will be the same whether they would have been invitees or licensees at common law. **Section 2(2)** requires the occupier 'to take such care as in all the circumstances of the case is reasonable to see that the visitor is reasonably safe in using the premises for the purposes for which he is invited or permitted by the occupier to be there'. [6.]The test for determining whether there has been a breach of that duty is the same as at common law, taking account of the degree of risk and the cost of taking precautions.

Kidikicks may be able to argue that they have discharged their duty of care by using an independent contractor to do the work within **s. 2(4)(b) OLA 1957**. They will have to show that they had acted reasonably in their choice of contractor and had checked that the work had been properly done. The facts say little about the competence of Sparky, but although electrical fittings require technical knowledge (*Haseldine v Daw*), a dangling light fitting may be considered something that the occupiers should have checked up on themselves (*Woodward v Mayor of Hastings*). If **s. 2(4)** has been satisfied then Kidikicks will have performed their duty and [7.]no liability on their part will arise.

Any potential liability of Sparky would be considered under negligence principles. It might be argued that by entering the ride, when he has exceeded the height limit, Adam has consented to the risk of injury under the **OLA 1957, s. 2(5)**. However, all Adam is aware of is a low ceiling, and he is injured by a low-hanging light fitting, so it is unlikely that he will be taken to have consented to that risk.

Kidikicks Ltd may argue that the warning notice at the entrance to the ride discharges their duty under the Act. However, **s. 2(4)(a)** requires a warning to enable a visitor to be reasonably safe taking account of all the circumstances of the case. [8.]In *Roles v Nathan* **[1963] 2 All ER 908**, two industrial chimney sweeps died after ignoring a warning that they should not work on certain boiler flues if the fire in the boiler was lit. The warning was held to have discharged the occupier's duty of care. By comparison, Kidikicks' warning does not indicate how a user of the ride can remain safe, so that it is unlikely to discharge the duty.

Kidikicks may be able to rely on the defence of contributory negligence: **OLA 1957, s. 2(3)**. This allows a court to consider 'the degree of care, and want of care, which would ordinarily be looked for in such a visitor'. Adam, as an adult, may have failed to take reasonable care for his own safety, so that any damages awarded may be reduced under the provisions of the **Law Reform (Contributory Negligence) Act 1945**. The defence will operate to reduce his damages only if the injury was due to, or was made worse by, his being too tall for the ride. However, as Bronwen, who is only 5 feet 3 inches tall, was also injured by the low-hanging light, it appears that Adam's height is not the cause of the problem.

If Adam is treated as a trespasser, he is a non-visitor, and therefore **OLA 1984** must be considered. This Act requires the non-visitor to establish that a duty is owed. Under **s. 1(3)** three conditions must be satisfied, namely that (i) the occupier knows or has reasonable grounds to believe that the danger exists, (ii) the occupier knows or has reasonable grounds to believe that the non-visitor is or will come into the vicinity of the danger, and (iii) the risk is one against which in all the circumstances it is reasonable to offer the other person some protection. Arguably, in respect of a simple maintenance matter, the occupier ought to have been aware of this danger.

Exclusion notices are permitted by the **OLA 1957** in relation to visitors, subject to **s. 65(1) Consumer Rights Act 2015** which specifies that a 'trader cannot by a term of a consumer contract or by a consumer notice exclude or restrict liability for death or personal injury resulting from negligence'; and further, under s. 65(2) that 'a person is not to be taken to have voluntarily accepted any risk merely because the person agreed to or knew about the term or notice'. In this respect, the warning notices at the entrance will not prohibit Bronwen and Adam from being successful with their claims.

[9.] Conclude by referring back to the question. Who were you asked to advise? What is your opinion of their situation? A strong conclusion leaves a favourable impression on your examiner.

[9.] In conclusion, in assessing overall liability, both Pleasureland Ltd and Kidikicks Ltd are 'controllers', although the facts indicate that Kidikicks has a greater degree of control on a day-to-day basis. A further consideration is whether Kidikicks has discharged its duty by carefully selecting an independent contractor to undertake the maintenance. If this is the case, the claimants may pursue a claim against Sparky, therefore releasing both Pleasureland and Kidikicks from any potential liability.

LOOKING FOR EXTRA MARKS?

■ Occupiers' liability problem questions tend to be rather lengthy, and it is easy to miss important information. Before starting your answer, you should ensure that you have identified all the key issues that the question sets you.

■ Issues of causation and remoteness of damage are likely to occur in these problem scenarios. If you have planned your time well, you may briefly address these points in your answer.

QUESTION | 2

Stepford College is managed by Mr Alldred the principal, under the governance of Westbrook County Council. The college grounds include a leisure complex comprising a gymnasium, a small theatre, and a swimming pool. Mr Alldred asks the council for permission to let out these facilities to outside organizations to raise money for the college, but he is told that this is not possible at present, as the college's insurance does not cover them for any liabilities that might thus arise.

Despite this Alldred agrees to let the theatre for one week to Empire Opera Company, an amateur operatic society, for their production of *The Mikado*. As he is aware of the insurance problem, Alldred posts a notice by the theatre doors, stating: 'The college accepts no responsibility for any injuries that may happen to any persons using this theatre.'

Alldred is also aware that theatre may be unsafe, as the aisles in the stalls have several steps which are neither illuminated nor marked in any way. He pays two students, Crazed and Dumbo, to put white tape on the edge of the steps. The students take his money but do not bother to do the job. Alldred does not check to see the work has been completed.

During a performance of the show, Bazza, who is helping out in the box office, receives an urgent message from a member of the audience. He creeps into the auditorium and down an aisle to locate the audience member in question. As the theatre is in darkness, except for the lights on the stage, he is walking very carefully, when he trips over one of the unmarked steps, falls, and breaks his arm.

During the interval of the show Ethan, aged 25 and who is rather bored by the production, goes to explore the leisure complex. He finds the swimming pool, which is very dimly lit and obviously closed. Although the doors are locked, he sees that there is a large window open and he easily climbs through it to gain access to the pool. He decides to go for a swim, so he underdresses and goes towards the end of the pool with the diving board, assuming it to be deep end. He dives in head first. Unfortunately the pool has been completely drained for cleaning and Ethan breaks his neck when he hits his head on the concrete floor.

Meanwhile Fay, aged seven, whose parents are both in the show, has been left by herself in the auditorium. Getting bored, she leaves the theatre and walks through some open doors into the gymnasium. This contains several items of portable weight-training equipment in one corner. There is a large sign near the equipment which says 'Caution: Misuse of this equipment can lead to serious injuries. Do not use unless you have been properly trained.' Fay attempts to lift a 16 kg kettle weight and is injured when she pulls a muscle in her back.

Advise Bazza, Ethan, and Fay of their rights, if any, in the law of occupiers' liability.

! CAUTION

- As with the previous question, make sure that you read the facts carefully before you start your answer.
- There are three different claimants, therefore you should anticipate three different answers, though there will be some overlap in your advice.

DIAGRAM ANSWER PLAN

Identify

Who is the occupier? (There is often more than one.)
What are considered to be premises in this scenario?
Is the claimant a 'visitor' or 'trespasser'?
Are there any defences?

Relevant law

Occupiers Liability Acts 1957 and 1984.
Consumer Rights Act 2015.
Wheat v Lacon Ltd [1966] AC 552.
Tomlinson v Congleton Borough Council [2003] UKHL 47.

Apply the law

Use OLA 1957 for Bazza. Has the common duty of care been discharged?
Ethan will need to be advised under OLA 1984. Can he prove that the three-point test is satisified?
Consider whether the occupier has taken 'reasonable care'.
Although Fay is technically a trespasser, might she been considered under OLA 1957?

Conclude

Alldred will be the occupier. The County Council may also be considered occupiers.
Bazza is likely to be successful in his claim, under OLA 1957.
Applying OLA 1984, Ethan is unlikely to be awarded damages.
Fay may have a claim, but her parents' actions may prevent a successful action.

SUGGESTED ANSWER

A 'night at the opera' has left Bazza, Fay, and Ethan suffering a variety of personal injuries. Consequently, we are asked to advise the various parties as to their rights in the law of occupiers' liability. The law in this area is predominantly defined by statute: the **Occupiers' Liability Act 1957** (OLA 1957) which deals with 'visitors' and includes claims for property as well as physical damage, and the **Occupiers' Liability Act 1984** (OLA 1984), which is confined to liability for 'trespassers'.

[1.] An essential step in the parties' claims will be to establish who the 'occupier' was. OLA 1957 s. 1(2) stipulates that an occupier under the Act is 'the same as the persons who would at common law be treated as an occupier'. We must therefore turn our attention to the common law. According to *Wheat v E Lacon & Co Ltd* [1966] AC 552,

[1.] Remember to start with the statute law in the area before moving on to case law.

to assess if someone is an 'occupier' one has to determine if he or she has 'a sufficient degree of control' over the premises. A person does not have to be in actual occupation of the premises to be considered an occupier (*Harris v Birkenhead Corporation* [1976] 1 WLR 279). There may also be more than one occupier (*Stone v Taffe* [1974] 3 All ER 1016). [2.]Referring back to our claimants, it seems then that we have two occupiers, Mr Alldred and also Westbrook County Council, as both have 'a sufficient degree of control' over the Stepford College.

2. If you are looking for extra marks, you may wish to discuss the legal relationship of the two occupiers.

For the claims to be assessed under the terms in OLA 1957, it is important to ascertain whether our claimants satisfy the criteria of 'visitor'. The definition in the statute is vague—under s. 1(2), visitors are those who 'would at common law be treated as . . . invitees or licensees'; in other words they have express or implied permission to be there. Initially, it appears that all claimants had express permission to enter the college theatre. It does not matter that their presence was strictly prohibited by the council, if the claimants, themselves, do not realize this (*Stone v Taffe*).

For the claim to be successful, it needs to be established that the injuries happened on 'premises'. There is no explicit definition of 'premises' contained in the statute, although s. 1(3)(a) refers to any 'fixed or moveable structure'. Consequently, the common law has a broad approach to this. Premises have included a lift (*Haseldine v Daw*), a ladder (*Wheeler v Copas*), and a bowling alley (*D v AMF Bowling*). [3.]Therefore, it will easy to establish that the scenes of the accidents—namely the stairs, the swimming pool, and the gym—are 'premises' for the purpose of the Act.

3. Try to match the facts of the question with identified case law.

Bazza

It is of no surprise to find that there are a number of cases involving falls down unlit stairs, and the case law turns on the individual facts. In *Stone v Taffe*, the court found for the claimant, but in *Wheat v Lacon*, it was held there was not sufficient evidence regarding the nature of the fall to prove liability [4.]In *Capitano v Leeds Eastern Health Authority* [1989] CLT 3522, a security guard was unsuccessful in his claim, being told that a torch was sufficient illumination by which to descend an unlit flight of metal stairs. Consequently, the provision of the torch was sufficient to discharge the duty of care. It would be worth establishing if a torch was available at the theatre.

4. There is an abundance of case law in this area. If you can find a more obscure case to mention, it will make your answer more colourful.

We are not told of the condition of the stairs. It might be that they are unusually slippery, or uneven. Section 2(2) of OLA 1957 defines the common duty of care. It should be noted that it is the visitor, rather than the premises, that must be reasonably safe. The occupier does not need to have created the danger in order to be liable. (In *Ward v Tesco Stores Ltd* [1976] 1 WLR 810, the company were found liable in negligence for not attending to a yoghurt spillage, of unknown origin, promptly.) It is possible that during the production, the steps may have become slippery due to the theatre production itself. This will not affect a potential claim, as it is the state of the premises rather than the activity that needs to be safe under the Act.

Bazza is a visitor to the box office, and it could be argued that when he leaves the box office he is no longer a visitor. However, as his mission is 'theatre business', it is likely that this argument would be dismissed. [5.] Could Bazza be contributorily negligent as he has embarked on an errand? Following *Brioland Ltd v Mary Searson* [2005] EWCA Civ 55, it could be said that even if Bazza was not fully concentrating on the steps, but on locating someone, it does not excuse the occupier for defective premises.

It may bode well for Bazza that Alldred has acknowledged that the premises were dangerous by employing Crazed and Dumbo to put white tape along the edge of the steps. As this is an unskilled job, as opposed to one requiring technical knowledge (*Haseldine v Daw* [1941] 2 KB 343), it will be no excuse for Alldred not to check that the work was done. As Parcq LJ stated in *Woodward v Mayor of Hastings*: [6.] 'The craft of the charwoman may have its mysteries, but there is no esoteric quality in the nature of the work which the cleaning of a snow-covered step demands.'

It may be possible for Bazza to be successful in his action.

Ethan

Although this person was given initial permission to enter the college, the situation has since changed.

Initial permission can be limited in three ways. The occupier may permit the visitor to only enter certain parts of the building (*Gould v McAuliffe* [1941] 2 All ER 527). Permission can also be limited to certain length of time, or for a particular purpose (*Hillen and Pettigrew v ICI (Alkaki) Ltd* [1936] AC 65).

Ethan, a 'victim of macho male diving syndrome' (*Tomlinson v Congleton Borough Council* [2003] 3 WLR 705), has blatantly strayed beyond his permitted boundary. [7.] Not so much a 'slide down the bannisters' (*The Calgarth* [1927] P 93 Coram) as a dive in the (empty) pool. Consequently, he will not meet the criteria of OLA 1957. Instead we need to turn our attention to the Occupiers' Liability Act of 1984.

[8.] Under s. 1(3)(a) of this Act, the occupier must be aware of the danger or have reasonable grounds to believe it exists. In *Rhind v Astbury Water Park Ltd*, the action failed as the claimant could not prove that the danger was visible. Here, the danger—an unfilled swimming pool—is clearly visible, and consequently within the occupier's knowledge.

Under s. 1(3)(b), however, the occupier must expect the trespasser to 'come into the vicinity'. The doors have been locked, and the only

---

[5.] Look for any possible defences that may arise.

[6.] Weaving in case quotes helps to bring your answer alive. You examiner will enjoy reading relevant quotes.

[7.] There are several recent cases which incorporate this famous phrase; you may like to consider using them alongside the original.

[8.] All aspects of the three-part test in OLA 1984 must be met if the claimant is to be successful.

method of entry to the pool area is through a window. In *Ratcliffe v McConnell*, the claimant failed, but not by reason of his unorthodox entry. Even the lack of a warning sign did not assist him. Their Lordships were of the opinion that the defendants were not under any duty to warn of the risk of diving into shallow water as this was 'a risk of which any adult would be aware' *per* Stuart-Smith LJ.

[9.] This was confirmed in *Tomlinson v Congleton Borough Council*, indicating that Ethan, one of approximately twenty-five 25-year-olds who break their necks each year in similar circumstances, will have very little chance of establishing Alldred's liability for his accident.

[9.] It is worth looking at the law in context in this area. This helps to make the statute and case law, that you have so carefully studied, relevant to everyday actions.

Fay

Fay has a more optimistic prospect. Although she has left her permitted area, and appears to be a trespasser, as she is a minor she may be afforded protection under OLA 1957 s. 2(3)(a), by virtue of the fact that children are 'less careful'. Under the common law, if there is an 'allurement' on the premises (*Glasgow Corporation v Taylor*), there will be a good cause of action. [10.] Lifting gym equipment, not dissimilar to raising abandoned boats (*Jolley v Sutton Borough Council* [2000] 1 WLR 1082), would certainly be considered a foreseeable of risk, with regards to children.

[10.] Discuss OLA 1984, but also look at current law in relation to children.

In tandem with this, to a certain extent the Act allows an occupier to limit his liability to visitors. However, **s. 65(2) Consumer Rights Act 2015** specifies that: 'a person is not to be taken to have voluntarily accepted any risk merely because the person agreed to or knew about the term or notice.' A locked door would have been a more suitable solution in these circumstances.

However, a potential problem for Fay is that the courts will expect parents to take responsibility for their children (*Phipps v Rochester Corporation* [1955] 1 QB 450, and more recently in *Bourne Leisure v Marsden* [2009] EWCA Civ 671). Despite Fay being older then the children in these cases, parental supervision has clearly not been sufficient, and this may jeopardize Fay's claim.

LOOKING FOR EXTRA MARKS?

■ There is an abundance of case law in this area, but do not forget to focus on the essential House of Lords/Supreme Court decisions.

■ You may wish to spend more time writing about the legal relationship of the two occupiers, and why, in an insurance-related way, it will be important to tie in the County Council.

■ Consider the relationship of the law in this area and children. There is an interesting overlap between the Acts and case law here. A sophisticated answer will spend some time considering this.

Multimillion plc own a building and contract with Shambles Ltd to demolish it. Shambles Ltd are responsible for the security of the site and they leave it unattended on Sundays when work is not in progress. The site is protected by a perimeter fence topped with razor wire.

During working hours, Sven, an electrician from another company, has been called to the site to repair a defective generator. He is told by a security guard that he must report to the site office in order to be provided with protective headgear to guard against any risks present on the demolition site, especially the possibility of debris falling from overhead operations which are in progress.

Sven sees the defective generator and decides to make a preliminary inspection before reporting to the site office. As he approaches the generator, Sven stumbles over a drainage pipe left on the ground and as he limps to the site office he is struck by a brick which falls off a wall.

As a result of these incidents Sven suffers head and leg injuries. A few days after the event, Shambles Ltd put up a notice near the site office which states clearly that visitors should keep their eyes on the ground to avoid tripping over articles left temporarily on the site.

On Sunday, Fabio, aged 20, decides to enter the site to take scrap metal to exchange for cash. He climbs over the tall fence but falls off because the top strand of wire is loose, and breaks an arm. As he tries to recover a handful of brass fittings, he slips into a deep trench and is injured.

Advise Multimillion plc and Shambles Ltd as to their potential liability under the OLA 1957 and the OLA 1984.

CAUTION

- In an examination, there is often the temptation to use a short version of each of the sections of the Acts. Concentrate on expressing the key elements of the sections, whilst writing your answer. For example, in **s. 2(4)(a)** the warning must be sufficient to enable the visitor to be *reasonably safe*, not to be *safe*. There is a significant legal difference here.
- Answers should contain reference to those cases which address broad issues of principle.

DIAGRAM ANSWER PLAN

Identify

Who is the occupier? (There is often more than one.)
What are considered to be premises in this scenario?
What duty is owed and to whom?
Are there any defences?

Relevant law

Occupiers Liability Acts 1957 and 1984.
Wheat v Lacon Ltd [1966] AC 552.
Tomlinson v Congleton Borough Council [2003] UKHL 47.

Apply the law

Consider whether the occupier is able to discharge (perform) their duty by using an independent contractor.
Does Sven meet the requirements to be advised under OLA 1957? If so, has the common duty of care been discharged?
Fabio is a non-visitor so will need to be advised under OLA 1984.
Can he prove that the three-point test is satisfied?

Conclude

Multimillion plc and Shambles Ltd are both occupiers.
Fabio is clearly a non-visitor.
Sven's position as visitor is in doubt.
Both claimants may be contributorily negligent.

SUGGESTED ANSWER

1. This question centres on the liability of contactors and whether their actions have been sufficient to avoid liability.

Both the **OLA 1957** and the **OLA 1984** deal with harm arising from dangers due to the state of the premises rather than activities on the premises: see *Fairchild v Glenhaven Funeral Services Ltd* [2002] **UKHL 22.** [1] Under the 1957 Act an occupier who employs a subcontractor will only be liable for damage caused by the contractor if it affects the state of the premises.

Both the **OLA 1957** and the **OLA 1984** require a danger arising from 'the state of the premises', which was said to signify something unusual and dangerous for that type of premises in *Tomlinson v Congleton Borough Council* [2003] **UKHL 47** with the result that it was held that no such risk was posed by a lake if it was just like any other lake, that is shallow at the margin with muddy water and uneven depth. But if the lake possesses some unusual feature it may pose such a risk: *Rhind v Astbury Water Park* [2004] **EWCA Civ 756**. Here, a building site could be regarded as no different to any other building site with no additional risks, but the fence had a loose strand of wire which suggests that it is defective and this could pose additional risk.

Under the **OLA 1957** a duty is automatically owed by an occupier to visitors, but under the **OLA 1984** the duty may be owed to non-visitors only provided certain preconditions are satisfied. In **Wheat v Lacon & Co [1966] AC 552** it was held that it is possible for there to be more than one occupier of premises as different people may con-trol different parts of the same premises. [2.]Here it is likely that both Multimillion plc and Shambles Ltd will be occupiers and that each will owe a duty dependent upon their degree of control and its nature.

[2.]Conclude as you are going along, so that you are not left with a series of unanswered issues at the end of your work.

Once it is decided that both parties may be occupiers then under the **OLA 1957** the common duty of care will be owed towards visitors. But is Sven a visitor? It is important that an implied licensee does only those activities the implied licence extends to, otherwise the occupier will owe no duty of care (**Harvey v Plymouth City Council [2010] EWCA Civ 860**). He has been told to report to the site office, but as he does not do so this may make him a non-visitor outside the scope of the **OLA 1957**. If Sven is a visitor, he is owed the common duty of care, under **s. 2(1)**. Under **s. 2(2)**, this is a duty to take such care as is neces-sary to see that the visitor is reasonably safe in using the premises for the purposes for which he is invited by the occupier to be there.

Multimillion plc are not answerable for damage caused by any work of construction, maintenance, or repair by an independent contractor if, in the circumstances of the case, it was reasonable to entrust the work to an independent contractor and if such steps as are reasonable have been taken to ascertain that the contractor was competent and the work was properly done: **OLA 1957, s. 2(4)(b)**.

[3.]In **Ferguson v Welsh [1987] 3 All ER 777**, it was held that demo-lition fell within the scope of **s. 2(4)(b)** so it will be reasonable to entrust demolition to an expert and Multimillion plc will have to show that they had exercised reasonable care in selecting the independent contractor. If the contractor does technical work which the occupier cannot be expected to check, the occupier can be expected to do no more than check that the contractor is competent: **Haseldine v Daw & Sons Ltd [1941] 2 KB 343**. However, very complex work, such as a major building project, may require specialist supervision: **AMF International Ltd v Magnet Bowling Ltd [1968] 2 All ER 789**. Accordingly it is suggested that Multimillion have discharged their duty of care since it would not be reasonable to expect them to em-ploy another contractor, such as an architect, to supervise the work.

[3.]This is a sophisticated issue to address, so back up your arguments with reference to a variety of case law.

Since Shambles Ltd, as demolition contractors, have responsibility for the security of the site, it is assumed that they have control of the prem-ises and are occupiers: **AMF International Ltd v Magnet Bowling Ltd**.

The duty under the **OLA 1957, s. 2(2)** is to take steps to ensure that the visitor is reasonably safe for the purposes for which he is invited or permitted to be there. A visitor can be made safe by means of a warning that a risk exists, but the warning must be such as would enable the visitor to be reasonably safe: **s. 2(4)(a)**. The warning given to Sven by Shambles regarding the risk of tripping over a pipe is non-specific. [4.]If Sven had gone to the site office, he would have been provided with a hat, which might have protected him from falling rubble, but it would have had little effect in relation to the risk of harm resulting from tripping over a pipe. The risk of tripping over a pipe might be regarded as obvious. However, Sven might argue that the subsequent erection of a notice warning of the danger which has resulted in his injury is some admission of liability.

[4.] You will see that the two different incidents raise different discussion points, so make the most of this when addressing your answer.

If Sven is a trespasser he will be in the same position as Fabio as a non-visitor outside the scope of the **OLA 1957**. Under the **OLA 1984, s. 1(3)** there are three criteria to be satisfied before a duty of care will be owed by an occupier to a non-visitor. First, Shambles Ltd must be aware of the danger or have reasonable grounds for believing that it exists: **s. 1(3)(a)**. Here the danger due to the state of the premises has already been identified (see *Tomlinson v Congleton Borough Council* [2003] UKHL 47 and *Rhind v Astbury Water Park* [2004] EWCA Civ 756). In Sven's case an occupier would be aware of the dangers inherent in a building site such as the falling brick and the pipe, whereas in *Rhind*, as a matter of objective fact, the occupier could not have been expected to be aware of the danger hidden at the bottom of the murky lake.

Secondly, Shambles Ltd must have known or must have had reasonable grounds to believe that the particular non-visitor is in, or may come into, the vicinity of the danger: **OLA 1984, s. 1(3)(b)**. They know that Sven is on site and must be aware that he is or may come into the vicinity of the danger. However, there would have to be evidence that a trespasser such as Fabio would have been anticipated at that time. In *Higgs v Foster* [2004] EWCA Civ 843 it was not anticipated that a trespassing police officer would enter a bus depot and come into the vicinity of an uncovered inspection chamber into which he fell.

[5.] If you are looking for extra marks, address issues of policy in your answer. Here would be a good place to incorporate academic literature.

[5.]The third requirement is that Shambles Ltd must be aware that the risk is one against which they could reasonably be expected to offer the particular non-visitor some protection: **s. 1(3)(c)**. This may require consideration of the practicality of taking greater precautions, the utility of the defendant's behaviour, and the nature of the claimant's behaviour: *Tomlinson v Congleton Borough Council*. In *Tomlinson*, diving into a lake was regarded as normal activity so that an occupier would not be expected to take special precautions for the benefit of visitors. It would seem to follow that the same should also be the case for non-visitors.

Where a duty is owed, it must also be shown that there has been a breach and under the **OLA 1984, s. 1(4)**. Shambles Ltd must take reasonable care to ensure that the non-visitors do not suffer personal injury or death due to the danger arising out of the state of the premises. For the purposes of lawful visitors, obvious risks, such as the presence of razor wire, do not need to be warned of, so the same ought to be the case for non-visitors.

[6.] You might want to consider the issue of *volenti non fit injuria* under OLA 1984. Could this be used as a defence in preference to contributory negligence in this scenario?

[6.] Shambles Ltd may argue that under the **OLA 1984, s. 1(5)** they have discharged their duty by taking sufficient steps to discourage Fabio from taking the risk in the first place. They have erected a fence which is topped with razor wire. Causation may also be an issue to the extent that Fabio may have been so intent on theft that he would not have been deterred even if the fence had not been faulty.

Finally, it could be argued that Fabio and Sven are contributorily negligent, having failed to take reasonable precautions for their own safety and having been in part a cause of the harm they suffer: *Jones v Livox Quarries* [1952] 2 QB 608.

LOOKING FOR EXTRA MARKS?

■ Remember that a claimant can sue in occupiers' liability alongside the tort of negligence and contract law if applicable. Be aware of a range of defences to use in these situations.

■ Incorporate policy rationale where you get an opportunity.

TAKING THINGS FURTHER

■ Buckley, R., 'Occupiers' Liability in England and Canada' (2006) 35 *Common Law World Review* 197.
This is an article which adopts a comparative approach to the law in England and Canada.

■ Jones, M., 'The Occupiers' Liability Act 1984' (1984) 47 MLR 359.

■ Law Commission Report No. 75, Report on liability for damage or injury to trespassers and related questions of occupiers' liability, Cmnd 6428, 1976.
Law Commission Reports are always useful to read. Although the law changed some time ago, the reasons for introducing the 1984 Act will become apparent from reading this.

■ British Transport Police, Trespass Statistics 2018 http://www.btp.police.uk/pdf/trespass%20 stats%202018.pdf
Recent statistics which highlight a contemporary problem.

Online Resources   www.oup.com/uk/qanda/

Go online for extra essay and problem questions, a glossary of key terms, online versions of all the answer plans and audio commentary on how selected ones were put together, and a range of podcasts which include advice on exam and coursework technique and advice for other assessment methods.

Intentional Torts

8

ARE YOU READY?

To answer questions on this topic, you need an understanding of the following:

- **Trespass to the person:**
  - assault
  - battery
  - false imprisonment
  - the rule in *Wilkinson v Downton*
  - Protection from Harassment Act 1997
- **Trespass to land**
- **Trespass to goods and the tort of conversion**
- **You should also have a knowledge of defences to intentional torts:**
  - necessity
  - lawful arrest
  - consent
  - self-defence

KEY DEBATES

The Supreme Court recently revisited the rule in *Wilkinson v Downton*, in the case *O v Rhodes* [2016] AC 219. How did the Supreme Court deal with the case? Has this clarified the law of tort?

Eric had just won a darts game in the Dog and Duck public house. As he returned to his seat he was cheered on by his friends; Jockey, his opponent, slapped his shoulder in a hearty fashion to congratulate him on his victory. Eric was off balance at the time and tumbled over, injuring himself. Eric shouted at Jockey, 'You swine, you did that on purpose, I'll see you outside in two minutes'.

Fearing the worst, Sid, the owner of the Dog and Duck, grabbed Eric by the shirt collar and frog-marched him to his office. Eric resisted violently.

Sid managed to calm Eric and persuaded him to remain in the office in order to avoid further trouble. Having left the office, Sid asked two burly friends, Peter and Phil, to ensure that Eric did not leave the ground-floor room. Four hours later, Sid called the police. In the meantime, Eric slept off the effect of the alcohol and was unaware that Peter and Phil were there.

Consider whether any causes of action in trespass to the person are revealed by these facts.

CAUTION

- The rubric (ie the instruction at the bottom of the problem) clearly indicates that you should advise in trespass to the person, so do not advise on any other tort that might appear on the facts.

- Check your syllabus so that you know precisely what torts might appear on your examination paper.

DIAGRAM ANSWER PLAN

Identify	What potential trespass actions occur? What are they? Are there any defences?
Relevant law	*Collins v Wilcock* [1984] 3 All ER 374. *Turbervell v Savage* (1669) 1 Mod Rep 3. *Bird v Jones* (1845) 7 QB 742. Section 24A Police and Criminal Evidence Act 1984.
Apply the law	What force has been applied and to whom? Is the force unlawful?
Conclude	Batteries may have been carried out by Jockey and Sid (on Eric). Eric may have committed an assault (on Jockey). Sid may have committed false imprisonment (on Eric).

A

Trespass to the person comprises three distinct torts (battery, assault, and false imprisonment). They all require direct, intentional acts and are actionable per se, that is complete without the need for proof of actual harm.

1. Try to back up every argument with case law or statute to explain where the principle is laid down.

[1.]When Jockey slapped Eric's shoulder, Jockey may have committed battery. Battery is the infliction of immediate, unlawful force to the person. For Eric to succeed in battery he will have to prove that Jockey intended the contact with him. There is no need to prove intention to any resulting harm (*Wilson v Pringle* **[1986] 2 All ER 440**); the merest touching will suffice (*Collins v Wilcock* **[1984] 3 All ER 374**). On the facts, slapping Eric on the shoulder intentionally is a battery, as the touching appears to be without the consent of the claimant (consent would make the action lawful). However, the courts might allow Jockey the defence of consent, in that backslapping, as an action of congratulations in the context of a sporting event, may be viewed as general touching acceptable in everyday life.

When Eric shouted at Jockey, 'You swine . . . I'll see you outside in two minutes', Eric may have assaulted Jockey. An assault was defined by Goff LJ in *Collins v Wilcock* as 'an act which causes another reasonably to apprehend the infliction of immediate, unlawful force on his person'. Despite the earlier authority of *R v Meade and Belt* **(1823) 1 Lew CC 184**, which indicated that words alone could not constitute an assault, the House of Lords held in *R v Ireland* **[1997] 4 All ER 225** that a silent telephone call (or one where words are spoken) may be an assault if it causes apprehension in the claimant's mind. Jockey would have to show that the words used and Eric's general behaviour disclose an immediate threat. Eric says he wishes to speak with Jockey in two minutes' time but the whole of his behaviour has to be considered in light of its impact on a reasonable person in the claimant's position.

2. This is a very popular case, both for tort law and criminal law, so make sure you know and understand the principle of this ancient case.

[2.]It is possible that the words used may negate assault, as in *Turbervell v Savage* **(1669) 1 Mod Rep 3**. Here, the defendant's words were deemed to mean, 'much as I would like to, I will not attack you now', and therefore the court believed that this was not an assault as there was no immediate risk of a physical attack.

Further, before anything can be done to carry out the threat, Sid intervenes. A threat, no matter how violent, cannot be an assault if the claimant does not believe he will be battered, because the claimant perceives that the defendant is unable to carry out the threat. Such a situation occurred in *Thomas v NUM (South Wales Area)* **[1986] Ch 20** where the claimants, although violently threatened, were safe

3. Here the situation has been summed up, but go further and conclude that no tort has therefore been committed.

inside a bus with a police escort. [3.] Accordingly, whilst Eric remains in Sid's office there seems little for Jockey to fear.

By contrast, Sid's grabbing Eric by the shirt collar and frogmarching him to his office is clearly the application of physical force. Further, Sid's actions are likely to be considered to be beyond what is generally acceptable in everyday life, and will therefore constitute a battery unless Sid can raise a defence. [4.]He might be able to raise the defence of self-defence but the facts suggest that when Sid grabbed Eric he was not threatening Sid. In contrast to criminal law the defendant, that is Sid, must have held an honest and reasonable belief that he would be attacked by the defendant (*Ashley v Chief Constable of Sussex* [2008] UKHL 25). At this stage Eric was not threatening Sid, but Jockey. [5.]There is a suggestion that, in line with criminal law, s. 3 of the Criminal Law Act 1967 extends to defence of another. This might well work for Sid. Further, Sid might raise the defence of necessity. This is a limited defence, which allows the defendant to pursue an action which is the lesser of two evils, that is to prevent harm to a third party. Sid might argue that in holding back Eric he has stopped Eric causing Jockey some significant harm (*Austin v Commissioner of Police for the Metropolis* [2009] UKHL 5). However, in taking hold of Eric and frogmarching him to and detaining him in his office, Sid may have committed a false imprisonment.

False imprisonment was defined by Goff LJ in **Collins v Wilcock** as: 'the unlawful imposition of constraint on another's freedom of movement from a particular place.' The restraint must be total: in **Bird v Jones (1845) 7 QB 742** the fact that the claimant could use an alternative, though more lengthy, route meant that he had not been subject to a tort and was not justified in using force to make his way past an obstruction. On the facts, Eric does not know that if he tries to leave the office he will be prevented from doing so by Peter and Phil. The House of Lords in **R v Bournewood Community and Mental Health NHS Trust ex parte L [1998] 1 All ER 634** concluded that there must be circumstances amounting to a factual detention of the claimant. [6.]The case concerned a voluntary mental health inpatient who would have been restrained had he attempted to leave a hospital and who was subject to ongoing supervision. This was held by the majority not to be false imprisonment, though subsequently the European Court of Human Rights in **HL v UK 45508/99 (2004) ECHR 471** held the same patient's detention to have been in breach of his Article 5 rights.

As Eric is first unaware of the men outside the office, and later falls asleep, it must be considered whether a claimant must be aware of his restraint for the tort to be committed. The House of Lords in **Murray v Ministry of Defence [1988] 1 WLR 692** decided that the claimant need not know of the fact of restraint.

[7.]The House of Lords in **Murray** concluded that there were good policy reasons why the tort should continue to protect the claimant irrespective of his knowledge of the detention. This analysis suggests that the basic elements of false imprisonment are made out.

4. This is a weak sentence because the issue of self-defence has been raised, without any further reference as to how it operates.

5. Again be more specific in your arguments. Define legal terms and then back them up with authorities before applying them to the facts.

6. This is interesting, but does it advance your argument? Due to your short time frame, do not go off on a tangent. Try to focus on what is relevant in the facts.

7. It might have been more cohesive to have added the final words 'on these facts' or 'in the situation before us'.

If this is so, the burden of proof lies on the defendant (Sid) to justify his actions in restraining Eric. [8]**Section 24A Police and Criminal Evidence Act 1984** provides two defences in respect of 'citizen's arrest'. These permit any person to arrest without a warrant anyone who either is committing an indictable offence (an offence tried by jury) or is reasonably believed to have committed an indictable offence. In this problem, there is no indication that such an offence has been committed. However, Sid may be able to argue that he acted on the basis of preventing physical injury to another, one of the four specified grounds under s. 24A(4). However, this only allows Sid to restrain Eric until a police officer can arrive on the scene. The facts clearly state that Sid called the police four hours later, which would be too long to avoid liability. [9]Sid could argue that Eric consented to his detention, but the length of time involved, and in addition the fact that he could not have left if he had wanted to, suggest that this defence will be unavailable also.

[8] This may be beyond the scope of your syllabus. Check your syllabus thoroughly when preparing for examinations, so that you do not waste time revising for subjects that will not come up.

[9] If you have time, write a short paragraph drawing together all the conclusions you have made throughout your answer.

LOOKING FOR EXTRA MARKS?

- Have you spotted all the issues? Remain focused on the relevant facts.
- Consider carefully how to best arrange your answer. Here, the torts are dealt with chronologically, but in Question 2 they are dealt with thematically. What method suits you best?

QUESTION | 2

Harry, a scruffy-looking young man, is chatting in the street with his friend Terry. Both are drinking from bottles of lager.

Gino, accompanied by his 15-year-old daughter, Bella, passes by on the other side of the street and makes loud, offensive comments on Harry's and Terry's appearance. Harry moves towards Gino, swearing loudly and brandishing his bottle in a menacing manner, but is unable to cross the road due to the volume of traffic.

Gino and Bella return ten minutes later, Gino carrying a baseball bat. Gino takes a swing at Harry, but misses and strikes Terry instead, knocking him unconscious. Harry, fearing for his own safety, strikes Gino over the head with his bottle, which breaks, causing a splinter of glass to cut Bella, who runs home. David, a witness to these events, grabs Harry by the neck and restrains him by means of a stranglehold until the police arrive. Terry, still unconscious, is taken to hospital where Dr John decides that emergency surgery is necessary, entailing a blood transfusion, to which Terry would have objected on religious grounds had he been conscious.

Bella is taken to hospital by her mother, Sophia. Dr John advises Sophia that it would be wise for Bella to have an antibiotic injection. Bella objects because she is passionately opposed to all drugs that have been developed using animal testing, but Sophia tells Dr John to ignore her daughter's objections. Accordingly, Dr John arranges for the injection to be given.

Advise all the parties of their potential liabilities in trespass to the person.

CAUTION

- It is very easy to repeat legal principles in problem questions with multiple parties and events. By dealing with matters thematically, as is done here, some repetition can be avoided, but be careful that you apply defences only after establishing a tort.
- The rubric (ie the instruction at the bottom of the problem) refers only to trespass to the person, so do not be tempted to discuss other torts.

DIAGRAM ANSWER PLAN

Identify	Have any assaults or batteries occurred? If so, to whom, by whom? Are there are any defences?
Relevant law	*Collins v Wilcock* [1984] 3 All ER 374. *Bici v Ministry of Defence* [2004] EWHC 786 (QB). Police and Criminal Evidence Act 1984 (PACE) s. 24. *F v West Berkshire Health Authority* [1989] 2 All ER 545.
Apply the law	Discuss the core content of assault and battery. Consider the ingredients of necessity, consent, self-defence, and lawful arrest.
Conclude	Various assaults may have occurred: Gino has committed battery, David has committed battery but may have a valid defence of lawful arrest. Dr John has valid defences of necessity (Terry) and consent (Bella).

SUGGESTED ANSWER

There are numerous potential trespass actions in this scenario. We will start by considering any assaults, before moving on to batteries, and then finally considering any defences.

Assault

[1] In this opening you have identified the issue, specified a legal principle, given its legal authority, and then applied it to the facts to reach a conclusion.

[1] Gino makes loud, offensive comments which may constitute an assault. Assault is as an act which causes another person reasonably to apprehend the infliction of immediate, unlawful force on his person (**Collins v Wilcock [1984] 3 All ER 374**). However, in our situation, Gino's comments are unlikely to convey any threat of force, therefore no assault would have occurred. When Harry swears and waves a

bottle in response to Gino's comments, his words may be insufficient to amount to a threat. [2.]Until recently, there was no clear legal authority that words alone could constitute an assault. Dicta went both ways (**R v Meade and Belt** (1823) 1 Lew CC 184 (no assault); **R v Wilson** [1955] 1 WLR 493 (assault)). However, the House of Lords in **R v Ireland** [1997] 4 All ER 225 took the view that even a silent phone call could amount to an assault. Lord Steyn noted that a thing said 'is also a thing done'. Therefore, the use of words alone may be an assault. However, where words are accompanied by a threatening act or gesture, as in the question, there is likely to be an assault (**Read v Coker** (1853) 13 CB 850).

If Harry has committed an assault, it needs to be proved that the threat is immediate and gives rise to a reasonable apprehension of the imminent infliction of a battery (**Thomas v NUM (South Wales Area)** [1986] Ch 20). [3.]The volume of traffic on the road dividing Harry from Gino may suggest that there is no reason to believe that a battery was imminent.

When Gino returns with the baseball bat and takes a swing at Harry there may well be an assault as it would be reasonable for Harry to anticipate an immediate battery in the circumstances. In this circumstance the swing may also be an assault on Terry who receives the blow.

Battery

Battery was defined by Goff LJ in **Collins v Wilcock** [1984] 3 All ER 374 as 'the actual infliction of unlawful force on another person', and requires a direct intentional contact. In the problem, the potential batteries are: first, when Gino strikes Terry with the baseball bat; secondly, the use of the bottle; thirdly, the arrest; and fourthly, the interventions by the doctor. [4.]In all of these instances there are direct intentional acts resulting in contact that go well beyond anything that could be regarded as acceptable in everyday life.

It would seem, then, that the issue in the question is one of intention. Gino intends to hit Harry, but in fact strikes Terry. It is important to remember that, for trespass, the intention should relate to the act rather than to the consequences of the act. **Bici v Ministry of Defence** [2004] EWHC 786 (QB) adopted the principle of transferred intent (akin to transferred malice in criminal law), applying dicta in the Northern Irish case **Livingstone v Ministry of Defence** [1984] NI 356. It seems logical that if Gino intends to strike Harry he should also be liable in damages for striking Terry.

[5.]Gino cannot successfully plead self-defence, as his act occurs after any threat has disappeared, and the defence needs to be a simultaneous event to the action. Further, the action must be considered proportionate to the threat (**Cross v Kirby** (2000) The Times,

[2.]If you are running out of time, do not involve yourself with historical discussions when answering problem questions. Just direct us to the current situation.

[3.]Use the facts of the question to reach your conclusions.

[4.]Dealing with all the potential batteries at the same time stops you from writing out the legal principle on every occasion.

[5.]If you have discussed the legal principles of a defence on one occasion within your answer, you do not need to go through them again at a later stage.

5 April). In Gino's case, the use of an offensive weapon is probably out of proportion to the threat posed by a bottle in the hands of 'a scruffy-looking young man' on the other side of a busy street.

By contrast, Harry's response to the threat posed by Gino may be justified in self-defence. In light of the threat posed by a person wielding a baseball bat, it is possible that the use of a bottle may be regarded as proportionate and he may be taken to have acted reasonably in all the circumstances, especially as Gino has already hit Terry with the bat. Moreover, a person who sets out to attack another but who 'gets more than he bargained for', as seems to be the case with Gino, may also find his claim barred on grounds of public policy as in

6. Make sure you conclude as you go along.

Murphy v Culhane **[1977] QB 94.** [6.] The so-called illegality defence, or *ex turpi causa non oritur actio*, operates to prevent a successful action by an individual whose claim depends for its success on an unlawful act of the claimant of a very serious nature. As a matter of public policy the courts will not be seen to be supporting a claim in such circumstances.

Applying a stranglehold is capable of amounting to a battery, and if it constitutes an 'unlawful imposition of constraint on another's freedom of movement from a particular place' (*Collins v Wilcock* **[1984] 3 All ER 374**) it may be a false imprisonment. The circumstances suggest that David does this by way of a citizen's arrest. The **Police and Criminal Evidence Act 1984 (PACE), s. 24** excuses a private individual who makes an arrest provided certain conditions are met. A person other than a police officer may arrest a person actually committing or reasonably suspected of committing an indictable offence, provided such an offence has taken place. A serious assault on an individual is an indictable offence and it is reasonably clear that an offence has been committed as David has witnessed the events. **Section 24A** also requires that arrest is necessary to prevent injury to another or to prevent the suspect escaping, and that it is not practicable to wait for a police officer to make the arrest. Under **s. 28**, the person arrested must be told that he is under arrest and the reason for his arrest, either at the time, or as soon as practicable thereafter. If the arrest is made by a person who is not a constable, as here, the common law rule is that the arrested person does not have to be informed of the reason for his arrest if the circumstances make the reason obvious—in *Christie v Leachinsky* **[1947] AC 573** the House of Lords suggested that this would be so if someone were caught red-handed. [7.] All of these requirements seem to be satisfied with the result that David probably has not committed a tort, with the worrying (for David) exception that if Harry's claim of self-defence is successful, no crime was actually committed.

7. This is a very sophisticated point but it is this level of sophistication which assists candidates to reach first-class marks.

Dr John's surgical treatment of Terry is, prima facie, a battery within the definition by Goff LJ quoted earlier in this suggested answer, and

8. Consent is not an option here, but invariably, if faced with this question, some students will discuss this defence in depth. If it does not advance your arguments, do not discuss it.

the usual defence in relation to medical treatment—**8.** consent—is not an option since Terry is unconscious. Clearly, it would not be in the public interest for the treatment of patients incapable of consenting to be an actionable battery, so there must be some other justification. In *F v West Berkshire Health Authority* **[1989] 2 All ER 545**, Lord Goff explained the nature of the defence of necessity, which permits, in the case of an emergency concerning a temporarily incapacitated patient, such treatment as is necessary in order to save life, ensure improvement, or prevent physical or mental deterioration, and no more. **Section 5 Mental Capacity Act 2005** requires that treatment of a person lacking capacity must be 'in their best interests', which according to **s. 4** includes considerations of the person's own beliefs, values, etc 'so far as reasonably ascertainable' and of the likelihood of the person regaining capacity. This approach is consistent with public policy, which recognizes a presumption in favour of the preservation of life. Since the operation on Terry is considered to be essential, the defence of necessity would seem to apply unless Dr John can be taken to have been aware of Terry's objection to receiving blood other than his own. On the facts, there is nothing to suggest that Dr John is aware of Terry's religious objections, so his actions will probably be justified.

9. Here is your chance to discuss consent.

9. In regard to Bella, the defence of necessity is not appropriate here as there are several potential sources of consent. First, as Bella is 15 years old, the question of her capacity to consent will be determined by reference to the *Gillick* test (*Gillick v West Norfolk and Wisbech Area Health Authority* **[1986] AC 112**). Under this test, provided Bella was of sufficient maturity to understand what is involved in having an injection, she could consent for herself. However, Bella is refusing to consent. In *Re W (a minor) (medical treatment)* **[1992] 4 All ER 627**, Lord Donaldson specified that: 'anyone who gives [a doctor] a flak jacket (ie consent) may take it back, but the doctor only needs one and so long as he continues to have one he has the legal right to proceed.' As Bella is under the age of 16, her mother can provide consent on her behalf. Provided Dr John has valid consent from Bella's mother, he commits no battery on Bella.

 LOOKING FOR EXTRA MARKS?

▨ Only discuss the legal principles which assist you to develop your arguments.

▨ Look out for any subtleties in the question. They have usually been put there to allow a good student to demonstrate their knowledge.

During a party at Yasser's house, Barney, a house guest and known prankster, jumped from the doorway in a darkened corridor with a sheet over his head just as Wilma, another guest, was passing, but he did not make physical contact with her. Wilma fainted with shock and banged her head causing bruising. Barney carried her into a room and left her there to recover.

One hour later, Barney went to see if Wilma had recovered, but found Wilma asleep. Barney shook her gently to ask if she was feeling better. Wilma awoke, and believing she was being attacked, struck violently at Barney with a poker from the fireplace. Barney suffered a fractured skull.

Consider the potential liability of the parties in trespass to the person and under the principle in *Wilkinson v Downton*.

CAUTION

- In addition to trespass to the person, the rubric also includes reference to the principle in ***Wilkinson v Downton***, so your answer should identify the original principle but also show how it has undergone more recent developments in the Supreme Court.

DIAGRAM ANSWER PLAN

Identify	What torts may have occurred: Assault? Battery? An action under *Wilkinson v Downton*? Are there any defences?
Relevant law	*Collins v Wilcock* [1984] 3 All ER 374. *Wilkinson v Downton* [1897] 2 QB 57. *O v Rhodes* [2016] AC 219. *Ashley v Chief Constable of Sussex Police* [2008] UKHL 25.
Apply the law	Do the actions constitute an assault? Battery? Or an action under *Wilkinson v Downton*? Consider the defences of self-defence/necessity.
Conclude	Barney may have committed an assault, but there is not likely to be a cause of action under *Wilkinson v Downton*. Both have committed a battery, but Barney may have the defence of necessity and Wilma may have the defence of self-defence.

SUGGESTED ANSWER

Barney may have committed an assault when he jumps out in front of Wilma. Assault was defined by Goff LJ in *Collins v Wilcock* **[1984] 3 All ER 374** as an act that causes another 'reasonably to apprehend the infliction of immediate, unlawful force on his person', so the question here is whether or not Wilma was placed in such a fear. If she was, then she may succeed in assault. Barney may say that he did not intend any harm, but while the act must be intentional, an intention to harm is not required. [1]Barney may also say that his action was only a joke. Again motive is irrelevant and the action should be judged objectively.

1. You may want to give a formal conclusion here before moving onto the next tort.

It may also be possible to establish that in respect of Barney's prank an action lies under the rule in *Wilkinson v Downton* **[1897] 2 QB 57** which has been recently clarified by the Supreme Court in *O v Rhodes* **[2016] AC 219**. Reconsidering this tort, their Lordships specified that it comprises three elements: a conduct element, the necessary mental element, and the consequence element. These three elements need to occur without any justification for the defendant's actions, if the tort is to be made out.

2. Consider whether you should devise a linking sentence between these two paragraphs.

[2]The conduct element, be it actions or words, should be an action directed towards the claimant, or a definable group of persons including the claimant, 'for which there is no justification or reasonable excuse'. The practical joke performed at a house party, may not be aimed directly at Wilma, but she would fall into the class of ascertainable persons. Further, there must be an intention in deliberately causing physical harm or psychiatric illness (not just distress). Since *O v Rhodes*, recklessness is no longer sufficient to qualify as the necessary mental element. Additionally, some injury must be the result of the actions.

3. This is a significant point of law, which might end any chance of Wilma being successful. However, ensure that you have discussed all aspects of the tort.

[3]Wilma's difficulty, should she pursue an action in this tort, is that since *O v Rhodes*, proof of actual intention to cause harm is required. On the facts in front of us, there is no evidence that Barney intended any harm.

If we consider first Wilma's injuries, she fainted with shock and sustained some bruising. In the circumstances, it is unlikely that the 'shock' will be considered anything more than distress and will therefore not be a cause of action. [4]Additionally, the faint may not be sufficient harm for these purposes, although there is authority in criminal law that a temporary loss of consciousness qualifies as actual bodily harm (*T v Director of Public Prosecutions* [2003] EWHC 266). Her head injury may also qualify, as that is clearly physical damage.

4. There are significant overlaps between tort law and criminal law here. You may refer to criminal law, but your priority is to advise in the law of tort.

Further, Barney may have a 'justification or reasonable excuse' for the conduct, as Barney may argue that he was merely engaging in well-intentioned horseplay to contribute to the party atmosphere.

However, Wilma may be able to pursue an action in battery. Battery was defined by Goff LJ in *Collins v Wilcock* **[1984] 3 All ER 374** as 'the actual infliction of unlawful force on another person', and requires a direct intentional contact. When Barney picked Wilma up and, later, when he shook her, Barney has inflicted physical force on Wilma. Therefore, Wilma may have an action for battery in respect of these touches, no matter how slight, unless a defence applies.

5. You may not have time to discuss any defence in detail, so just specify briefly how the defence works and then apply it.

5. When Barney picks up Wilma, he may have the defence of necessity. This was explored in *F v West Berkshire Health Authority*, which acknowledged a distinction between permanently incapacitated patients for whom the guiding principle was what was in the best interests of the patient judged according to the principle in *Bolam v Friern Hospital Management Committee* **[1957] 1 WLR 582**, and the temporarily incapacitated where the principle justifies only such treatment as is necessary for saving and conserving life. For such patients, the principle of autonomy dictates that they should not be deprived, while unconscious, of their overriding right to self-determination. On this basis, Barney's actions may appear to be justified.

6. You can use authorities from other areas of trespass if they assist your arguments, but point out to your examiner that you know this is not a trespass to land case.

6. However, it was held in *Rigby v Chief Constable of Northamptonshire Police* **[1985] 2 All ER 985** (a case on trespass to land) that the defence of necessity cannot be relied on where that necessity arose from the defendant's tortious behaviour. If Barney's original act of scaring Wilma was a tort then necessity may not be available as a defence. On this basis, Barney could be liable unless he can show that picking Wilma up after the prank was 'generally acceptable in the ordinary conduct of daily life'. Similarly, when Barney shook Wilma, the gentleness of the shake is not the key point, but whether the shake could be described as generally acceptable in everyday life. In *Mepstead v DPP* **[1996] COD 13** the gentle holding of the arm of a motorist to calm him down when a fixed penalty notice had been given was not sufficient to amount to a battery.

When Wilma lashes out violently at Barney and causes substantial harm this is prima facie a battery. The issue here is the availability of self-defence for her actions. Wilma has acted in self-defence based on a mistake.

7. Discuss the legal principles then apply them to the facts.

7. In *Ashley v Chief Constable of Sussex Police* **[2008] UKHL 25** the House of Lords confirmed the decision of the Court of Appeal that the necessity must be judged on the facts as the defendant honestly believed them to be, but if he made a mistake of fact then it would have to be shown to be a reasonable mistake. On the facts in front of us, the circumstances might suggest that it was reasonable to suppose that there was an attack in progress and there is no suggestion this was not an honest belief.

As regards the degree of force used, the law demands that this should be reasonable and proportionate to the perceived threat, but the courts are keen to ensure that this is not weighed too finely. For example, in *Cross v Kirby* (2000) *The Times*, 5 April the Court of Appeal held that a defendant who had been struck several times by a baseball bat-wielding assailant had not reacted disproportionately by using the bat to strike the claimant, breaking his skull.[8] So although Wilma's use of the poker has caused a serious injury, this may be regarded as reasonable in all the circumstances, and therefore she will have a valid defence to battery.

8. Conclude after discussing the law and applying.

QUESTION | 4

Paresh owns a farm in the country and a disused plot of land in central London. The farm is situated near to an airfield used by a gliding club. Some of the gliders have occasionally landed in the fields of surrounding farms, damaging the crops, but the gliding club has always paid compensation to the farmers in such circumstances. The plot of land in central London is adjacent to a building site owned by Bipin and on which he is building a new office block. The jib of a tall crane constantly oversails into the airspace above Paresh's plot. Bipin has offered to buy the plot of land from Paresh, but Paresh has always asked for more than Bipin is prepared to pay.

Paresh is now seeking to obtain an injunction against the gliding club, preventing it from flying over his farm, and against the developers of the building site, preventing them from intruding into the airspace above his land with their crane, even though it will be very difficult for them to redevelop their land without doing this.

Advise Paresh as to any actions he may have in trespass to land.

CAUTION

■ You are not asked to consider the application of private nuisance here, so keep any reference to it very brief. Deal with the cases on airspace fully, to demonstrate your knowledge of the legal reasoning.

DIAGRAM ANSWER PLAN

Identify	The relevant action—trespass as a result of interference with airspace. Has Paresh the lawful right to sue?
Relevant law	*Kelsen v Imperial Tobacco Co* [1957] 2 QB 334. *Bernstein v Skyviews & General Ltd* [1978] QB 479. *Anchor Brewhouse Developments Ltd v Berkley House Ltd* [1978] 2 EGLR 173.
Apply the law	Are the gliders, or the crane, trespassing on Paresh's property?
Conclude	Paresh appears to have exclusive possession of the property. Gliders: no trespass, therefore no injunction. The crane: trespass. The courts may award damages in lieu rather than an injunction.

SUGGESTED ANSWER

¹· This is an important principle of law, which often takes students by surprise.

²· Look carefully at the facts. If the paper owner has leased out his property, it is the tenant, not the owner who has the right to sue in trespass.

¹Paresh should be advised that trespass to land involves direct and unjustifiable interference with the claimant's possession of land. It requires there to be an intention, but the intention is to the entry onto the land, rather than an intention to trespass. Therefore, as long as the entry was voluntary, trespass can occur, even if the defendant was not aware of the fact (*Conway v George Wimpey & Co Ltd* [1951] 2 KB 266). So, in Paresh's case, the defendants may have trespassed even if they have no intention to actually do so.

As with all trespasses, trespass to land is actionable per se, that is it is complete without proof of actual harm.

In order to sue in trespass, it is essential to be in possession of the land (*Nicholls v Ely Beet Sugar Factory* [1931] 2 Ch 84). The facts of the question tell us that Paresh owns the land concerned. However, an interest in land without possession will not be enough to sue, as would be the case, for example, if Paresh had rented out his land.

²Referring to the facts, there is nothing to suggest that he does not have exclusive possession of these properties, and in the 'absence of evidence to the contrary, the owner of the land with the paper title is deemed to be in possession of the land' (*Powell v McFarlane* (1977) 38 P & CR 452 per Slade J; *Star Energy Weald Basin Ltd v Bocardo SA*

[2010] UKSC 35). The fact that he does not live on the London land does not matter as he does not need to be physically on the land at the time that the trespass occurred.

Having established Paresh's right to sue, we will consider the necessary cause of action.

The Gliders

To obtain an injunction to prevent the gliders flying over his land, Paresh needs to establish that there has been an interference with airspace. In *Kelsen v Imperial Tobacco Co* **[1957] 2 QB 334** an overhanging advertising sign that intruded by no more than a few centimetres, well above the claimant's roof, was held to be capable of amounting to a trespass. Further in *Liaquat v Majid* [2005] EWHC 1305 (QB), a 75 cm projection 4.5 metres above the claimant's ground was considered a trespass. In principle, there is an action. However, in these cases, the invasion was at a relatively low height by a fixture and not an aircraft or a crane.

In *Bernstein v Skyviews & General Ltd* **[1978] QB 479**, it was held there would be no trespass by an overflying aeroplane unless the aeroplane flies so low that it penetrates the airspace at a height which could be thought to interfere with the rights of the 'normal user of the land'. [3.] Griffiths J in *Bernstein* concluded that there had to be a balance drawn between the private rights of the owner and the interests of the public to take advantage of scientific developments in travel and communications. Therefore an owner has rights in the land extending only to such height as is necessary for the ordinary use and enjoyment of the land. As *Bernstein* informs us that there was no trespass at height, therefore, regarding the gliders (if airborne) there may be no trespass into Paresh's airspace. The situation might be different if, for example, the gliders were a method of taking aerial photographs of Paresh's farm or were being deliberately landed on his farm. In this situation Paresh may have a claim under the Protection of Harassment Act 1997; however, the facts do not suggest this to be the case.

[4.]Paresh may have more success in an action for nuisance. However, overflying and possible noise nuisance may be subject to immunity under the **Civil Aviation Act 1982, ss. 76** and **77**. This immunity extends both to trespass to airspace and to nuisance, but it only arises if the club was complying with an air navigation order made under **s. 60.** [5.]However, even if nuisance is made out, the court is likely to balance the social value of the gliding club with the need to protect property (*Miller v Jackson* [1977] 1 QB 966; *Coventry v Lawrence* [2014] UKSC 13), and to award damages in lieu of an injunction.

[3.] Remember that tort law pays attention to social utility, so be prepared to discuss this in any tort answer.

[4.] A detailed knowledge of this statutory provision would not normally be required, but check with your examiner.

[5.] You will often find that examination questions set on the tort of nuisance also include aspects of trespass. Make sure that you are able to spot the difference and advise on both.

The Crane

The jib of Bipin's crane will intrude Paresh's airspace at a lower level than the gliders, but does this interfere with the rights of the 'normal user of land'? In *Anchor Brewhouse Developments Ltd v Berkley House Ltd* [1978] 2 EGLR 173, the defendant company had sought to argue that their cranes, which overhung the claimant's land, were not a trespass because of the public interest in developing a major site in London and the unreasonable cost to them of re-siting them and constructing a building with a smaller 'footprint'. It was held that the decision in *Bernstein v Skyviews* had not altered the law, so that where there was an invasion by a structure adjoining the land of the claimant then there would be a trespass. The defendant was taking into possession, no matter how briefly, airspace which the claimant was entitled to reduce into actual possession. There was no scope for balancing interests in the way adopted in *Bernstein v Skyviews*, since that case was concerned with protecting the interests of society at large rather than the interests of an individual airline operator. Accordingly, the invasion by Bipin's crane will amount to a trespass.

Will Bipin be allowed a defence?

[6.]Under the **Access to Neighbouring Land Act 1992**, the court may make an order (upon application) allowing for reasonably necessary works to be performed for the purpose of the preservation of adjacent land. The Act does not apply to works for the alterations and so forth, unless those operations are incidental to works of 'preservation'. Since Bipin is building something completely new he cannot take advantage of the legislation.

Normally an injunction (which is an equitable remedy) will be granted subject to the normal equitable rules such as the behaviour of the claimant; s/he must not, for example, have encouraged the defendant to believe that the work was permitted, nor must s/he have delayed. [7.]In *Woolerton & Wilson v Costain* [1970] 1 WLR 411 an injunction to restrain a developer from trespassing with a crane was suspended for such time as effectively denied the remedy to a claimant who had adopted a wholly unreasonable attitude towards consenting to the proposed aerial invasion. However, this approach has been disapproved of in later cases, including *Anchor Brewhouse*. This case confirmed that the claimant was entitled to an injunction as a matter of course if the trespass was going to be repeated. It does not seem to matter that the claimant might be acting as a 'dog in a manger' (per Scott J in *Anchor Brewhouse*).

However, Bipin may argue that damages would suffice. [8.]The general principles governing the grant of damages were set out in *Shelfer v City of London Electric Lighting Co* [1895] 1 Ch 287. These were that the injury to the claimant's rights is small; the injury can be estimated in financial terms; the injury can be adequately

[6.] Every now and again you are asked to consider this Act in an answer. Make sure you are familiar with the overriding features.

[7.] In most cases of trespass to land, what the claimant wants is an injunction preventing the activity, so it is right to spend some time discussing this.

[8.] It is well worth spending some time looking at the relationship between injunctions and damages, before you sit your exam.

compensated in money terms; and it would be oppressive to the defendant to grant an injunction.

However, *Enfield LBC v Outdoor Plus Ltd* [2012] EWCA Civ 608 indicated that damages should be calculated by reference to all the factors. In that case, the defendant had benefited commercially from the use of the hoarding for advertising purposes. Arguably the commercial profits to be made by a building developer might equally suggest a substantial sum.

LOOKING FOR EXTRA MARKS?

- This is a narrow question, and as such you will need to demonstrate a deeper understanding of the law in this area.
- Do not be tempted to discuss other torts, just because you feel that you do not have much to say. Sometimes you can obtain a high mark by producing a narrow answer, if it is accurate and focused on the problem.

QUESTION | 5

Chris, a keen golfer, hits his ball into the lake on the Victoria Park golf course. This belongs to Phester Borough Council. He wades into his lake to find his ball. He does not find his ball, but instead he finds a skeleton wearing a heavy gold chain around its neck.

Chris lends the skeleton to his friend Atika, a medical student, to assist her with her studies. The skeleton is deliberately damaged by Brett, Atika's flatmate, during a party.

The necklace is in good condition, except for the clasp which needs repairing, so Chris asks JJ, a jeweller, to mend the clasp. JJ repairs it and sells the chain to Rohan for £500, claiming that it belongs to a friend of his who has given him authority to sell it. Rohan gives the chain to his friend, Hayley, as a birthday present. Hayley, a dealer in antiques, has now displayed the repaired chain in her shop window at a price of £1,500.

Advise the parties whether there is any action for conversion.

CAUTION

- This question requires consideration of the tort of conversion, in particular looking at defences available to a person alleged to have converted chattels where another person has a higher claim. This is a complex area and answers should not be rushed.

DIAGRAM ANSWER PLAN

Identify	Is the action one of trespass or conversion? Can the skeleton be the subject of conversion? If so, who has standing to sue? Who owns the chain? What remedies are available in respect of the tort of conversion?
Relevant law	Torts (Interference with Goods) Act 1977. *OBG Ltd v Allan* [2007] UKHL 21. *Yearworth v North Bristol NHS Trust* [2010] QB. *Parker v British Airways Board* [1982] QB 1004.
Apply the law	Where was the property found? Does this make a difference to Chris's claim? What effect does the existence of a bailment relationship have on the liability of the bailee? For each new possessor of the chain, assess their legal status and their right to dispose of the property. What effect does the common law defence *jus tertii* have in light of s. 8 of the European Convention of Human Rights?
Conclude	It is questionable that the skeleton is 'property', and if it is not it cannot be the object in an action of conversion. The chain is property, but its original ownership is in doubt, so that any action that Chris brings may not be successful. If he is deemed to be the owner, he may receive damages.

SUGGESTED ANSWER

This question requires a consideration of the torts of conversion and trespass to goods.

[1] Conversion is the intentional dealing with goods (physical property, rather than intangible personal property rights, ***OBG Ltd v Allan* [2007] UKHL 21**) which is seriously inconsistent to another's possession, or right to immediate possession. By comparison, trespass to goods involves a direct and intentional (or negligent) interference with goods which are physically in the possession of the claimant at the time the interference occurs.

[2] Looking at the question, it appears that Chris's action lies in conversion, since he does not have physical possession of the goods at the time of the acts of interference, and therefore cannot launch an action in trespass to goods. Conversion can occur in many ways, but

[1] Concentrate on the central requirements of conversion, namely an intentional act depriving an owner of the use or possession of his property.

[2] This is the crucial distinction of the torts.

the goods concerned must be moveable chattels that can be owned and possessed. We are informed that Chris has found a skeleton with a chain. A chain clearly falls into the category of 'moveable chattels', but the skeleton may cause some difficulty.

The Skeleton

It has been held that while there can be no property in a corpse (*Dobson v North Tyneside Health Authority* [1996] 4 All ER 474), aspects of the body may be regarded as property. For example, body parts (*R v Kelly* [1999] QB 621), sperm (*Yearworth v North Bristol NHS Trust* [2010] QB 1), and urine (*R v Welsh [1974]* RTR 478 (CA)). Generally, if some type of special skill or process has been applied to the body product, it has become property.[3] However, here a skeleton found at the bottom of a lake in a public area with a chain around its neck suggests that there has not been any application of special skill. It is possibly the remains of a victim of crime, and if that is the case it is unlikely to be a preserved specimen, and therefore will not be property that can be the subject of conversion.

[3] Remember the key issue for conversion is the dealing of another's property.

For Brett to be liable, he must have committed an act of conversion. This requires intention. By merely damaging the skeleton, Brett does not appear to meet the requirements of conversion (*Fouldes v Willoughby* (1841) 8 M & W 540). Neither would accidental destruction of the skeleton (*Simmons v Lillystone* (1853) 8 Exch 431) count. However, if his intentional damage has changed the identity of the property, so that it loses its former usefulness, the courts might find that conversion has occurred (*Jones de Marchant* (1916) 28 DLR 561, approved of in *Foskett v McKeown* [2001] 1 AC 102). This might be the case as the skeleton's usefulness as an anatomy study might have been eradicated.

[4] Look at who has the right to sue.

[4] If the skeleton is capable of possession, it is technically in the possession of both Chris (bailee) and Atika (possessor), but only one of them can sue, and whichever of the two elects to sue Brett first will have to account to the other possible claimant in respect of his interest (*Nicolls v Bastard* (1835) 2 Cr M & R 659; *Islamic Republic of Iran v Bakarat Galleries Ltd* [2009] QB 22).

The Chain

As the chain was found at the bottom of a lake on land owned by another, it must be established that Chris has a right to possession. In *Parker v British Airways Board* [1982] QB 1004, it was held that the finder of a chattel acquires rights over it if the true owner is unknown, the chattel appears to be abandoned or lost, and the finder takes the chattel into care or possession. The finder's right will be valid against everyone except the true owner, or a person who asserts a prior right to the goods (*Armory v Delamirie* (1722) 1 Stra 505).

The finder has a better interest in the goods if they are merely on the land rather than being attached to it.

The facts suggest that the chain has been found below the surface of the water but on the bed of the lake, which may allow Phester County Council to assert a superior interest. Things embedded in land are deemed to belong to the landowner, as can be seen in *Waverley Borough Council v Fletcher* [1995] 4 All ER 756 where the local authority was considered to have a superior right to that of the defendant who found a buried gold brooch by using a metal detector on the claimant's land.

Chris has not had to dig in order to find the chain, but the surface of the water may be regarded as the top of the County Council's land, in which case the chain may be regarded as equivalent to being buried. This was the case in *South Staffordshire Water Co v Sharman* [1896] 2 QB 44, where two gold rings found at the bottom of a pool were said to be owned by the local authority (who owned the pool) rather than their employee who found the rings. In any event, it should be noted that the finder, that is Chris, is under an obligation to attempt to find the true owner. He does not appear to have done so.

After finding the chain, Chris hands it to JJ for repair. This creates a bailment relationship under which JJ, as a bailee, has a lien over goods entrusted to him for repair, but only in respect of his right to payment for the work he has done. Once a bailee wrongly parts with possession, he loses his lien. He does this by selling the chain to Rohan. Moreover, his act also amounts to conversion, thereby entitling the owner to sue him (*Mulliner v Florence* (1878) 3 QBD 484).

JJ intends to deal in the chain in a manner which is inconsistent with Chris's right of possession, and as JJ has possession only for the purposes of repair there will not be a sale with the consent of the owner for the purposes of the **Factors Act 1889, s. 2.**

^{5.} Keep this in mind all the way through your answer.

^{5.}Conversion requires an intentional act which results in an interference with the claimant's goods (*Ashby v Tolhurst* [1937] 2 KB 242). It is irrelevant that a person is unaware that s/he has challenged the true owner's right to property or possession (*Caxton Publishing Ltd v Sutherland Publishing Ltd* [1939] AC 178). Therefore as Rohan has acted intentionally by delivering the chain to Hayley, the fact that he is unaware that he has challenged Chris's right to possession is irrelevant. There is no defence of mistake or acting in good faith in regards to the tort of conversion (*Hollins v Fowler* (1875)).

Hayley has invited offers for the purchase of the chain, but it has yet to be sold. However, even by trying to sell an article Hayley may be liable for conversion. Certainly if Hayley has 'used' the chain as her own (eg by wearing it), this may be conversion: *Petre v Hemeage* (1701) 12 Mod Rep 519.

Remedies

6. The claimant may not be able to retrieve his or her property, so a damages award is the correct remedy.

6. A claimant can recover damages to the extent of the value of the goods converted, namely the market value of the converted goods at the date of conversion: ***Uzinterimpex JSC v Standard Bank plc* [2007] EWHC 1151 (Comm)**. In this case, if Hayley's price for the chain represents its market value, that amount will be £1,500. However, the relevant date for assessment of damages is the date of conversion (***BBMB Finance Ltd v Eda Holdings Ltd* [1991] 2 All ER 129**). In *Kuwait Airways Corp v Iraqi Airways Co (Nos 4 and 5)*, Lord Nicholls drew a distinction between deliberate conversion and conversion, noting that the latter will create liability for consequential losses only to the extent that they were reasonably foreseeable, whereas a deliberate act creates liability for all damage flowing 'directly and naturally' from the tort.

By repairing the chain, JJ may have increased its value, but the enhanced value is not normally recoverable (***Caxton Publishing Ltd v Sutherland Publishing Ltd***). If the act of conversion occurs after the improvement, as in JJ's case, the **Torts (Interference with Goods) Act 1977, s. 6(1)** applies, allowing a defendant who has improved the goods in the mistaken belief that he has a good title to recover an allowance, but this is unlikely to assist JJ. Under **s. 6(2)** of the Act, a similar allowance may also be made in favour of subsequent purchasers, such as Rohan, provided they act in good faith. **7.** Hayley is unlikely to be able to use **s. 6** in her favour, since it only applies to a subsequent purchaser, and, as Rohan gave her the chain as a present, she is a volunteer.

7. Title can only pass if a person buys the goods; a person receiving the goods as a gift does not acquire title to property if conversion has occurred beforehand.

It should be noted that the **Torts (Interference with Goods) Act 1977, s. 8(1)** allows a third party to plead his better title at the time of conversion as a defence (***De Franco v Metropolitan Police Commissioner* (1987) The Times, 8 May**). So, ironically, if Phester County Council have a better title to the chain, then, by virtue of *jus tertii* (third party rights) Chris's action in conversion against JJ, Rohan, or Hayley is likely to fail.

+ LOOKING FOR EXTRA MARKS?

■ Look closely at the facts. Establish who the rightful owner is, and then see where the owner's rights have been usurped. This is a time-consuming process, so make sure you plan thoroughly before you start to answer the question.

■ It often helps to draw a diagram to remind yourself of what passed to whom.

TAKING THINGS FURTHER

Below is a selection of journal articles which examine various intentional torts.

- Austin, R. C., 'The New Powers of Arrest: Plus ça change: More of the Same or Major Change?' [2007] Crim LR 459.
- Curwen, N., 'The Remedy in Conversion: Confusing Property and Obligation' (2006) 26 Legal Studies 570.
- Feldman, D., 'Containment, deprivation of liberty and breach of the peace' 68(2) [2009] CLJ 243.
- McBride, N., 'Trespass to the Person: The Effect of Mistakes and Alternative Remedies on Liability' 67(3) [2008] CLJ 461.
- Tan, F. K., 'A Misconceived Issue in the Tort of False Imprisonment' (1981) 44 MLR 166.

Online Resources

www.oup.com/uk/qanda/

Go online for extra essay and problem questions, a glossary of key terms, online versions of all the answer plans and audio commentary on how selected ones were put together, and a range of podcasts which include advice on exam and coursework technique and advice for other assessment methods.

Nuisance and *Rylands v Fletcher*

9

ARE YOU READY?

In order to answer questions on this topic, you need an understanding of the following:

- **Private nuisance:**
  - who can sue in private nuisance?
  - who can be sued?
  - categories of nuisance (ie noise, vibrations, smells, etc)
- **Public nuisance**
- **The rule in *Rylands v Fletcher* (1866) LR1 Exch 265**
- **Specific defences to claims of nuisance**
- **Remedies available in nuisance**

KEY DEBATES

The House of Lords decisions of *Cambridge Water Co Ltd v Eastern Counties Leather plc* [1994] 1 All ER 53 and *Transco plc v Stockport MBC* [2003] UKHL 61 considered the rule in *Rylands v Fletcher* (1868) LR 3 HL 330. Since then, it appears to have been assumed into the law of nuisance, but should *Rylands v Fletcher* remain an action in its own right? This is considered in the final question of the chapter.

QUESTION | 1

Elsa owns an estate in London comprising a plot of land with two large houses on it. One of the houses, and its large garden, is leased to Che. The other house is divided into three flats, which are

(▶)

leased to Bertrand on the top floor, Anisa on the middle floor, and Edward on the ground floor. Che complained when he discovered that the garden he had leased from Elsa had been contaminated over the years by a leaking sewage pipe under the ground, which Elsa knew about but made no effort to repair. Although this did not present a health hazard, it made the ground unsuitable for growing vegetables, a particular hobby of Che's. As he cannot cultivate the land, Che has sublet part of the garden to Donna, a traveller, who has parked her caravan on the land. Donna often stands on Che's garden wall throwing stones and bricks at the windows of Edward's flat, occasionally breaking them. Anisa is often disturbed by Bertrand, who has the flat above hers, as the floors and ceilings are not very well soundproofed, and when she is in her flat, she can hear him walking about, talking and running water in his flat. It is particularly bad when he is in his kitchen, which is above her bedroom, as Bertrand has ceramic tiles which amplify the noise of his footsteps. Edward, who lives in the flat below Anisa's, also upsets her by occasionally using his flat as a studio to make films to promote various charities. She can hear the noise of the actors and crew stomping about and shouting, and some of the electronic equipment attached to Edward's ceilings makes the floors of Anisa's flat vibrate. All this is particularly bothersome to Anisa's daughter Zara, as she likes to sleep for most of the daytime so that she can paint at night. Furthermore, the electrical impulses from the filming equipment cause a disturbance to Anisa's television signal so that she cannot watch any live transmissions whilst Edward is working in his flat. Anisa asked Edward to stop. When he ignored her, she bought a powerful portable radio. She now stands outside his flat in the street, waiting for filming to start. Whenever it does so, she turns the radio up to its full volume so that Edward is unable to continue recording. Anisa and Edward have also complained to Bertrand because he has allowed the roof of the house to fall into disrepair, resulting in water damage to all the flats. Although Bertrand is responsible under the lease for the repairs to the roof, he has told the other tenants he cannot pay for them as he is unemployed and it is all he can do to afford the rent.

Advise the parties as to their rights in the tort of private nuisance.

CAUTION

- This question requires you to consider private nuisance only. Do not be tempted to discuss negligence or other categories of nuisance.

- Nuisance questions can appear quite complex, so spend some time organizing your material before you begin. If you rely on the question to set your structure you may repeat principles of law, which is time-consuming and will not increase your grade.

DIAGRAM ANSWER PLAN

Identify	Who are the potential claimants? Can they sue in private nuisance? Is there any actionable nuisance being caused? Who are the defendants? Any defences? What remedies might be available?
Relevant law	Private nuisance is a common law tort. Cases to consider include: *Sturges v Bridgman* [1879] 11 Ch D 852; *Halsey v Esso Petroleum Co Ltd* [1961] 1 WLR 685; *Hunter v Canary Wharf Ltd* [1997] 2WLR 684; *Baxter v Camden LBC (No 2)* [1999] 3 WLR 939; *Coventry v Lawrence (No 2)* [2014] UKSC 46.
Apply the law	All but Zara appear to be Elsa's tenants. As they will have a leasehold interest, they will be eligible to sue (*Hunter v Canary Wharf Ltd*). Consider what they are complaining of. Have the courts previously considered sewage, noise, and/or property damage, to be potential nuisances? If so, are the facts suggestive that the noise etc is 'unlawful'?
Conclude	Che is faced with an actionable nuisance, but may not be able to sue due to the principle of caveat lessee. Zara may not be able to sue as she appears to have no proprietary rights. Anisa cannot sue for loss of TV signals, and further, her actions appear to be malicious, and therefore more likely to be considered unlawful should Edward sue. Bertrand is responsible for the leaking roof but the courts order the costs to be split between all parties.

[1.]SUGGESTED ANSWER

[1.] Remember that all the answers in this book are suggested answers to assist you. You may wish to adapt the answers to better suit your writing style.

[2.] Define legal terms and back up with legal authority.

[3.] Students are often confused about this point, but remember the tort is designed to give a remedy to your land rather than to you personally.

We have been asked to advise various parties as to their rights in the tort of private nuisance. [2.] Private nuisance is a land-based tort. It is 'the unlawful interference with a person's enjoyment of land, or some right of way over, or in connection with it' (*Read v J Lyons & Co Ltd* [1945] KB 216 (CA) *per* Scott LJ). Potential remedies are an injunction and/or damages.

As the tort is concerned with land, to be able to sue in private nuisance a person must have an [3.] 'interest in land' (usually a free-hold or leasehold title), not just a personal licence (*Hunter v Canary Wharf Ltd* [1997] 2 WLR 684). Most of the potential claimants are Elsa's tenants, and therefore appear to have a leasehold interest. They should thus be eligible to sue. We will consider each claimant in turn.

[4.] Che

[4.] In this answer, claimants have been addressed in the order they appear in the question, but this will not always be the best approach to answer questions.

Regarding Che, his garden is suffering due to sewage contamination. Leaking sewage, a nuisance to anyone's mind, has been judicially recognized as that (*Fawcett v Phoenix Inns Ltd* [2003] EWCA Civ 128). Therefore he appears to have an actionable nuisance. So the question is, who might he be able to sue?

As a rule, one should sue the person responsible for the nuisance. Che would be able to sue a neighbour if their inactions have led to some type of encroachment on his land (*Lemmon v Webb* [1895] AC 1; *Delaware Mansions Ltd v City of Westminster* [2002] 1 AC 321). However, in this scenario the person responsible for the potential nuisance is his landlord. In this respect Che is unlikely to receive the support from the court, as the general principle in these situations is caveat lessee, as discussed in *Erskine v Adeane* [1873] LR 8 CH 756. In other words, Che should have investigated the land thoroughly before signing his tenancy, as he will be assumed to have taken on the property as seen. The situation might be different if the contamination was a recent event, [5.] but the facts clearly stipulate that the sewage contamination has occurred 'over the years', that is prior to Che moving in to his house.

[5.] Remember that you are advising on the facts given, so ensure you weave these into your answer.

Anisa

Regarding Anisa, she is claiming that her property is being interfered with by Bertrand's walking, talking, and running water. These appear to be everyday activities. Therefore although noise is a nuisance (*Tetley v Chitty* [1986] 1 All ER 663), according to the case of *Baxter v Camden LBC (No 2)* [1999] 3 WLR 939, to be an actionable nuisance, the noise will have to be considered both annoying and unusual. As the facts suggest that what Bertrand is doing is not 'annoying and unusual', this would not as a rule lead to a successful claim. However, Anisa may have a claim as Bertrand has ceramic tiles in his flat. Depending on the layout of the flat, that is if the ceramic tiles had been placed by Bertrand directly above Anisa's bedroom, the court might consider this to be unusual (*Stannard v Charles Pitcher Ltd* (2003) Env LR 10), although in a general way it is quite common to have ceramic tiling as flooring; therefore, although annoying, it is not 'unusual'.

Regarding Anisa's complaints against Edward, in respect of television interference, as the general rule such interference is not an actionable tort (*Bridlington Relay Ltd v Yorkshire Electricity Board* [1965] Ch 436; *Hunter v Canary Wharf*). However, following the case of *Network Rail Infrastructure Ltd v CJ Morris (t/a Soundstar Studio)* [2004] EWCA Civ 172, it has been accepted that electromagnetic interference can be an actionable nuisance. In this situation, as it is live transmissions that are suffering from interference rather than a video recording, the courts are likely to take the view that Anisa can find an alternative remedy to the situation.

However, Edward does appear to be creating noises which are both 'annoying and unusual', by working with actors, and causing her floors to vibrate. [6.] Vibrations can constitute actionable nuisance (*Sturges v Bridgman* [1879] 11 Ch D 852; *Halsey v Esso Petroleum Co Ltd* [1961] 1 WLR 685). In this respect, a defence of undertaking charity work will not assist Edward. The general rule is that even if a process or business is considered useful, as charity work should be considered, no matter how useful this might be, it will not prevent an action being considered 'unreasonable' by the courts, who may then issue an injunction. Such was the situation in *Adams v Ursell* [1913] 1 Ch 269, when an injunction was granted against a fried fish shop. By contrast, in *Miller v Jackson* [1977] 3 WLR 20 an injunction was not issued as the defendants (a village cricket club) were carrying out a useful activity. Damages were awarded instead. In our situation, it is possible that Anisa would be awarded damages rather than an injunction. However, it does not appear that it is Anisa herself that is affected, but her daughter, Zara.

Zara

To advise Zara, we must consider her interest in land. We are not informed as to whether she has an independent letting from Anisa, or just a mere personal licence to live in Anisa's flat. [7.] It as a matter of principle that it is not necessary for rent to be paid in order to have a valid lease (Law of Property Act 1925, s. 205, confirmed by *Ashburn Anstalt v Arnold* [1989] Ch 1), but this looks as though it is a mere licence. If this is the case, Zara will be unable to sue in her own right (*Malone v Laskey* [1907] 2 KB 141; *Hunter v Canary Wharf*). Even if she has an interest in land, it is likely that she would be considered a sensitive claimant (*Robinson v Kilvert* [1889] 41 Ch 88). The general rule is that a claimant will not succeed if s/he is adversely affected by a nuisance which would not affect a normal person. In this respect, even if Zara did have an interest in the land, it is unlikely that her sensitivity would allow her to be able to pursue an action against Edward.

An action for private nuisance may be brought against anyone with a degree of responsibility for the nuisance (**Sedleigh-Denfield v O'Callaghan [1940] AC 880**), whether they have control of the land or not. Edward is now complaining of the interference caused by Anisa. Although the interference is caused when she is standing in the street, rather than on her own property, a person can be sued in nuisance if their actions are affecting another's enjoyment of land (*Church of Jesus Christ of Latter Day Saints v Price* [2004] EWHC 3245). This appears to be the case here.

Further, not only is Anisa being disruptive, she is acting maliciously. While malice is not usually relevant to liability in tort, it may convert an otherwise reasonable act into one which is unreasonable (*Christie*

6. Ensure you have mastered all the subcategories of nuisance that might appear on your exam paper. The case of **Halsey v Esso Petroleum** discusses several types of nuisance.

7. If you are looking for extra marks, consider incorporating other areas of law.

v Davey [1893] 1 Ch 316; *Hollywood Silver Fox Farm Ltd v Emmett* [1936] 2 KB 468). In such a situation, the judge is likely to take an unfavourable view of Anisa's actions and Edward may be granted an injunction against her.

Edward also has an actionable nuisance in terms of Donna, as she has broken his window. Property damage is always an actionable nuisance (*St Helen's Smelting Co v Tipping* [1865] 12 LT 776) even as a one-off event (*Crown River Cruises Ltd v Kimbolton Fireworks Ltd* [1996] 2 Lloyd's Rep 533). It appears that Che has authorized the nuisance by letting Donna on to the land (*Lippiatt v South Gloucestershire Council* (1999) 3 WLR 137). Edward may be able to sue Che for allowing this unacceptable behaviour to continue (*Southwark London Borough Council v Tanner* [1999] 3 WLR 939).[8] However, in **Coventry v Lawrence (No 2) [2014] UKSC 46** the Supreme Court held, by a 3 : 2 majority, that a landlord should be liable only where they had directly participated in the nuisance (mere encouragement of the activity was not enough); or where an actionable nuisance was a 'virtual certainty'.

Regarding Bertrand's repairs, or lack of them, water entering a building and causing property damage will always be a nuisance (*Marcic v Thames Water Utilities Ltd* [2003] 3 WLR 1603). His lease stipulates that he is responsible for repairs. Consequently, Anisa and Edward have every right to sue him on this ground. Saying that, it has been decided that where through no fault of one party, a nuisance has arisen from their land, and that nuisance cannot be paid for, that person should look for alternative accommodation (*Abbahall v Smee* [2002]1 All ER 465). Otherwise, it may be that the court orders there to be a splitting of the costs between all the parties.

[8] As you will have seen there is an abundance of case law in this answer. Make sure you include recent Supreme Court decisions.

LOOKING FOR EXTRA MARKS?

- Use a variety of case law to advise on both sides of the argument. Ensure you incorporate recent (and relevant!) Supreme Court decisions.
- If appropriate, incorporate legal principles that are not strictly speaking from 'tort' law, to display your knowledge of the interface of tort law with these other areas.

QUESTION 2

Cockroach plc produce chemicals. As part of their operation, they use a fume-suppression device which is extremely noisy. The device is widely regarded as efficient and reliable but, occasionally, noxious fumes are nonetheless discharged into the atmosphere. Numerous residents in the locality have complained of the noise and the fumes produced by Cockroach plc's operations. These residents allege it is impossible to sleep with the windows open and that they cannot now sunbathe in their back gardens.

Ellen, one of the local residents, complains that her highly sensitive African violets, grown in her greenhouse, have all died as a result of the pollution caused by Cockroach plc. Moreover, Tom, a lodger in Ellen's house, complains that the combined effect of the noise and the fumes has caused him to suffer from a respiratory illness and extreme fatigue brought on through loss of sleep so that he has become permanently incapable of work.

Advise the parties in the law of nuisance.

CAUTION

■ The question concerns private nuisance, but it also raises the possibility of an action in public nuisance, and an action under the rule in *Rylands v Fletcher*. Unless your examiner specifies otherwise, make sure you address all the potential actions, albeit briefly.

DIAGRAM ANSWER PLAN

Identify

Who are the complainants? Do they qualify to sue in private nuisance and/or public nuisance?
Who do they sue?
What damage have the complainants suffered?
How is the issue of personal injury dealt with in private nuisance?
Does Rylands v Fletcher have an application?

Relevant law

Hunter v Canary Wharf Ltd [1997] 2WLR 684.
Coventry v Lawrence (No 2) [2014] UKSC 46.
Attorney-General v PYA Quarries Ltd [1957] 2 QB 169.
Rylands v Fletcher (1868) LR 3 HL 330.

Apply the law

Cockroach plc is both the occupier of land and the creator of the potential nuisance, but are the complainants eligible to sue in private nuisance?
What other courses of action do they have?
Has Tom suffered special damage, and does he thus qualify for an action in public nuisance?
In the circumstances what remedies are available?

Conclude

Ellen appears to have a proprietary interest and can therefore sue in private nuisance, but is more likely to be awarded damages rather than an injunction.
As a lodger, Tom is not able to sue in private nuisance. He may have a claim under public nuisance.

Private nuisance is the unreasonable, and therefore illegal, interference to someone's enjoyment of their real property (land or proprietary rights) (*Read v Lyons & Co Ltd* [1945] KB 216 *per* Scott LJ). To be able to sue for private nuisance, Ellen must have a proprietary interest in the land affected (eg as owner or tenant or a licensee with exclusive possession (*Malone v Laskey* [1907] 2 KB 141; *Hunter v Canary Wharf Ltd* [1997] 2 All ER 426)). [1.]There is nothing in the facts to suggest that Ellen lacks such an interest.

An action for private nuisance may be brought against anyone with a degree of responsibility for the nuisance, including the creator of the nuisance and, in certain circumstances, the occupier of the land from which the nuisance emanates (*Sedleigh-Denfield v O'Callaghan* [1940] AC 880). [2.]Since Cockroach plc is both the creator and the occupier, it appears to be the only possible defendant.

In *Kennaway v Thompson* [1981] QB 88, the Court of Appeal highlighted the point that private nuisance is based on the principle of give and take and that the role of the court is to try to reach a balance between the competing interests of neighbours. Usually the activity complained of is not in itself unlawful, but it will become so when carried out to an extent which the law regards as unreasonable due to its negative effect on the claimant's property. Reasonableness is to be measured against a number of relevant criteria.

Although the issue of locality is often relevant, in *St Helens Smelting Co v Tipping* (1865) 11 HL Cas 642 a distinction was drawn between property damage and 'sensible personal discomfort'. Locality is relevant to the latter, but not the former since damage to property cannot be regarded as reasonable. Thus since Ellen complains of damage to property (her African violets), the character of the neighbourhood will be irrelevant. However, Cockroach plc will raise the argument that the African violets are 'hypersensitive'. If Ellen's violets are unusually sensitive and there is evidence that other plants would not be damaged in the same way, there is no nuisance (*Robinson v Kilvert* (1889) 41 Ch D 88). But, if Cockroach's activity would have interfered with ordinary land use, the fact the claimant is unusually sensitive will make no difference (*McKinnon Industries v Walker* (1951) 3 DLR 557). [3.]Evidence from other residents who have been affected by the fumes will assist Ellen's case in this respect.

Cockroach may well seek to argue that they have taken all reasonable steps to avoid creating a nuisance—specifically their choice of equipment that is widely regarded as efficient and reliable. While this might be enough to avoid liability in negligence, liability in nuisance differs. It was said in *Wagon Mound (No 1)* [1961] AC 388 that

1. If the facts of a question do not give you all the information that you need, you may make the mistake of spending too long justifying your approach. This sentence demonstrates a quick way of addressing this problem.

2. Highlight key conclusions as soon as possible.

3. Make sure you look at both sides of any legal argument. We are looking for balancing of arguments rather than a definitive conclusion.

negligence in the narrow sense is not necessary in a nuisance action. But negligence in the wider sense of foresight of harm under the remoteness test is a requirement. ⁴·Thus, if it is foreseeable to Cockroach that Ellen might suffer damage through the emission of fumes, an action may lie (*Wagon Mound (No 2)* **[1967] 1 AC 617**). On this basis, it is probably foreseeable that the fumes emitted from Cockroach's factory could cause damage of the kind actually suffered. These and other factors will also apply to the other local residents referred to in the question.

⁴· This is a sophisticated paragraph. This is not needed if you want to achieve a 'good mark', but it is if you are hoping to achieve an 'exceptional mark'.

Tom is a lodger, which suggests that he does not have a sufficient interest in the land affected. In *Hunter v Canary Wharf Ltd* **[1997] 2 All ER 426**, it was held that since the tort of private nuisance is directed at protecting the claimant's enjoyment of his rights over land, the action must be confined to a person with a sufficient interest, ⁵· in which case Tom is unlikely to be able to claim in the law of nuisance.

⁵· Remember to consider the general principles of law, and then apply them to your situation.

So far as the other residents' discomfort is concerned, locality is a factor. Where there is an inconvenience nuisance (eg noise, smells, etc), it is relevant to consider where the alleged nuisance takes place. It was said in *Sturges v Bridgman* **(1879) 11 Ch D 852** that 'what would be a nuisance in Belgrave Square would not necessarily be so in Bermondsey'. The facts reveal that others in the area have had to close their windows, indicating that the interference is widespread.

Regarding the noise, the courts have previously indicated that loss of sleep is far from trivial (*Halsey v Esso Petroleum* **[1961] 2 All ER 145**). Duration is another factor. What matters for private nuisance is that the defendant's activity must be capable of causing a continuing, unreasonable state of affairs, although a one-off dangerous occurrence is still capable of being a nuisance (*Crown River Cruises Ltd v Kimbolton Fireworks Ltd* [1996] 2 Lloyd's Rep 533).

As private nuisance is concerned with damage to an interest in land, respiratory ailments and fatigue do not come into this category; therefore there is no cause of action in nuisance for damages for personal injury (*Read v Lyons* **[1947] AC 156** confirmed in *Hunter v Canary Wharf Ltd*). Thus any claims by residents in respect of personal injury, such as Tom's respiratory illness and extreme fatigue, are actionable only in negligence, or possibly public nuisance.

⁶· As always, explain to your examiner what the proposed action is, and its legal authority.

⁶· Public nuisance is a crime actionable as a tort on proof of special damage, and is defined as an act or omission which materially affects the reasonable comfort and convenience of life of a class of Her Majesty's subjects (*Attorney-General v PYA Quarries Ltd* **[1957] 2 QB 169**). A class of people has to be affected. The fact that other residents have complained suggests an effect on a class of people, but Tom has to prove special damage, that is damage over and above that suffered by others in the class, if he is to be successful. Here the inconvenience caused by the fumes is suffered by everyone, but

only Tom appears to have suffered respiratory illness and consequential loss of earnings. According to *Walsh v Ervin* **[1952] VLR 361**, the damage must be substantial, direct, and not consequential, although it may cover general damage. [7.] There remains the question whether Tom's respiratory illness and collapse from exhaustion, being forms of personal injury, may be compensated under public nuisance, or whether his claim should lie in the tort of negligence (*Hunter v Canary Wharf Ltd*).

[7.] If you identify any type of physical illness in a question which appears to be based in the law of nuisance, this is an indication that you should consider the law of public nuisance.

Assuming a nuisance is established, which is more likely in Ellen's case than in Tom's, the appropriate remedy must be considered. The options are damages and/or an injunction. In general there are four guiding principles, as identified in *Shelfer v City of London Electric Lighting Co* **[1895] 1 Ch 287**. Damages will be awarded instead of an injunction if the injury to the claimant's legal rights is: (i) small; and (ii) can be estimated in money terms; and (iii) can be adequately compensated by a small money payment; and (iv) it would be oppressive to grant an injunction. However, in the more recent decision of *Coventry v Lawrence (No 2)* **[2014] UKSC 46**, Lord Neuberger noted that the court should not be fettered by these four principles, and the mood of the court generally seemed to indicate that an award of damages was preferable to an injunction as a remedy.

[8.] In general, public interest may be relevant to the grant of an injunction, although the cases are divided on this issue. For example, the fact that heavy job losses might result from the closure of a factory was ignored in granting a temporary injunction on a factory in *Bellew v Cement Co* **[1948] IR 61**; but in *Miller v Jackson* **[1977] QB 966** an injunction was refused against a cricket club on the ground that there was a public interest in preserving playing fields for recreation. The fairness and utility arguments may prevent a full injunction from being granted provided the interference is not excessive, though a partial injunction might be used to limit the timing of the defendant's activities and maintain a balance between the legitimate interests of both parties (*Kennaway v Thompson* **[1981] QB 88**; *Halsey v Esso Petroleum* **[1961] 2 All ER 145**). Overall, it is suggested that damages rather than an injunction will be awarded.

[8.] Start with general principles, then narrow down to focus on the facts in front of you. This is an opportunity to consider policy issues.

On the facts given, an action under the rule in *Rylands v Fletcher* **(1868) LR 3 HL 330** seems unlikely to be successful as the rule requires the accumulation of something tangible that is likely to do mischief if it escapes. Fumes and smells do not normally satisfy this requirement, so a *Rylands* action is unlikely to apply.

LOOKING FOR EXTRA MARKS?

- Remember that the law of nuisance is an issue of give and take, and as such discussing issues of policy can add merit to your answer, if you have time.
- Your 'potential claimant' will want a remedy to their problem. Therefore, it is worthwhile discussing remedies in depth. There is scope to bring in academic literature here.

QUESTION | 3

Chromoshine Ltd, a cleaning firm, stores large quantities of a toxic industrial cleaning chemical on its land on an industrial estate close to a residential housing estate. Evidence shows that a group of badly behaved teenagers has been seen in the area on various occasions over the past two months. Mysteriously, a barrel of the toxic fluid is overturned and breaks open with the following results.

Sharma, a catering assistant who works in Chromoshine's canteen, steps in the spilled fluid. Her legs are badly burned and her shoes are seriously damaged.

A quantity of the fluid seeps into an underground water supply used by the South Downs Water Company with the result that the latter must find an alternative source of supply in order to meet its statutory obligations to water consumers in the area.

The fluid flows into the street outside Chromoshine Ltd's premises. Traffic in the street sprays the fluid on to Enya's front garden rendering it in need of decontamination. The smell of the fluid causes Enya physical illness and she also has to vacate her house for two weeks while remedial action is taken.

Consider the liability of Chromoshine Ltd under the rule in *Rylands v Fletcher*.

CAUTION

- This question calls for a detailed knowledge and application of the principles contained within the rule in ***Rylands v Fletcher* (1868) LR 3 HL 330**, so you should not stray into the law relating to private nuisance generally or any other torts.
- It also allows for some comment upon the continued usefulness of the rule in ***Rylands v Fletcher***, which was thoroughly discussed in the case of ***Transco plc v Stockport MBC* [2003] UKHL 61**.

DIAGRAM ANSWER PLAN

Identify	Is the substance within the *Rylands v Fletcher* rule, that is was it brought on to the land for the defendant's benefit and might it do mischief? Has there been an escape? Was the defendant company engaged in a 'non-natural use' of its land? Is the harm suffered an actionable loss? Are there any defences available?
Relevant law	*Rylands v Fletcher* (1868) LR 3 HL 330. *Rickards v Lothian* [1913] AC 263. *Read v Lyons* [1947] AC 156. *Cambridge Water Co v Eastern Counties Leather plc* [1994] 1 All ER 53. *Transco plc v Stockport MBC* [2003] UKHL 61.
Apply the law	Do any of the claimants have a potential claim? What might be the difficulties with each claim? If one of the potential claimants is qualified to pursue a claim, consider each of the rules comprising the tort. Are all of the conditions met? What are the rules on remoteness of damage?
Conclude	Sharma will have no claim in *Rylands v Fletcher*, as she was on the defendant's land at the relevant time, therefore there was no 'escape' from that land. Enya may have a claim for property damage, but not for her physical illness. The water company may be able to claim, depending on the nature of the scientific knowledge at the time. The defendants may raise the defence of 'unforeseeable act of a third party'.

 SUGGESTED ANSWER

[1.] As the question asks you to advise under the rule in *Rylands v Fletcher* you should explain what this is at the beginning of your answer.

[1.] The rule in *Rylands v Fletcher* (1868) LR 3 HL 330 applies when a defendant, in the course of the non-natural use of his or her land, brings on to that land, and keeps or collects there, something which, if it escapes, is likely to do mischief. The tort is one of strict, but not absolute, liability. This means that where an escape occurs and causes relevant harm, the defendant is prima facie liable for that harm, but may nevertheless successfully defend an action if s/he is able to raise one of several recognized defences.

<table>
</table>

2. Discuss the general issues, then expand on them. After this, apply to the facts.

3. If you jump straight to your application, you will miss an opportunity to demonstrate your knowledge in this area.

4. You can discuss facts of cases, but remember that they are to help highlight the legal principles. We do not want to read a case summary, as such.

2. First, there has to be an accumulation by the defendant for the defendant's own benefit of something likely to cause harm if it escapes. The strictness of this requirement was emphasized by Lord Bingham in the case of *Transco plc v Stockport MBC* **[2003] UKHL 61**, so that the 'something' has to be an accumulation which is recognized either subjectively, by the defendant, or objectively, as creating an exceptionally high degree of risk.

Historically, the court has decided that water (*Rylands* itself), gypsies (*Attorney-General v Corke* **[1933] Ch 89**), and a flagpole (*Schiffman v Order of St John* **[1936] 1 KB 557**) all fall into this category, although the correctness of the latter two may be doubted following the decision in *Transco plc v Stockport*, where the importing into the site of water for domestic purposes, even in bulk in a large-diameter pipe, did not meet that criterion. **3.** Consequently, the core element appears to be accumulation rather than the operation of nature. In the facts above, there is a deliberate accumulation and if the cleaning chemical is known (or ought to be known) to be likely to do 'mischief' if it escapes, then liability may follow.

Secondly, the accumulation must involve a non-natural use of land. This point has proved to be the most crucial of the control mechanisms available to the courts in extending or reducing the scope of the rule. **4.** Lord Bingham in *Transco plc v Stockport MBC* thought that 'ordinary user' is preferable to 'natural user', and that the rule applied only where the defendant's use is shown to be extraordinary and unusual. In that case the use of a large-bore pipe to take domestic water to a tower block was an ordinary use of its land. However, Lord Goff in the House of Lords in *Cambridge Water Co v Eastern Counties Leather plc* **[1994] 1 All ER 53** made it clear that the storage of substantial quantities of chemicals on industrial premises was almost a classic case of non-natural use and that it could not be thought objectionable to impose strict liability for escape. Several cases including *Transco* and *Cambridge Water* have rejected the idea in *Read v Lyons* **[1947] AC 156** that the manufacture of munitions in wartime could be a 'natural' or ordinary use of land. Applying these principles, it would seem likely that a court would be entitled to hold that the storage of the chemicals by Chromoshine was a non-natural use of land. This would be so even though it was an industrial area, as was the land in the *Cambridge Water* case, and even though it provided employment in the area.

Thirdly, there must be an 'escape from a place where the defendant has occupation of, or control over, to land which is outside his occupation or control'. On this basis, it seems clear that Sharma could not pursue an action in *Rylands*, since, at the material time, she was still on the premises of Chromoshine Ltd, as was the claimant in *Read v Lyons* who was injured by exploding munitions whilst still on the defendant's premises.

Fourthly, the relevant type of harm must be suffered. Since *Rylands* involved damage caused to a neighbour's land the question might be asked whether damage to chattels and personal injury are protected by the tort. Cases such as *Transco* and *Cambridge Water* seem to suggest that *Rylands v Fletcher* liability is a subset of nuisance liability, and thus the tort is concerned with protecting interests in land. Therefore, damage to chattels and personal injury harm would be beyond the scope of the rule. [5.] In *Transco* Lord Bingham (albeit obiter) drew support from *Cambridge Water* and *Hunter v Canary Wharf Ltd* [1997] 2 All ER 426 to reach this conclusion. Thus, Sharma will also be unable to recover for this reason.

[5.] Some examiners are keen to see you include obiter dicta, as part of your reasoning. This is an opportunity to display your knowledge of leading authorities, and also an opportunity to incorporate academic literature.

In contrast, Enya, while not being able to claim for personal injury, may be able to recover for the diminution in value of her property and the loss of use of the land. The calculation will involve assessing the cost of reinstatement of the property and the cost of alternative accommodation.

Fifth, recovery of damages is dependent upon reasonable foreseeability of the type of harm. The *Cambridge Water* case decided that the test for the remoteness of damage in *Rylands* is the same as that in negligence: *Wagon Mound (No 1)* [1961] AC 388 (reasonable foresight of the kind of harm suffered). In *Cambridge Water* the impact of the escaping chemicals on the water supply of the claimant was unforeseeable in the light of scientific knowledge current at the time of the escape and there was no recovery for this unforeseeable harm. Therefore, it is the harm which has to be foreseeable and not the escape. So it is arguable that the type of loss that Enya suffered would be regarded as not too remote a consequence of the spillage of some of the toxic fluid into a street down which motor traffic passes.

The position of the South Downs Water Company will have to depend on the scientific evidence available. It is known that the chemical is 'toxic' but we are not informed of the precise nature of its behaviour. In the *Cambridge Water* case the type of chemical spilled was thought to evaporate into the atmosphere and that it could not be absorbed into the ground and thence to the water-bearing rocks. If such contamination is foreseeable then Chromoshine will be liable for the diminution in the value of the land which will reflect the consequential economic loss.

[6.] As with all questions, look out for relevant defences which allow you to discuss case law not involved in your answer up to that point.

[6.] Regarding any defences that may be open to Chromoshine Ltd, the only one that might be available is 'act of a stranger'. A defendant may avoid liability where the escape is attributable to the act of a third party over whom the defendant had no control. The defence will fail if the claimant can show that the act which caused the escape was an act of the kind which the owner could reasonably have contemplated and guarded against. In *Rickards v Lothian*, property was damaged by water. The overflow of the water was caused by an unknown third party blocking the waste pipe in a sink. It was held that this provided a defence akin to the defence of 'act of God' or sudden overwhelming force such as an attack by enemies of the state. By contrast, in *Hale v Jennings* [1938] **1 All ER 579**, the court held that the defendant should have foreseen the possibility of third-party interference with a fairground ride. The facts simply say the spillage occurred mysteriously, though it may not be unreasonable to suppose an element of human interference, in which case the defence may well be invoked.

LOOKING FOR EXTRA MARKS?

- If you have a narrow question, such as this one, your examiner will expect you to know the law in depth, so make sure you take the opportunity to refer to the judgments in detail.
- If a cause of action or a judgment is controversial, you should read academic literature beforehand, so that you have a variety of arguments to use in your answer.

QUESTION | 4

Atif buys a farmhouse and the surrounding farm buildings in Toddington. He plans to convert the house into a 50-bed private nursing home, retaining an apartment for his private use. Planning permission to convert the land from agricultural use has been granted by Toddington District Council.

During the building works, Desmond, a neighbouring landowner, complains that dust produced by Bashitt Ltd, the building contractors employed by Atif to convert the farm buildings, has blocked a drain on Desmond's land. When the nursing home opens, Desmond objects to the increased traffic to the premises and retaliates by frequently firing guns, day and night, on his own land. Desmond claims this is necessary in order to control the rabbit population and to frighten off birds.

Some weeks after Atif's nursing home receives its first residents, Desmond lets some of his outbuildings to John, who organizes a 'rave' on one night only. Many of the residents at the home are unable to sleep and one of them, Mary, suffers a broken arm when she falls down some stairs on her way to complain to Atif about the noise. Many of the residents find other nursing homes, resulting in loss of income to Atif.

Advise Atif, Bashitt Ltd, Desmond, and John of their liability in tort and how, if at all, Atif can prevent raves from taking place in future.

CAUTION

- This question deals with the problem of disputes between neighbouring landowners and requires consideration of both public and private nuisance. Keep in mind the different forms of action, in terms of legal standing, type of damage covered, and remedy sought, throughout your answer.

DIAGRAM ANSWER PLAN

Identify	Who are the defendants? Who are the claimants? Can they sue in public nuisance? Can they sue in private nuisance? What remedies are available?
Relevant law	*Attorney-General v PYA Quarries Ltd* [1957] 2 QB 169. *Corby Group Litigation v Corby BC* [2008] EWCA Civ 463. *Hunter v Canary Wharf Ltd* [1997] 2 All ER 426. *Dennis v Ministry of Defence* [2003] EWHC 793 (QB). *Coventry v Lawrence (No 2)* [2014] UKSC 46.
Apply the law	Do Atif and Mary qualify as claimants in public nuisance? Atif and Desmond are owners and may sue in private nuisance. Are any of their complaints actionable in nuisance?
Conclude	The 'rave' may be considered public nuisance. Atif should seek an injunction to prevent future events. Desmond's action for damage caused by the dust should succeed, but his actions with a shotgun appear to be malicious and therefore an actionable nuisance.

SUGGESTED ANSWER

1. The structure of this answer may not appear to match the question set. You might plan to advise each individual in turn and/or start with private nuisance, but write your answer in a logical order, whatever you decide to do (see notes 7 and 8).

2. Note here that the question does not ask you to advise Mary, although she is clearly in the facts of the question. Do not waste time discussing her.

1. The 'rave' might give rise to an action in public nuisance. Public nuisance is generally a crime which is actionable as a tort on proof of special damage, and is defined as an act or omission which materially affects the reasonable comfort and convenience of life of a class of Her Majesty's subjects (***Attorney-General v PYA Quarries Ltd* [1957] 2 QB 169**). A class of people has to be affected, and although this usually refers to a neighbourhood, the 50 residents and Atif may well be a sufficiently large group. In regard to a public nuisance, there is no need for claimants to have an interest in land in order to be able to sue. **2.** This will be important to Mary as she has no remedy in private nuisance.

To succeed in a private action for damages arising out of a public nuisance, it must be shown that the claimant has suffered damage over and above that suffered by others. It is unclear whether the specific damage must be a different kind, or whether a difference in terms of extent will suffice. Here the inconvenience caused by the noise is suffered by everyone, but Mary's broken arm and the loss of income to Atif are specific to the claimants. According to ***Walsh v Ervin* [1952] VLR 361**, the damage must be substantial, direct, and not consequential, although it may include general damage. It was believed, following the decision and reasoning in *Hunter v Canary Wharf Ltd* **[1997] 2 All ER 426**, that personal injury claims should be considered under the 'now fully developed law of negligence'. However, in *Claimants in Corby Group Litigation v Corby BC* **[2008] EWCA Civ 463** the Court of Appeal held that personal injury is recoverable in public nuisance. Despite this, given the circumstances in which Mary's arm was broken, the injury might be regarded as consequential rather than direct damage, and Mary will not be able to claim. Financial loss such as loss of income is also recognized as special damage (*Benjamin v Storr* **(1874) LR 9 CP 400**).

^{3.}The dust produced by Atif's contractors may also give rise to public nuisance liability, if the damage is sufficiently widespread (*Hunter v Canary Wharf*). However, there is no evidence here that anyone other than Desmond has been affected.

By contrast, private nuisance is unreasonable interference with a person's use or enjoyment of land (*Read v Lyons & Co Ltd* [1945] KB 216). To be able to sue for a private nuisance, the claimant must have a proprietary interest in the land affected (*Malone v Laskey* [1907] **2 KB 141**; *Hunter v Canary Wharf Ltd*). Atif and Desmond have no problems in this respect as they are both owners. However, Mary, as 'a resident', is likely to be no more than a contractual visitor.

^{4.}An action for private nuisance may be brought against anyone with a degree of responsibility for the nuisance (*Sedleigh-Denfield v O'Callaghan* **[1940] AC 880**). Thus John and Bashitt Ltd (as creators) may be sued even though they have no interest in the land (*Southport Corp v Esso Petroleum Ltd* **[1953] 3 WLR 773**). The occupier can also be sued in respect of a nuisance committed by an independent contractor. However, temporary building works will not generally give rise to an action in private nuisance unless they are carried out in an unreasonable manner. Generating sufficient dust to block a drain suggests carelessness on the part of the builders, so Desmond may succeed in claiming damages to cover the cost of clearing the drain. Furthermore, a landlord can be sued where he lets premises and in doing so authorizes an activity which amounts to a nuisance, although in *Coventry v Lawrence (No 2)* **[2014] UKSC 46** the majority held that a landlord should be liable only where they had directly participated in the nuisance or where an actionable nuisance was a 'virtual certainty'. Applying this to Desmond, there is no evidence of his participation in organizing the rave, nor is it clear that an actionable nuisance was an inevitable outcome.

In *St Helens Smelting Co v Tipping* **(1865) 11 HL Cas 642**, and approved in *Hunter v Canary Wharf Ltd*, nuisances were said to fall into three main categories: encroachments; physical damage; and unreasonable interferences. Of these three, the first two will almost always be automatically unreasonable, whereas the reasonableness (and thus

^{3.} Try to conclude one aspect of the scenario, before moving on to another set of facts.

^{4.} Discuss general principles then move on to your facts to apply the law.

lawfulness) of the third is a question of degree and calls for a complex balancing of relevant factors, including the locality within which the activity takes place. **5.** Thus it was said in *Sturges v Bridgman* **(1879) 11 Ch D 852** that 'what would be a nuisance in Belgrave Square would not necessarily be so in Bermondsey'. In the question, the general locality is a rural area within which a noisy event such as a rave might not be regarded as falling within what is normally acceptable.

5. This is a famous quote, which frequently appears in answers on private nuisance.

So far as Desmond's objection to the nursing home is concerned, Atif might argue that he has planning permission for the changed use of the land; however, this will not afford him an outright defence. In *Gillingham Borough Council v Medway (Chatham) Dock Co Ltd* **[1992] 3 WLR 449**, planning permission was granted to convert a naval dockyard into a commercial port, causing a substantial increase in heavy traffic, especially at night. It was held that no nuisance was committed given the altered character of the locality. **6.** By contrast, in *Wheeler v JJ Saunders Ltd* **[1995] 2 All ER 697**, planning permission granted to a farmer to build two pig housing units on land next to the claimant's was held not to have changed the nature of the entire locality. Further, *Coventry v Lawrence* **[2014] UKSC 13** calls for an evaluation of the locality as though it were not affected by the nuisance aspects of the planning changes. Altogether, the question seems largely to be one of scale. However, it is clear that locality is irrelevant where material property damage is caused by the alleged nuisance (*St Helens Smelting Co v Tipping*). Therefore Desmond's action for damage caused by the dust should succeed.

6. Think carefully before writing down too many facts; they should be succinct and purposeful.

A second important factor is the duration of the interference. Generally a 'one-off' event will not be sufficient to establish a nuisance. Having said this, it may suffice if it arises from an underlying state of affairs (*Sedleigh-Denfield v O'Callaghan* **[1940] AC 880**; *Castle v St Augustine's Links* **(1922) 38 TLR 615**). In this case, there has been no indication that a series of similar events will be arranged in future; **7.** therefore on balance, a single rave party is unlikely to be actionable in private nuisance, though it could well be a public nuisance, as in *R v Shorrock* **[1993] 3 All ER 917**, in which case the residents would all benefit from any injunction to prevent a recurrence.

7. Consider whether this would have been a better place to start your section on public nuisance. The time to decide this is before you start your answer, not halfway through.

While malice is not usually relevant to liability in tort, it may convert an otherwise reasonable act into one which is unreasonable. This covers deliberately making a noise with a view to annoying one's neighbour (*Christie v Davey* **[1893] 1 Ch 316**) or deliberately causing damage (*Hollywood Silver Fox Farm Ltd v Emmett* **[1936] 2 KB 468**). On the facts of this scenario, Desmond, in deliberately firing guns all day and night, has created an unreasonable state of affairs. In line with the reasoning (and the facts) in *Hollywood Silver Fox Farm v Emmett*, although the sound of gunshots may be expected in a rural area, the fact that Desmond's activity is intended to cause a nuisance may be enough to make it actionable.

Generally, the more useful the defendant's activity, the less likely the court is to grant an injunction. In ***Dennis v Ministry of Defence [2003] EWHC 793 (QB)***, low-level training flights by military aircraft were held to be a nuisance but an injunction was withheld on the basis of public interest. Here, the construction of a nursing home seems to reflect the defendant's own commercial interest rather than offering any important public amenity.

[8.] Consider whether this paragraph is in the wrong place. You can usually use an asterisk to insert a paragraph, but if you do make sure you are informing your examiner precisely where it goes.

[8.] Two remedies are available in the event of a private nuisance—damages and an injunction. A claimant such as Atif may well be seeking both: damages for past losses; and an injunction to order a continuing nuisance to cease and to prevent a recurrence in the future. Damages being the legal remedy, they will be awarded as of right once the nuisance is made out; but injunctions are a discretionary remedy, allowing for a fairly sophisticated approach to balancing the parties' rights. Although this may well apply as between Atif and Desmond, none of this reasoning would seem to assist John.

➕ LOOKING FOR EXTRA MARKS?

■ Before starting your answer, it is often worthwhile drawing a flow diagram of what you intend to cover and the order you intend to cover it in. The more logical the structure of your essay, the more it will please your examiner.

■ Ensure that you clearly convey any conclusions you have reached in your arguments.

Ⓠ QUESTION | 5

'It would ...lead to a more coherent body of common law principles if the rule [in *Rylands v Fletcher*] were to be regarded as essentially an extension of the law of nuisance to isolated escapes from land.

Lord Goff in ***Cambridge Water Co Ltd v Eastern Counties Leather plc*** [1994] 1 All ER 53.

Discuss the interrelationship between the two torts in light of this statement. Should the rule in *Rylands v Fletcher* remain an action in its own right?

❗ CAUTION

■ The answer also requires consideration of the principles underlying the imposition of liability in nuisance and under the rule in ***Rylands v Fletcher***, with emphasis being placed upon both shared and distinguishing features.

■ In particular this question requires discussion of the House of Lords' decisions in ***Cambridge Water Co Ltd v Eastern Counties Leather plc*** [1994] 1 All ER 53 (in which Lord Goff subjected the interrelationship between these two torts to detailed examination) and, to a lesser extent, ***Transco plc v Stockport MBC*** [2003] UKHL 61.

DIAGRAM ANSWER PLAN

> Identify the rule.

> Consider the cases of *Cambridge Water Co Ltd v Eastern Counties Leather plc* and *Transco plc v Stockport MBC* and how they might have impacted on the rule.

> Identify the similarities and distinctions to private nuisance.

> Consider any distinctions that merit keeping the rule as a separate action in tort.

> Back up conclusions with reference to academic literature.

SUGGESTED ANSWER

Liability under the rule in **_Rylands v Fletcher_ (1868) LR 3 HL 330** is imposed on a defendant where in the course of non-natural use of his land he accumulates upon it for his own purposes anything likely to do mischief if it escapes, and which does escape and cause damage.
[1.] In **_Rylands_**, the defendants had employed independent contractors to construct a reservoir on their land for their factory. The contractors negligently failed to discover and block a disused mineshaft, and consequently water from the reservoir burst through the shafts and flooded the claimant's mine. The defendants were held personally liable despite the absence of fault on their part and no apparent remedy from the existing law.

[1.] Consider how much time you wish to spend discussing the facts of the case, if at all.

At the time, it appeared that Blackburn J did not believe he was laying down any new principle of law. However, during the early twentieth century, the rule seemed to take on a life of its own, until the case of **_Read v Lyons_ [1947] AC 156** prevented the rule from being a marker for strict liability for ultrahazardous activities.

The more recent decisions of the House of Lords in **_Cambridge Water Co Ltd v Eastern Counties Leather plc_ [1994] 1 All ER 53** and **_Transco plc v Stockport MBC_ [2003] UKHL 61** have clarified the confusion which has marked the development of the tort. In *Cambridge Water*, it was held that strict liability under the rule in **_Rylands v Fletcher_** only arose if the defendant knew or ought reasonably to have foreseen that the escape would cause damage.

2. If there are essential facts which the courts used to devise the ratio, then discuss them.

3. As these are important cases, your examiner will be looking to see if you have included quotes from them. However, only include quotes that easily fit into your structure.

4. Tort law is frequently approached to supply a remedy where other laws do not provide one, but the court is unlikely to devise a completely new tort.

5. As with all answers, we are looking for a balancing of arguments. If you address a question from one side only, you are unlikely to achieve a high mark.

2. In *Cambridge Water*, the defendant could not have reasonably foreseen that the seepage of the chemical through the factory floor would cause the pollution to the claimants' borehole, and was not therefore liable under the rule in *Rylands v Fletcher*.

The gist of Lord Goff's treatment of this point was that *Rylands v Fletcher* and private nuisance derived from the same core and that since the authoritative cases on private nuisance led to the conclusion that reasonable foreseeability of damage was an essential element of private nuisance, it must also be an essential element under the rule in *Rylands*. **3.** Further, in *Transco*, Lord Bingham stated clearly that '[t]he rule in *Rylands v Fletcher* is a sub-species of nuisance'. This approach suggests that the place of *Rylands* is within private nuisance. This is more so as private nuisance does not include recovery of damages for personal injury (*Malone v Laskey*; *Hunter v Canary Wharf*) and it now seems likely that personal injury damages will not be recoverable under *Rylands* either.

Further, it is apparent, particularly in more recent decisions culminating in *Cambridge Water*, that the judges are steadily eroding non-fault-based liability. Further, the importance of fault-based liability in nuisance was recognized by Lord Reid in *Wagon Mound (No 2)* **[1967] 1 AC 617** when he stated that 'fault of some kind is almost always necessary and fault involves foreseeability'. **4.** As Lord Goff noted in *Cambridge Water*, strict liability for operations of high risk would be better served by statute law than the rule in *Rylands*, and this is perhaps what the courts would desire.

In fact, there are several overlaps between *Rylands* and the tort of nuisance, which may mean that the rule could be disposed of with no detriment to English law. For example, liability for nuisance arises where there has been an unreasonable interference with the claimant's proprietary interest in land. In *Read v Lyons* **[1947] AC 156**, Lord Simonds indicated that in most cases the law of nuisance and the rule in *Rylands v Fletcher* may be 'invoked indifferently'. Also, the principle of reasonable user in nuisance means that a defendant acting reasonably will not be liable for harm to his/her neighbour's enjoyment of his/her land. This is closely allied to the principle of natural use found in the rule in *Rylands v Fletcher*, albeit that in *Transco plc v Stockport MBC* **[2003] UKHL 61** Lord Bingham considered that the principle would be better described as ordinary rather than natural, applying the Privy Council analysis in *Rickards v Lothian* **[1913] AC 263**. Lord Bingham also restated the proposition that Blackburn J had regarded *Rylands v Fletcher* itself as a simple case of nuisance.

5. However, there are marked distinctions between the torts, and consequently, removing the rule may cause an injustice. *Rylands* is founded upon the non-natural accumulation of something by the defendant on his land which is likely to do damage if it escapes. The 'something' has to be dangerous in itself. For example, combustible material, in itself, is insufficient should a fire ignite spreading to another's property. (*Stannard v Gore* [2012] EWCA Civ 1248). This clearly excludes things naturally found on the defendant's land, such as trees; growing a tree is a natural use of soil (***Noble v Harrison* [1926] 2 KB 332**). However, in ***Crowhurst v Amersham Burial Board* (1878) 4 Ex D 5**, a yew tree on the defendant's land projected over land belonging to the claimant on which cattle grazed. The leaves of yew trees are poisonous, and the claimant's horse died after eating some of them. The defendant was held liable under the rule in ***Rylands v Fletcher*** on the basis that it was not a natural use of land to plant a poisonous tree on it.

A further distinction that can be drawn between the rule in ***Rylands v Fletcher*** and the tort of nuisance relates to 'standing to sue'. With respect to the former, it was stated by Lawton J in ***British Celanese v A H Hunt* [1969] 1 WLR 959** that once an escape is established, anyone who suffers consequential damage may claim irrespective of whether or not they are occupiers of adjoining land. However, nuisance is premised upon protecting proprietary interests in land. Since the claimant must satisfy the requirement of having a proprietary interest in order to bring an action in nuisance, members of his family who lack this interest will be precluded from suing even though they have suffered the nuisance as a result of the defendant's activity, as in ***Malone v Laskey* [1907] 2 KB 141**. The correctness of the decision in ***Malone*** was confirmed by the House of Lords in ***Hunter v Canary Wharf Ltd* [1997] 2 WLR 684**, which held that an action in nuisance can only be brought by a person in 'exclusive possession' of the affected land, or by an owner without exclusive possession.

[6.] However, as pointed out by John Murphy in 'The Merits of *Rylands v Fletcher*', ***Rylands*** has never formally required a claimant to hold a proprietary interest, and further, comments in ***Transco*** regarding such a need were obiter. Murphy also points out that Article 8 of the European Convention of Human Rights grants all citizens equal respect for their private lives; therefore, to base an action on proprietary interest alone seems at odds with Convention rights. This might be an important aspect in maintaining ***Rylands*** as an actionable tort.

[7.] The question, then, left to be answered is whether ***Rylands v Fletcher*** has any legal merit on its own. Academic opinion, in the light of the recent House of Lords cases is divided. In 'The distinctiveness of *Rylands v Fletcher*', Donal Nolan argues that since ***Cambridge Water*** and ***Transco***, ***Rylands*** is but 'a shadow of its former self, lacking either rationale or practical significance'. Further, in 'Deconstructing the Rule in *Rylands v Fletcher*', A. J. Waite argues that legislation will be required if ***Rylands v Fletcher*** is to become legally potent.

[6.] If you are hoping to achieve a high mark, you need to incorporate academic literature into your answers, particularly for essay-style questions.

[7.] As with case law, your academic commentary should be balanced to provide a debate for the merits of both sides of any argument.

However, Murphy argues that ***Rylands*** 'forms a useful residual mechanism for securing environmental protection by individuals affected by harmful escapes from polluting heavyweight industrialists'. This is built on by Róisín Áine Costello, who notes that in regard to fracking, ***Rylands*** might be a 'powerful deterrent against irresponsible practices through the threat of both monetary and reputational damage'.

8. We are looking to see if your conclusion flows logically from your well-balanced discussion of relevant law and academic commentary.

8. As society has recently seen the promotion of human rights, and also of fracking, it may well be that ***Rylands v Fletcher***, although currently dormant, will be awakened for use in future litigation. For this reason the rule should be maintained as a separate tort.

LOOKING FOR EXTRA MARKS?

- In essay questions, remember that your examiner will be assessing your detailed knowledge of the cases, along with your use of academic commentary. This requires in-depth preparation in your subject, but the benefits are that you can structure your essay to incorporate your knowledge in a way that suits you.
- Be bold and innovative with your arguments. As long as they are legally sound, they will be rewarded.

TAKING THINGS FURTHER

The articles below consider **Rylands v Fletcher***. Taken as a whole, they examine its effect and how it might be used in contemporary circumstances.*

- Costello, R. A., 'Reviving *Rylands*: How the Doctrine Could Be Used to Claim Compensation for Environmental Damages Caused by Fracking' RECIEL 23 (1) 2014. ISSN 2050-0386.
- Murphy, J., 'The Merits of *Rylands v Fletcher*' Oxford Journal of Legal Studies 24 (2004), 643–69.
- Nolan, D., 'The Distinctiveness of *Rylands v Fletcher*' LQR 121 (2005) 421.
- Waite, A. J., 'Deconstructing the Rule in *Rylands v Fletcher*' J Environmental Law (2006) 18(3) 423–42.

Online Resources   www.oup.com/uk/qanda/

Go online for extra essay and problem questions, a glossary of key terms, online versions of all the answer plans and audio commentary on how selected ones were put together, and a range of podcasts which include advice on exam and coursework technique and advice for other assessment methods.

10 Defamation and Privacy

ARE YOU READY?

To answer questions on defamation, you need an understanding of the following:

- Categories of defamation:
  - libel
  - slander
- What constitutes a defamatory statement:
  - innuendo
- Defences to defamation:
  - absolute privilege
  - qualified privilege
- The Defamation Act 2013:
  - section 2: Truth
  - section 3: Honest Opinion
  - section 4: Publication on matter of public interest
- Offer of Amends, Defamation Act 1996 sections 2–4

To answer questions on privacy, you need an understanding of the following:

- The nature of privacy
- The overlap between the torts of misuse of private information, and other causes of action
- Trespass
- Negligence
- The Human Rights Act 1998
- The Protection from Harassment Act 1997

KEY DEBATES

The Defamation Act 2013 has received mixed reviews. Whilst it is approved of for trying to balance issues of Human Rights, at present there are some areas of the statute which require further enlightenment from the court. In particular, does libel still remain actionable per se, or does it now need quantifiable evidence of some kind? Mullis and Scott, writing before recent Court of Appeal decisions, offer some useful analysis.

 QUESTION | 1

Fatima is a student of the Du Maurier College of Melodrama. She believes that she is being sexually harassed by Omar, one of the lecturers at the college. She writes a letter, addressed to all the governors and lecturers at the college, which includes the statement: 'Omar sexually harasses female students'.

Fatima takes the letter to the public library, where she makes 200 copies of it. By mistake, she leaves the original letter in the photocopier, where it is found by Nosey, who reads the letter and posts it, anonymously, to Omar's wife.

Fatima sends copies of her letter to every governor and lecturer at the college, using the internal post. Each letter is in a brown envelope, addressed to the recipient and marked 'confidential'. Two days later, one of these letters is found pinned to a noticeboard in the students' common room. Omar denies the allegation of sexual harassment.

Advise Omar as to his cause of action, if any, in defamation. You should ignore any issues of vicarious liability.

 CAUTION

■ Problem questions on defamation often require you to discuss whether defamation has occurred and what defences are available. Make sure you balance your answer to incorporate both aspects.

DIAGRAM ANSWER PLAN

Identify	Has a defamatory statement been made? If so what type of cause is this? Does the claimant meet the requirements to sue? What defences are available?
Relevant law	Defamation Act 2013. *Lachoux v Independent Print Ltd* [2017] EWCA Civ 1334. *Sim v Stretch* [1936] 2 All ER 1237.
Apply the law	Is the statement about the claimant? Does it 'tend to lower the claimant in the estimation of right-thinking members of society'? If so, has it been published? The defence of truth Defamation Act 2013 s. 2 or qualified privilege are potentially available.
Conclude	A defamatory statement has been made in permanent form (ie libel). However, Fatima may be able to raise a defence to this.

SUGGESTED ANSWER

[1.] This is the three-part test for defamation, so in any question on defamation you need to be able to articulate this, identify relevant authorities, and apply it to your problem.

[1.] To pursue an action in defamation, Omar will have to establish that words used about him were defamatory, that the statement referred to him, and that it was published to a third party. Omar does not have to establish that the Fatima's statement was untrue, as the law presumes that a defamatory statement is false, but by virtue of s. 1(1) Defamation Act 2013, a 'statement is not defamatory unless its publication has caused or is likely to cause serious harm to the claimant'. Clearly allegations of 'sexual harassment' will have the potential to cause serious harm to the claimant.

[2.] Remain focused on your answer throughout. Do not waste time going through the rules of slander when there is clearly no need to do so. (Even if you have spent a long time revising it!)

[2.] Defamation comes in two forms: libel and slander. Here, as the words were written, this would be an action in libel which technically remains actionable per se, although the courts may look for evidence of pecuniary damage by the time of hearing (*Lachoux v Independent Print Ltd* [2015] EWHC 2242; *Ames v Spamhouse Project Ltd* [2015] 1 WLR 3409). However, the judgment in *Lachoux v Independent Print Ltd* [2017] EWCA Civ 1334 appears to be more liberal.

There is no single test for when words are defamatory, but if the words 'lower the claimant in the estimation of right thinking members of society' (*Sim v Stretch* [1936] 2 All ER 1237), they are likely to be classed as defamatory. Further, it does not matter whether the words are true or false for them to be considered defamatory (*Daniels v British Broadcasting Corporation*) [2010] EWHC 3057).

[3.] Make your application as clear as possible. It helps your examiner follow your argument.

[3.] Applying this knowledge, a statement specifying that someone sexually harasses female students is clearly defamatory, even more so given Omar's profession, since it suggests he abuses a position of trust. Further, the statement clearly refers to Omar by name.

Regarding the third requirement, that is publication, in defamation, publication means simply the communication of the statement to a third party (ie a party other than the claimant). Each fresh publication is a new libel and will be a major factor to be considered when assessing the amount of any damages to be awarded. Fatima has clearly published the defamatory material to the governors and lecturers at the college. Omar will also argue that the letter left on the photocopier has been published to Nosey, because a publication may occur even if the maker of a statement negligently allows a third party to read it (*Theaker v Richardson* [1962] 1 WLR 151).

Nosey has published the letter to Omar's wife, but Omar may be able to sue Fatima for this unauthorized publication. In *Cutler v McPhail* [1962] 2 QB 292, it was held that the author of a defamatory letter sent to a newspaper was also responsible for its subsequent publication by that newspaper. [4.] In *Slipper v BBC* [1991] 1 QB 283, it was held that the makers of a defamatory television programme should have foreseen that it would be reviewed in a national newspaper, thereby spreading the allegations to a wider audience. The Court of Appeal, however, took the view that the actions of an unauthorized person could break the chain of causation, thereby releasing the original maker of the statement from any responsibility for its further publication, that is as a matter of remoteness of harm. However, as Fatima has negligently left a document in a public place, Omar may still be able to sue Fatima for this publication.

[4.] Discuss relevant authorities to lead up to the conclusion that you wish to make.

Omar may also allege that the college is responsible for the publication of the letter on the students' noticeboard. It is not clear how the letter appeared on the board, but Omar will allege that the college is responsible because the college authorities should have removed the copy and that, by failing to do so, they adopted the defamatory statement and published it to the users of the common room. To have removed the letter would have involved no expense, and no damage to the structure of the building. This accords with the reasoning in *Byrne v Deane* [1937] 1 KB 818, in which the manager of a clubhouse had failed to remove an allegedly defamatory notice. Omar must show, however, that the college authorities had a reasonable opportunity to discover the letter and to remove it from the noticeboard.

5. You will need to be prepared to tackle relevant defences in an answer to a defamation question. Allow yourself plenty of time to do so.

5. Omar should be made aware that Fatima may have a valid defence. She is likely to argue that her statements are true (**Defamation Act 2013, s. 2(1)**). In order to succeed with this defence, Fatima must prove that, while it does not have to be 100 per cent accurate, the 'sting' of the defamatory statement must be substantially true. This statutory defence has replaced the former common law defence of justification, but appears to have maintained the essence of the defence.

6. Although you should try to keep case facts to a minimum, they can help you get across the parallel arguments to your problem.

6. So, for example, in *Alexander v North Eastern Railway Co* (1865) 34 LJQB 152, the defendant was able to show that the claimant had been convicted of an offence and sent to prison and had served two weeks. The jury was entitled to regard the original statement (that he had served three weeks) as having been justified. However, in *Wakley v Cooke & Healey* (1849) 4 Exch 511, the defendant could not justify the statement that the claimant journalist was a 'libellous journalist' as this was taken to mean that he made a habit of writing libels, not just on the one established occasion. Even if Fatima can demonstrate that she, herself, had been harassed, she may not be able to prove the 'sting' of the allegations that

7. To ensure a good 'flow' in your answer, conclude your paragraph and write a sentence leading onto the next paragraph.

7. Omar is consistently harassing female students, and therefore this defence will not work. In which case, she may argue the defence of qualified privilege.

The governors and the lecturers of the college are the intended recipients of Fatima's letter. Fatima may invoke qualified privilege. In this defence the law recognizes that it is in the public interest to protect some communications provided there is no malice and the communication is published no more widely than is necessary. If Omar can show that Fatima was motivated by malice, she will not be able to invoke the defence, (*Horrocks v Lowe* [1975] AC 135). However, the facts do not suggest there is malice in this case.

Omar may argue that Fatima has circulated her allegations too widely to invoke this defence. In *Adam v Ward* [1917] AC 309 it was suggested that a publication to the public at large could be protected by the defence of qualified privilege if it related to a matter of the widest public importance, but the defence of privilege will be lost if the defendant exceeds the privilege by communicating the allegations to those with no legitimate interest.

8. Remember who you are advising and try to write your answer with this in mind. Here there is a danger that you may start advising Fatima rather than Omar.

8. Fatima has an interest to protect in complaining about Omar to the proper authorities within the college, and the college authorities have a reciprocal duty or interest to receive it. The courts have taken the view that where there is a pre-existing relationship then there is no need to establish the exact nature of the duty–interest involved: *Kearns v General Council of the Bar* [2003] EWCA Civ 331. However, in *Chapman v Lord Ellesmere* [1932] 2 KB 431 it was held that the publication of a disciplinary decision of the jockey club was privileged when it appeared in *The Racing Calendar*, but not privileged when it appeared in *The Times* newspaper. Likewise, in *De Buse*

v McCarthy [1942] **1 All ER 19** the court found that a report that was posted in public libraries had been circulated too widely. By contrast, in *Kearns v General Council of the Bar*, the Bar Council had circulated to all barristers incorrect and defamatory material about a firm of solicitors. This was retracted two days later but the claimants sued. The Court of Appeal held that the communication was between parties in an established relationship which required the flow of free and frank communications and that qualified privilege applied.

Applying *Kearns*, any communication between a student and the governors of the college ought to entitle the student to rely on the defence of qualified privilege if it relates to the conduct of a member of staff. There is a clear incidence of the duty–interest relationship identified in *Adam v Ward*. The fact that the governing body might be a large number of people does not matter. In *Horrocks v Lowe*, the House of Lords held that qualified privilege extended to a complaint made against a town councillor published to all the other councillors.

[9.] Make sure that you conclude by advising the relevant party. What about Omar? What remedies are available if his action is successful?

[9.] However, did Fatima have any right to circulate her allegations amongst the academic staff? If the articles of government of the college show that all the lecturers have the right to participate in the running of the college the net of qualified privilege will reach further; otherwise, she will have published too widely.

LOOKING FOR EXTRA MARKS?

■ Keep your focus on the question, and who you are asked to advise. You can lose marks by not advising the right person.

■ Consider any remedies available to an action in defamation. You do not need to spend long discussing them, but they should be in your answer somewhere.

QUESTION | 2

Sanjay Selloff, the Member of Parliament for Wessex North, is in the process of introducing a Private Member's Bill in Parliament authorizing the redesignation of agricultural lands in his constituency for industrial development. This would allow Mover Cars Ltd to build a manufacturing plant in the area. During the Parliamentary debate, the MP for a neighbouring constituency, Peter Piper, who belongs to the Wessex Alliance Party, emerged as the Bill's loudest opponent.

On hearing of the debate, Nick Whippet, the Chairman and Chief Executive of Mover, wrote to Selloff stating:

> Mover Cars' principal opponent in the House is a hypocrite like the party he belongs to and whose opposition to the scheme has more to do with the fact that he has recently purchased several farms in Wessex North which he stands to lose than with his apparent concern for the preservation of the countryside.

Selloff confronts Piper with the allegations during a Parliamentary debate and accuses him of abusing his position by failing to disclose his personal interests. The *Wessex Daily Globe* is interested in this matter and publishes a detailed report of the debate. Selloff has also written to the *Wessex Daily Globe* stating that 'Peter Piper MP is a liar whose only interest is to protect his own property at the expense of bringing employment into the region'. Using this information, which it does not check with Peter Piper, the newspaper prints an editorial criticizing Peter Piper in similar terms. In fact Peter Piper does not own property in the Wessex North constituency.

Consider the law of defamation as it applies to the potential liability of the parties.

! CAUTION

- Your answer should try to balance the issue of the statement with any defences available.

- The new defence of publication on a matter of public interest replaces the **Reynolds** defence (**Reynolds v Times Newspapers [1999] 4 All ER 609**). A strong answer will consider how the statutory approach reflects principles previously evolved through case law extending the boundaries of qualified privilege.

DIAGRAM ANSWER PLAN

Identify	Has a defamatory statement been made? If so, is it libel or slander? Does the claimant meet the requirements to sue? What defences are available?
Relevant law	Defamation Act 2013, Defamation Act 1996, and Defamation Act 1952. *Lachoux v Independent Print Ltd* [2017] EWCA Civ 1334. *Sim v Stretch* [1936] 2 All ER 1237.
Apply the law	Is the statement about the claimant? Does it 'tend to lower the claimant in the estimation of right-thinking members of society'? If so, has it been published? Consider the defences of truth (Defamation Act 2013 s. 2), absolute privilege and qualified privilege, and publication on a matter of public interest.
Conclude	Defamatory statements have been made (both in libel and slander). However, defences may be available for the various parties, although Selloff is unlikely to have a defence for his words written outside the House.

Peter Piper may be able to bring an action in the tort of defamation against Nick Whippet, Selloff, and the *Wessex Daily Globe*. [1.]If the defamatory statement is conveyed in a permanent form it is libel, whereas if it is in a temporary form, it is slander. Peter Piper must prove the three elements of the tort of defamation: that the particular words used were defamatory; that they referred to him; and that they were published to a third party by the defendant.

1. Consider if this is the most logical place to put this sentence. It might be better placed in the following paragraph.

Nick Whippet

Whippet's letter is potentially a libel. Peter Piper will have to prove that the words are defamatory. In addition, the **Defamation Act 2013, s. 1(1)** states that a statement must cause or be likely to cause 'serious harm' to the claimant's reputation to qualify as defamatory. [2.]There is some question these days as to whether libel used to be actionable per se. *Lachoux v Independent Print Ltd* [2015] EWHC 2242 suggested this was no longer the case. However, in the following appeal, *Lachoux v Independent Print Ltd* [2017] EWCA Civ 1334, the Court of Appeal gave a more liberal judgment in this respect.

2. This is a recent ruling, and it is important to keep up to date with court decisions that have followed the Defamation Act 2013's coming into force.

A definition of defamation was suggested by Parke B in *Parmiter v Coupland* [1840] 6 M & W 105, in which he said that a defamatory publication is one which 'is calculated to injure the reputation of another by exposing him to hatred, contempt or ridicule'. In *Sim v Stretch* [1936] 2 All ER 1237 this was reformulated to: 'Would the words tend to lower the claimant in the estimation of right-thinking members of society generally?' [3.]More recently, in *Monroe v Hopkins* [2017] 4 WLR 68 it was said that there must be 'room for differing views to be expressed. . . . [A] statement is not defamatory if it would only tend to have an adverse effect on the attitudes . . . of a certain section of society.' Applying this to the facts, the description of Peter Piper as a 'hypocrite' may not appear to be libellous on its ordinary meaning, but taken alongside the statement referring to 'several farms' then this does suggest a person without scruples and may be considered defamatory.

3. You will have noticed that many defamation cases are quite old and seem out of step with the views of society today. It is worthwhile making this point to examiners.

The second element requires the words to refer to Piper. Although the words do not refer to Piper by name, he can introduce evidence to show that he was the person referred to in the letter. In *Morgan v Odhams Press Ltd* [1971] 1 WLR 1239 the test was said to be the impression that would be conveyed to an ordinary sensible man having knowledge of the circumstances.

The third element of the tort is publication, which has been defined as the communication of defamatory words to a third party (ie to some person other than the claimant). It is evident, therefore, that Whippet has published the statement to Selloff. Having established that the statement is defamatory, we will now consider any potential defences.

[4.] The defence of truth (**Defamation Act 2013, s. 2(1)**) is not available to Nick Whippet, as he would have to prove the truth of the imputation in the defamatory statement, and generalized evidence of behaviour is insufficient. In *Wakley v Cooke & Healey* (1849) 4 **Exch 511**, the statement that the claimant journalist was a libellous journalist was taken to mean that he made a habit of libels and not that he had done so once (which was true)—the defendant could therefore not justify the statement. Given that Peter Piper does not own the farmland claimed, there is no truth in the statement that he is a hypocrite seeking to protect his property.

Similarly, honest opinion (**Defamation Act 2013, s. 3(1)**) is not available to Whippet as a defence since it requires a statement of opinion about fact that can be proven to be true.

There is a defence of qualified privilege in situations where inaccurate information may be passed on but where the public interest in maintaining the free flow of information (even inaccurate information) outweighs the interest in the reputation of the claimant wronged by such a statement, provided that there is no malice behind the statement. Provided Whippet is able to demonstrate that he has a legitimate interest in bringing the matter to the attention of the MP and Selloff has a corresponding duty to receive the information, this defence may work. There must be a reasonable belief in the truth of what is said, although the actual truth need not be established.

Sanjay Selloff

Selloff has made vocal criticisms of Peter Piper. Therefore this is slander.

[5.] Slander is actionable only upon proof of actual damage, or if it meets a specific imputation. The **Defamation Act 1952, s. 2** provides that where the words are calculated to disparage the claimant in any professional capacity, there is no need to prove special damage, 'whether or not the words are spoken of the claimant in the way of his office, profession, calling, trade or business'. Therefore, Selloff's statement regarding Piper's concealment of business interests would be an actionable imputation.

However, as the statement was made during a Parliamentary debate it enjoys the defence of absolute privilege both at common law (*Ex parte Wason* (1869) LR 4 QB 573) as stated in the **Bill of Rights 1688, Article 9**, and under statute (**Defamation Act 1996, s. 13(4)**), so no action will lie in respect of it.

The situation will change, however, if a member repeats outside Parliament what he said in the course of a debate. (*Buchanan v Jennings* [2004] UKPC 36). Therefore, Selloff's letter to the *Wessex Daily Globe* calling Peter Piper a liar is clearly libellous. It has been published to a third party, the newspaper, and, as with Whippet, since the statement is based on the false assertion that Peter Piper is motivated by protecting his property interests, the defences of truth and honest opinion are not available to him. Qualified privilege would depend upon the existence of a duty–interest relationship. Relationships which fall within this defence are narrowly confined. For example, in *Beach v Freeson* **[1972] 1 QB 14** an MP wrote to the Law Society and the Lord Chancellor and his letter repeated defamatory statements made to him by a constituent about a solicitor. It was held that he had a duty to make the statement and that the recipients were under a duty to receive these. Selloff's letter to the paper may not be justified on this basis.

By statute and at common law there is qualified privilege in newspaper or other reports of proceedings in Parliament provided that the reports are fair and accurate. Proof of malice would remove the privilege. However, in respect of the *Globe*'s story, referencing a statement as a rumour offers no protection as it is taken by the courts to be an assertion that the rumour is true. Similarly, the newspaper will be liable for libel even if it has expressly stated in the editorial that it is merely reproducing what the editors have been told by Selloff. Accordingly, the writer of the editorial, the newspaper proprietor, and its printers will each be held liable for its publication.

^{6.} Prepare yourself by reading this Act **before** your examination. Ensure that you understand how the various defences work.

^{6.} The **Defamation Act 2013** introduced a new defence—publication on a matter of public importance (**s. 4**). This defence attempts to balance potentially competing human rights both to freedom of expression (**ECHR, Art. 10**) and to respect for one's private and family life (**ECHR, Art. 8**), which includes protection of reputation. It also recognizes the crucial role of a free press within any truly democratic society. Previously, a similar approach had been upheld by the House of Lords in *Reynolds v Times Newspapers* **[1999] 4 All ER 609**, (the *Reynolds* defence). The *Reynolds* defence was abolished by the **Defamation Act 2013, s. 4(6)**. Now a defendant must show that the statement was on a matter of public interest, and that he reasonably believed that publishing it was in the public interest. **Section 4** also provides guidance to courts in assessing 'reasonable belief', including circumstances in which a failure to check the facts will not be fatal to the defence, and such allowance for editorial judgement as the court 'considers appropriate'. Here, the hypocrisy of an MP would seem to be a legitimate matter of public interest, but Selloff's letter in an editorial appears to be poor professional practice and should undermine the *Globe*'s use of the defence.

^{7.} Advise with the relevant remedy in mind. What does the claimant want? Are they seeking damages?

^{7.} The newspaper may make an 'offer of amends' to Peter Piper by offering to publish an apology or correction and pay him damages even before the writ is served (**Defamation Act 1996, ss. 2–4**). If Peter Piper accepts such an offer the issue must be settled by agreement

between him and the newspaper. The court will only intervene, if necessary, to adjudicate as to the amount of compensation or on the nature of the apology or correction. Acceptance of an offer will operate to terminate the defamation proceedings.

LOOKING FOR EXTRA MARKS?

- Keep up to date with latest case law in this area, and incorporate it in your answer.
- Look out for issues of conflicts in human rights. If you get a chance, weave them into the discussion.

QUESTION | 3

'The trouble with English tort law is that it fails to provide sufficient protection to each citizen's right to privacy in any shape or form.'
Discuss.

CAUTION

- Although this question centres upon the extent to which there is a right of privacy in English law, it will be important to have a knowledge of other torts to explain how they have been used in the past to support aspects of privacy.

DIAGRAM ANSWER PLAN

Introduction – no definitive tort of privacy.

Limits of the tort of trespass for the protection of privacy.

Scope of the Protection from Harassment Act 1997.

The difficulties using an action in defamation.

The effect of the Human Rights Act 1998, and the balancing of competing rights.

The desire for a tort of privacy is no recent phenomenon. For over two hundred years, individuals have gone to court to establish their right 'to be let alone' [1.](*Wheaton v Peters*, 33 US 591, 634 (1834); *Entick v Carrington* [1765] EWHC J98 (KB)). Unsurprisingly, for more than a century jurisprudents have been advocating the right to privacy (see T. M. Cooley, *A Treatise on the Law of Torts* 29 (2nd edn 1888); S. D. Warren and L. D. Brandeis, *The Right to Privacy*, 4 Harvard LR 193 (1890)). The desire for privacy is clearly an international one; for example, in 2014 the Australian Law Reform Commission (ALRC) made the recommendation that the Commonwealth create a right to sue for a serious invasion of privacy.

[2.]Over the years, many judges and academics have commented on the lack of legal protection for a person's liberty. This finally appears to be changing. Until very recently, common law rules have not recognized a specific right to privacy (***Wainwright v Home Office* [2003] UKHL 53; *Wong v Parkside NHS Trust* [2001] EWCA Civ 1721**), nor was harassment a discrete tort (***Kaye v Robertson* [1991] FSR 62**). However, aspects of several different torts did have the effect of protecting a person's privacy, provided the specific ingredients of that tort were satisfied. In addition, the coming into force of the **Human Rights Act 1998** made it easier for a claimant to sue in respect of the wrongful disclosure of private information.

[3.]The case of *Kay v Robertson* highlighted that there was no direct tort of privacy. Kay therefore had to bring his claims under malicious falsehood and trespass. In this respect, trespass to land can protect an individual's privacy, but the actions are limited. ***Bernstein v Skyviews* and *General Ltd* [1978] QB 479** informs us that there is no right of privacy in airspace. This means that it may not be possible to sue if photographs of yourself were taken at an extreme height, with a long-range-lens camera, which were later published without your permission.

It might be thought that the Protection from Harassment Act 1997 would help to solve the difficulty in protecting individual privacy. Unfortunately, the Act has strict stipulations which may mean it is not a benefit to everyone. Specifically, **s. 7(3)** requires there to be a course of action. This is interpreted as meaning two or more occasions. Therefore, it is possible for individuals to exploit the legislation and prevent prosecution, by ensuring that they have infringed the person's privacy on one occasion only! This will be particularly pertinent if that 'one-off' event is a wedding (*Douglas v Hello! Magazine* [2005] EWCA Civ 595).

Additionally, the tort of private nuisance, in certain circumstances, may provide a solution. In ***Hunter v Canary Wharf* [1997] 2 All**

[1.] Under examination conditions, you are unlikely to be able to write down all the details of publications, but do try to specify the author's name and the name of the article.

[2.] This question gives you wide scope to incorporate a number of cases. Make the most of your opportunity.

[3.] Plan your answer before you start to write. Does this paragraph make a point? Does it offer you evidence? What is your analysis?

ER 426 it was held that an act of harassment might amount to a private nuisance if there was an unreasonable interference with the claimant's proprietary interest in the land subject to the act of harassment; but that action would not protect a person with no protected proprietary interest. However, it was suggested in *McKenna v British Aluminium Ltd* **[2002] Env LR 30** that a person with no proprietary interest might have an arguable case under the **Human Rights Act 1988** if there is an interference with family and private life.

The tort of defamation also provides some protection, particularly under the recent Defamation Act 2013. However, even if a statement is defamatory, the claimant will not be successful in their action, if it proves that the statement is true (s. 2). The very essence of privacy is to keep things quiet, whereas an action in defamation brings everything into the spotlight. If a journalist uncovers some unpleasant or salacious (true) fact about a celebrity, then the celebrity has two options. Ignore the publication, and hope that it will not be noticed (which is unlikely), or sue in defamation, and hope to win.

[4.]During the 1990s, some cases were heard which arguably did more harm to the claimant than the original accusations did (*Gillian Taylforth v The Sun* **(1994) unreported**). Therefore an action in defamation is unlikely to provide a remedy for privacy.

Since 2000, the protection of a person's right to privacy must be considered in line with the **Human Rights Act (HRA) 1998 s. 3**, which requires, where possible, that legislation must be interpreted in a way that is compatible with rights provided for in the **European Convention on Human Rights (ECHR)**. Furthermore, it is also unlawful for a public authority to act in a manner that is incompatible with a Convention right (**HRA, s. 6**). One of the rights provided for in the Convention is a right to respect for private and family life (**ECHR, Art. 8**), suggesting that the approach to privacy adopted at common law might change, at least where the actions of public authorities are concerned. Actions on the part of the Home Office would fit this description, but the Convention also covers 'persons whose functions are functions of a public nature' (**HRA, s. 6(3)(b)**), which include the actions of universities, local authorities, and possibly a tabloid newspaper, insofar as information provision can be regarded as a 'public function'. This means that courts must balance two distinct human rights: the publisher's right to freedom of expression (**ECHR, Art. 10**) and the claimant's right not to have private information about him or her unjustifiably disclosed to a third party (**ECHR, Art. 8**).

[5.]According to Lord Nicholls and Baroness Hale in *Campbell v MGN Ltd* **[2004] UKHL 22**, which was the genesis for the tort of misuse of private information, the test to apply is whether the claimant has a reasonable expectation that his privacy will be protected. However, the 'reasonable person's reaction test' may be criticized

[4.] You have made a point and then mentioned a case. Does this create a compelling argument? Try to highlight aspects of the case which offer you evidence to back up your points.

[5.] Consider if you would have developed a better answer if you had started with issues of human rights, that is made the focus of your essay narrower, but gone into more depth.

particularly where the information relates to a disturbed adult or a very young child (see *T v BBC* [2007] EWHC 1683 (QB); *Murray v Express Newspapers plc* [2008] EWCA Civ 446).

An important consideration is whether or not the information is of a type that the claimant would want to control such as a person's health (*Campbell v MGN*), sexual behaviour (*PJS v News Group Newspapers Ltd* [2016] AC 1081), or financial information. However, some such information may have become so widely available as to render privacy virtually irrelevant (*Lord Browne of Madingley v Associated Newspapers Ltd* [2007] EWCA Civ 295).

On the other side of the balance, it needs to be determined what constitutes freedom of expression. For these purposes, political speech in a democratic society deserves protection. Other factors to consider include whether it is in the public interest to disclose the information.

Moreover, it would appear that public figures, including famous football players and other types of celebrity, may have to expect a greater degree of exposure as they have chosen to place themselves in the 'public eye', especially if the 'celebrity' has made untrue public denials relating to extramarital affairs (see *A v B & C* [2002] **EWCA Civ 337**). However, the decision in *Campbell* does indicate that public figures should not be faced with the prospect that all information concerning their private lives should be publishable. This is especially the case where publication might have an adverse impact on a child or stepchild of the public figure: *Rocknroll v News Group Newspaper Ltd* [2013] **EWHC 24**.

[6.] Pay special attention to recent cases, and research academic literature which discusses points of law.

[6.] Those who value privacy highly will have been heartened by recent decisions. In *Vidal-Hall & Ors v Google Inc* [2014] EWHC 13 (QB) Tugendhat J was asked to consider whether misuse of private information, breach of confidence, and breach of DPA statutory duties amount to a claim in tort. He found that they did. On appeal in *Google Inc v Vidal-Hall & Ors* [2015] EWCA Civ 311, the Court of Appeal confirmed that misuse of private information is a tort and moreover that the meaning of damage in the DPA, s. 13 permitted a claim for compensation where there was no pecuniary loss.

[7.] Make sure that you do refer back to the question during your work. You may have found yourself answering a completely different question otherwise!

[7.] Referring back to the question, it is clear that the statement is inaccurate. Although there is not a singular law of protection of privacy, there are mechanisms in place. In fact, a further step was taken in *PJS v News Group Newspapers Ltd* [2016] **UKSC 26**, when it was decided that there was a tort of intrusion into private life. The Supreme Court's decision to keep an injunction in place saw the inevitable disgruntlement of the press. However, as Lord Neuberger explained, that Court was applying the current law, and he added that 'if Parliament takes the view that the courts have not adapted the law to fit current realities, then, of course, it can change the law' [71]. Whether it will or not is another matter.

TAKING THINGS FURTHER

The Defamation Act 2013 changed the law on defamation significantly. Likewise, the issue of privacy is seen in court more frequently. Below is a sample of journal articles which look at these areas.

- Barendt, E., 'Problems with the 'Reasonable Expectation of Privacy' Test' (2016) Journal of Media Law, 8:2, 129–37, DOI: 10.1080/17577632.2016.1209326.
- Descheemaeker, E., 'Protecting Reputation: Defamation and Negligence' (2009) 29 OJLS 603.
- Howarth, D., 'Libel: Its Purpose and Reform' (2011) 74 MLR 845.
- Moreham, N., 'Beyond Information: Physical Privacy in English Law' (2014) 73 Cambridge Law Journal.
- Mullis, A. and Scott, A., 'Tilting at Windmills: The Defamation Act 2013' (2014) 77 Modern Law Review 87.
- Trindade, F. A., 'Defamatory Statements and Political Discussion' (2000) 116 LQR 185.
- Williams, K., 'Defaming Politicians: The Not So Common Law' (2003) 63 MLR 748.

Online Resources

www.oup.com/uk/qanda/

Go online for extra essay and problem questions, a glossary of key terms, online versions of all the answer plans and audio commentary on how selected ones were put together, and a range of podcasts which include advice on exam and coursework technique and advice for other assessment methods.

General Defences

ARE YOU READY?

To answer questions on this topic, you need an understanding of the following:

- The concept of negligence
- The Occupier's Liability Acts
- The defence of *volenti non fit injuria*
- The defence of contributory negligence and the Law Reform (Contributory Negligence) Act 1945
- The defence of illegality—*ex turpi causa non oritur actio*

KEY DEBATES

In *Patel v Mizra* [2017] AC 467, the Supreme Court investigated the defence of illegality (*ex turpi causa non oritur action*) and held that issues of policy can be considered when deciding whether to allow the defence. This has led to considerable discussion in the academic field, not least because, as Robert Sullivan points out in 'Private Rights versus Public Values': 'the jurisprudential boldness of Lord Toulson's judgment, as remarked by Lord Mance and Lord Sumption, raises some uncertainty whether the majority approach will ultimately prevail.'

What are your views on this defence?

QUESTION | 1

'In regard to defences to torts, the defence *volenti non fit injuria* is difficult to utilize and is in need of an overhaul, that is if there is any need for it at all.'

Discuss.

CAUTION

- This question requires an explanation the defence of *volenti*. Although you will need a consideration of its relationship with contributory negligence, keep *volenti* the focus of your answer.

- If you have not studied the defence in depth, do not try to attempt an examination question on it during your exam!

DIAGRAM ANSWER PLAN

> The meaning and operation of the defence of *volenti non fit injuria*.

▼

> Where the defence will work, and where it will not be applicable.

▼

> Contradictions in the deference itself.

▼

> Overlap with contributory negligence, and the Law Reform (Contributory Negligence) Act 1945.

▼

> Conclude.

(A)   SUGGESTED ANSWER

The defence of *volenti non fit injuria* (to one who is willing, no harm is done) is based on the claimant's consent to a situation, which consequently displaces the duty which the defendant would otherwise owe.

[1.] If it succeeds, *volenti* is a complete defence and absolves the defendant from all liability. Because of this, the conditions for its application are quite stringent, and at times difficult to follow.

[1.] If you are writing on any defence, remember to explain how the defence works, and its overall effect on liability.

Volenti encompasses the principle of autonomy, which in a medical ethics context is usually referred to as 'bodily integrity'. As Herring and Wal note in [2.] 'The Nature and Significance of the Right to Bodily Integrity': 'Every human being's right to life carries with it, as an intrinsic part of it, rights of bodily integrity and autonomy.' Further, it has been described by Hale LJ as 'the first and most important of the interests protected by the law of tort' (*Parkinson v St James NHS Trust* [2001] EWCA 530).

[2.] An essay question gives you the chance to demonstrate your wider reading, so make the most of the opportunity. If your lecturer directs you to an article, find time to read it.

But this is a double-edged sword. If the law allows rights of autonomy for a claimant, the defendant has a right to argue that it was the claimant's own self- rule (or free choice) that led to the injury and thus reduces or erases the defendant's liability.

[3.] The significant difficulty with the operation of defence is that it appears to vary according to the defendant's potential tortious liability. How the courts view *volenti* in the context of an action of trespass appears to be different to claims in negligence. Further, overlaps with other defences make the application of any defence to a tort more complex than might first appear. In this respect the quotation is correct.

The principal ingredients of *volenti* are that the claimant must have made a voluntary choice to accept the risk of harm with full knowledge of the nature and extent of that risk. It is therefore necessary to examine three elements: the legal meaning of voluntary; how we determine the claimant has accepted the risk; and the degree of knowledge required before the defence is made out.

The requirement of voluntary choice means that the claimant must be in an autonomous position to make a free informed choice, be legally and mentally competent, and be free from all outside interference. For example, if economic duress caused a defendant to act the way he did, this would not be an autonomous choice. This is particularly pertinent in the employment sphere. The courts have decided that an employee is not *volens* to the risk of injury at work even if he is aware of dangerous practices. In **Smith v Baker [1891] AC 325**, for example, the House of Lords recognized the need to earn a living. Moreover, as a matter of policy the courts recognize that employees, such as rescuers, are exposed to a risk of injury during their working hours. But the risk of injury is a potential 'side-effect' of undertaking their duty, not a risk that they have voluntarily assumed (**Haynes v Harwood [1935] 1 KB 146**).

[4.] Another area where *volenti* is raised is in the context of suicides. The defence has been defeated in a number of so-called custody cases, in which a negligent failure on the part of the defendant has created an opportunity for suicide (**Kirkham v Chief Constable of Greater Manchester Police [1990] 3 All ER 246; Reeves v Metropolitan Police Commissioner [2000] 1 AC 360**) on grounds, in most cases, of impaired autonomy, and also on the policy grounds that a duty to guard against potential suicide should not be negated by the act itself. Similarly, in cases of suicide consequent on physical injury caused due to negligence in the work sphere (**Corr v IBC Vehicles Ltd [2008] UKHL 13**), the courts have recognized that an impairment of autonomy may be such as to defeat *volenti*, even though the deceased had been able, in many ways, to function normally.

As it is based on consent, it has been said that the defence of *volenti* requires some degree of agreement. In regard to intentional torts, particularly medical treatment or participation in sports, this 'agreement' is easier to define. However, the situation is different when considering actions in negligence. Therefore, it is more appropriate in negligence to describe the defence in terms of a 'voluntary assumption of risk'. [5.] This mirrors the wording of the defence found in the **Occupiers' Liability Act 1957, s. 2(5)**, which refers to ' risks willingly accepted as his'.

Despite the terminology, any defence which deprives the claimant of a remedy is taken seriously by the courts and the defendant is required to prove that the claimant's conduct amounts to a clear waiver of any legal rights that may arise from the harm that is risked. In **Wooldridge v Sumner [1963] 2 QB 43** it was said that *volenti* should not be available in the absence of express consent to the legal risk of harm. Further, [6.] in **Nettleship v Weston [1971] 2 QB 691**, Lord Denning said that: 'Nothing will suffice short of an agreement to waive any claim for negligence.' By contrast, there are cases in which it has been held that the defence is available where the claimant merely encounters an existing danger, as in **Titchener v British Railways Board [1983] 3 All ER 770**, where the presence of a 15-year-old on a railway track was taken as evidence of her willingness to undertake the risk of being hit by a train.

6. Use case law to demonstrate your answer.

In reality, an 'agreement', may be inferred from the claimant's conduct, most often manifesting itself by their willing participation in some kind of risky joint venture. In **ICI Ltd v Shatwell [1965] AC 656**, for example, two experienced shot-firers were injured following a joint decision to use detonators against all safety rules. The House of Lords inferred from the claimants' equal knowledge and joint decision that the defence was made out, despite the lack of any apparent 'agreement'.

For the defence of *volenti* to succeed, the defendant must show that the claimant was aware of both nature and extent of the risk of harm. In **Dann v Hamilton [1939] 1 KB 509**, knowledge and apparent acceptance of the range of risks inherent in travelling with a drunk driver in a car was held to be insufficient to support a defence of *volenti*. This was qualified by Asquith J who indicated that it may apply where the risk was so glaringly obvious as to be the equivalent of 'intermeddling with an unexploded bomb' [7.] nowadays, *volenti* is not available for road traffic accidents: **s. 149(3) Road Traffic Act 1988**). By contrast, the claimant in **Morris v Murray [1990] 3 All ER 801** was found to have actively participated in the venture of flying a plane after imbibing a significant amount of alcohol. The claimant therefore knew that the pilot was intoxicated, but regardless of this, he assisted the pilot to prepare the plane for takeoff.

7. Consider whether the answer should have discussed this is more depth.

Prior to the **Law Reform (Contributory Negligence) Act 1945**, contributory negligence could be offered as a complete defence to negligence claims. Since the passing of the Act, the courts have the discretion to reduce damages to take into account the partial responsibility of the claimant in failing to take reasonable care for his own safety. The courts will use this discretion to the full, in order to achieve a calculation which appears to the court as 'just and equitable' (*Jackson v Murray* [2015] UKSC 5).

In this respect, it is clear why contributory negligence is preferred to *volenti*. Only in extreme cases such as **Morris v Murray [1990] 3 All ER 801** should the claimant be denied damages altogether. Moreover, where the denial of liability is considered necessary, in most cases this is justified by public policy rather than by the fact that the claimant has assented to the risk of injury. Case law seems to indicate a general unwillingness on the part of the courts to see a negligent defendant's liability altogether extinguished. [8.]However, It should be noted that contributory negligence is not available to a claim in trespass; *Co-operative Group (CWS) Ltd v Pritchard [2011] EWCA Civ 329* in this respect *volenti* must remain available.

[8.] As always, conclude your essay. However, this might be a starting point to discuss the defence of *ex turpi causa*, which has not been mentioned in the essay itself.

LOOKING FOR EXTRA MARKS?

- Although the focus of your answer should be *volenti*, you have scope to discuss other defences. This could be restructured to allocate some time to discussing the overlap with *ex turpi causa*.

- There is no set answer for essay questions; for extra marks what we are looking for is a demonstration of detailed research and comprehension, written in an original way.

QUESTION | 2

Anya and Tomas, two students, having completed their final examinations, decide to spend a night out at the Mucky Duck, a public house. At the end of the evening, Tomas offers Anya a lift home. They are both extremely drunk. Tomas drives his car down the middle of the road, occasionally swerving to frighten other road users. Anya enthusiastically encourages Tomas in this venture.

Tomas drives through a red traffic light at speed and collides with a car driven by Gary. Gary, who is not wearing a seat belt, is crushed behind the steering wheel of his car. Anya is also seriously injured in the collision.

Advise Tomas of his potential liability in tort. He is keen to learn of any defences that he may have available.

CAUTION

■ This question clearly wants you to focus on defences. In this type of question, you should establish the tort very quickly, as the best defence is that he has not committed a tort! After this, take the remaining time to discuss and apply defences available.

DIAGRAM ANSWER PLAN

Identify	Has Tomas committed a tort? Who are the potential claimants? What defences can Tomas raise?
Relevant law	*Nettleship v Weston* [1971] 2 QB 691. *Road Traffic Act* 1988, s. 149. *Law Reform (Contributory Negligence) Act* 1945, s. 1(1). *Jones v Livox Quarries Ltd* [1952] 2 QB 608. *Pitts v Hunt* [1990] 3 All ER 344. *Froom v Butcher* [1976] QB 286.
Apply the law	Negligence is made out—Tomas has breached his duty of care, causing damage. *Volenti* is not applicable. *Ex turpi causa* might work; if not, consider contributory negligence.
Conclude	Anya will see a reduction in her damages if she is considered contributorily negligent. She may not receive any damages if the court decides this is a situation of *ex turpi causa*. Gary's damages award will also be reduced for not wearing a seat belt.

SUGGESTED ANSWER

Tomas should be advised that Anya and Gary will wish to pursue an action in negligence.

[1] In order to sue in negligence, the claimants have to prove not only that the defendant owed them a duty of care, but that he breached his duty and the breach caused the claimants' damage.

There is no doubt that, as a driver, Tomas would owe a duty of care to both Anya and Gary, since any person who uses the road owes a

[1] Make sure that you discuss the components of the tort. You will have to prove each of these to make an initial finding that a tort has been committed.

2. In this question your focus should be on defences, so do not spend much time discussing contradictory case law to prove the tort.

duty of care to other road users. ²·Moreover, the way Tomas drives suggests that he breached his duty of care, since, by driving through a red light and crashing into another's vehicle, he has clearly not reached the standard ordinarily expected of a reasonably competent driver (*Nettleship v Weston* [1971] 2 QB 691). However, Tomas may be able to advance defences which reduce, or even negate, his potential liability.

Anya

3. Take each defence in turn; identify the defence, discuss it, and apply it. It should not matter which order you choose to write about these, but do not try to discuss them all in one go.

³·Anya's own involvement in the events of the evening may allow Tomas to argue that the defence of *volenti non fit injuria* applies; in other words that the claimant had undertaken a voluntary assumption of risk of injury. In *Titchener v British Railways Board* [1983] 3 All ER 770 the House of Lords took the view that a 15-year-old on railway tracks consented to the risk of injury from a train. In the present case, it may be more difficult to prove Anya's consent to the risk of injury, as, being 'extremely drunk', she may not be deemed to have the mental capacity required to make an informed decision. More to the point,

4. If you are short of time, it would be acceptable to limit your discussion to the Road Traffic Act 1988, s. 149, and its effect.

⁴·Tomas should be advised that the Road Traffic Act 1988, s. 149 prevents reliance on the defence of *volenti* where the compulsory insurance provisions of that Act apply. Here Tomas is driving on a public highway so he is subject to the requirement of compulsory third-party insurance and therefore is unable to rely on *volenti* as a defence.

Although Tomas does not have the defence of *volenti* available, he may be able to rely on the defence of contributory negligence. To establish contributory negligence, Tomas must prove that Anya has failed to take reasonable care for her own safety. First, it must be asked whether harm of this kind to Anya was reasonably foreseeable. The test is objective so that even if Anya is so drunk as to be incapable of making a rational judgement, this will not matter for the purposes of this defence (*Owens v Brimmell* [1977] QB 859).

While the claimant's conduct does not have to be the cause of the collision, it must be causally connected to the harm suffered. It will be enough if the claimant places herself in a dangerous position which increases the chance that harm of this kind will foreseeably be caused (*Jones v Livox Quarries Ltd* [1952] 2 QB 608).

If Anya accepts a lift from a person who is incapable of driving safely, she appears not to have acted as a reasonably prudent person would in respect of their own safety (*Jones v Livox Quarries Ltd*). Therefore, it is submitted that the court will find her contributorily negligent, and reduce her damages accordingly. ⁵·If the defence applies, the Law Reform (Contributory Negligence) Act 1945, s. 1(1) provides that the court must apportion damages to such extent as it thinks 'just and equitable' (*Jackson v Murray* [2015] UKSC 5) having regard to the claimant's share in the responsibility for the damage.

5. As this defence applies, spend more time analysing it. You will notice that there are a number of recent cases to consider. Make sure you incorporate these to give yourself a full answer.

The factors likely to be taken into consideration by the court are the levels of injuries (and other damage), causation, and blameworthiness. This varies significantly. So for example, in *Owens v Brimmell* [1977] QB 859, a 20 per cent reduction was made for the claimant accepting a risk from an intoxicated driver, whereas in *Donelan v Donelan and General Accident Fire & Life Insurance Co Ltd* [1993] PIQR 205, a 75 per cent reduction was applied where the defendant drove the car at the claimant's insistence even though the claimant knew that the defendant was inexperienced and drunk. As Anya has been drinking with Tomas all night, it is submitted that the defendant will argue that Anya knew he was drunk, but the court will have to decide what level of capacity both parties had at the time before they can settle on any reduction of damages.

If the court considers Anya's behaviour has been the cause of her own injuries, they may wish to deny her any damages at all. The most likely way of doing this is through an application of the 'illegality' defence *ex turpi causa non oritur actio*—'no action arises from a bad deed'. In negligence cases, the basis on which the defence works is that the claimant's 'illegal' involvement is such that the court may choose not to recognize the existence of a duty of care. [6.] In *Patel v Mizra* [2017] AC 467, the Supreme Court held that issues of policy were allowed to be considered when deciding whether to allow the defence. Additionally, the nature of the illegality must be of a serious nature, which would engage the interest of the public (*Les Laboratoires Servier v Apotex Inc* [2014] UKSC 55). For example, an application of *ex turpi causa* was allowed in **Joyce v O'Brien [2013] EWCA Civ 546**. The claimant was injured by the defendant's negligent driving when both were fleeing with stolen goods. Similarly, in *Pitts v Hunt* [1990] 3 All ER 344, the claimant was a pillion passenger on a motorcycle driven by the defendant, who was drunk. The vehicle was driven recklessly, but the claimant had encouraged him to drive in that fashion. The Court of Appeal held that the claimant's injuries arose directly out of the illegal venture and were not merely incidental.

In our situation, Anya appears to have encouraged Tomas to drive carelessly, in which case, following *Pitts v Hunt*, the court may rule out her claim. However, on balance it is more likely that contributory negligence would be the preferred defence, allowing the court to reduce her damages to the extent that its feels is appropriate.

Gary

Tomas clearly owes Gary a duty of care, and on a balance of probabilities it appears that Tomas has breached that, causing Gary injuries. However, Gary may not be able to claim the full award of damages, since he was not wearing his seat belt. This is a well-established

[6.] You will see policy at work in this section. Remember tort law is frequently policy driven, so read around the cases and be aware of any legal undercurrents that are there.

example of contributory negligence since it involves a failure by Gary to take reasonable care for his own safety (*Froom v Butcher* [1976] QB 286)—the failure to wear the seat belt is likely to materially increase the risk of injury should there be a traffic accident.

In *Froom v Butcher*, the Court of Appeal sought to lay down guidelines regarding the failure to wear seat belts. It was held that if wearing a seat belt would have prevented altogether the damage suffered, an appropriate reduction in damages would be 25 per cent. If the injury would have been less severe, the reduction should be 15 per cent, but if the injury would have been the same whether a belt was worn or not, there should be no reduction at all. These guidelines have been confirmed in more recent years by *Stanton v Collinson* [2010] EWCA Civ 81. [7] The fact that *Froom* was decided before the wearing of seat belts was made compulsory is irrelevant, since the defence is based on a claimant's failure to take care for his or her own safety and not simply a failure to abide by the law.

[7] This is a crucial point, and one that students often misunderstand. The defence operates on the basis of a failure to take reasonable care for oneself.

Gary is crushed behind the steering wheel. Whether he was wearing a seat belt or not, this is a kind of injury likely to be suffered by the driver of a car hit, at speed, by another vehicle. This would seem to suggest a maximum reduction in damages of 15 per cent, but if it is shown that the extent of injury would have been the same whether a seat belt was worn or not, then Gary's damages should not be reduced at all.

LOOKING FOR EXTRA MARKS?

- Make sure you discuss any relevant defence, even if you can tell straight away that it will not work. This is to ensure that you give a 'full answer'.
- Keep policy decision to the forefront of your mind, particularly when considering *ex turpi causa*. Be prepared to justify your arguments with reference to academic material.

QUESTION | 3

Adam arranges to meet his girlfriend, Sally, at the Roxy cinema. As he is walking to the cinema he is texting her on his mobile phone and steps into the road. He is struck and seriously injured by a car driven negligently and at grossly excessive speed by Ranjit, a 17-year-old. His mobile phone is crushed.

Ranjit, who has just passed his driving test, has taken his aunt's car without her consent. He is showing off to Manjit, his 12-year-old niece, who is a passenger in the car and who encouraged him to go for the 'joyride'.

Manjit is smashed against the dashboard of the car and is seriously injured. Manjit was not wearing a seat belt at the time of the accident, despite Ranjit telling her to.

Advise Adam and Manjit as to any potential claims in tort law, and in particular any defences.

CAUTION

■ There are a several issues in this scenario so you need to be sure to address them thoroughly. A strong answer will work systematically through the elements of the defences to negligence. Advise only in tort law!

DIAGRAM ANSWER PLAN

Identify	What is the cause of action? Who are the claimants and the tortfeasor? What are the potential remedies and defences?
Relevant law	*Nettleship v Weston* [1971] 2 QB 691. *Road Traffic Act* 1988, s. 149. Law Reform (Contributory Negligence) Act 1945, s. 1(1). *Jones v Livox Quarries Ltd* [1952] 2 QB 608. *Pitts v Hunt* [1990] 3 All ER 344. *Froom v Butcher* [1976] QB 286.
Apply the law	Ranjit is the potential tortfeasor. Has he breached his duty of care? What standard of care can be expected of a newly qualified driver? What is contributory negligence and what rules attach to this defence? Do the defences of *volenti* and *ex turpi causa non oritur actio* apply?
Conclude	Ranjit has breached his duty of care to both claimants, but any award of damages will be reduced by virtue of contributory negligence (for both claimants). The court might decide that Ranjit has the defence of *ex turpi causa* in regard to Manjit.

SUGGESTED ANSWER

Adam

[1.] There is no need to mention duty in detail here. As always, look at the rubric very carefully; it says 'in particular any defences'.

[1.] Looking at the facts of the question, the primary responsibility for the accident appears to lie with Ranjit, as it is well established that one road user owes a duty of care to anyone who also uses the road—this includes pedestrians such as Adam. Adam will have to show that Ranjit was in breach of that duty of care, and that the breach caused his injuries.

Regarding the breach of duty, the test is to ask what a reasonable person would do or would not do in the circumstances: ***Blyth*** *v Birmingham Waterworks Co* **(1856) 11 Ex 781.** 2. The standard to apply is that of the reasonably competent qualified driver (*Nettleship v Weston* **[1971] 2 QB 691**) and the fact that Ranjit is young and inexperienced will make no difference to this. The facts inform us that the car 'was driven at grossly excessive speed'. By driving too fast, Ranjit has breached his duty of care to other road users as the reasonable driver does not drive 'grossly at speed'. However, has Ranjit caused Adam's injuries? On a strict application of the 'but-for' test (*Barnett v Chelsea & Kensington Hospital Management Committee* **[1968] 3 All ER 1068**), it appears that if Adam had not walked into the road the collision would not have happened. In this respect, Ranjit may have a defence of contributory negligence.

The **Law Reform (Contributory Negligence) Act 1945** allows for an apportionment of responsibility in actions of negligence. Where negligence has been established, but the claimant has suffered damage partly as a result of their own fault, the Act gives the court a discretion to reduce the damages to the extent the court thinks just and equitable having regard to the claimant's share in the responsibility.

Looking at the facts, Adam failed to take reasonable care for his own safety (*Jones v Livox Quarries* **[1952] 2 QB 608**), as by focusing on texting his girlfriend, rather than keeping on the pavement, he has strayed into the zone of danger. In terms of causation, it would be assumed that a person who was not texting would have stayed on the pavement, and Adam must therefore be held partly to blame.

3. The third issue in contributory negligence cases is the matter of apportionment of damages. If the blameworthiness of Adam is small, as seems to be the case, even if he is in the road, a low reduction of, say 10–20 per cent may be likely under the **Law Reform (Contributory Negligence) Act 1945, s. 1(1)**. Alternatively, if Adam's fault is great, one might analyse the incident in terms of joint causation, as in *Fitzgerald v Lane* **[1988] 2 All ER 961** in which a negligent pedestrian was struck and injured by two negligent motorists. However, recent case law has concerned that fact that a car has a greater potency for causation of harm to a pedestrian than a pedestrian does to a car (*Jackson v Murray* [2015] UKSC 5). In this respect, it would be unjust to reduce damages by too great a degree particularly as Ranjit was driving at excessive speed.

Since Manjit is a passenger in the car, she is owed a duty of care in the same way as any other road user. As this is a road traffic accident, the defence of *volenti* is ruled out by statute where the vehicle must be compulsorily insured against third-party risks: **Road Traffic Act 1988, s. 149(3)**.

4. Manjit's involvement in 'joyriding' may be sufficient to invoke the public policy defence of *ex turpi causa non oritur actio* (although strictly it is a bar to an action proceeding rather than a defence). The precise scope of the *ex turpi causa* is difficult to ascertain.

In *Pitts v Hunt* **[1990] 3 All ER 344**, the claimant had actively encouraged the defendant to drive in an extremely dangerous manner and the principle was applied.

More recently in *Vellino v Chief Constable of Greater Manchester* **[2001] EWCA Civ 1249**, the claimant had attempted to evade arrest by jumping from a second-floor window, but he was severely injured. He claimed that the police officers had acted negligently. In the Court of Appeal the majority found that escape from custody was a sufficiently serious criminal offence to permit the principle to be applied. Therefore, the police did not owe an arrested person a duty to take care that he was not injured in a foreseeable attempt to escape police custody. [5.] Sir Murray Stuart-Smith said that:

> The operation of the principle arises where the claimant's claim is founded upon his own criminal or immoral act. The facts which give rise to the claim must be inextricably linked with the criminal activity. It is not sufficient if the criminal activity merely gives occasion for tortious conduct of the defendant . . . this has to be sufficiently serious to merit the application of the principle.

On the facts of the problem, although Manjit has actively encouraged Ranjit to take the car, she has not encouraged him to drive in a dangerous fashion. Further, it seems likely that Manjit's age may be significant, since she may be considered too young to appreciate the risks involved, and therefore that the *ex turpi causa* defence will not operate against her.

However, Manjit may have been contributorily negligent in getting into the car with Ranjit. Manjit's age, once again, will be relevant, as the courts are protective of young claimants (*Mullin v Richards* **[1997] EWCA Civ 2662**). It is a question of the claimant's age and the how obvious any risks were. In *N (A Child) v Newham LBC* **[2007] CLY 2931**, a seven-year-old schoolboy who was injured when he punched the glass panel in a classroom door was held 60 per cent to blame. This was because N knew right from wrong; that it was wrong to punch; and that when punched, glass was likely to break and injure him. On this reasoning, Manjit is old enough for the defence to apply since, although she may not be aware of the risk of Ranjit's careless driving, the need to wear seat belts is well known, even to very young children.

By not wearing her seat belt, despite being told to by Ranjit, she has materially increased the risk of injury. The case of *Froom v Butcher* **[1976] QB 286** suggests a 25 per cent reduction if no injury would have been suffered had the seat belt been worn, a 15 per cent reduction if the injury would have been less severe had the seat belt been worn, and no reduction at all if the same injury

[5.] Here is an opportunity to discuss case law, but under exam conditions a sentence of the judgment will suffice to put across your argument.

would have been suffered whether or not a seat belt was worn. Being thrown out of her seat suggests at least a 15 per cent if not a 25 per cent reduction in damages. We will now consider who will pay the damages.

[6.] In addition to learning defences, you are advised to revise calculations for damages. This is considered in the next chapter.

[6.] In normal proceedings, Ranjit's insurance company would pay any necessary damages. Unfortunately, in this scenario, it is suggested that Ranjit may have driven without insurance, on the grounds that it was not his car, and at the relevant time he did not have the owner's consent to drive it, even if his name was attached to the policy. If this is the case, it is likely that the Motor Insurers' Bureau, under its agreement with the Department of Transport, will be called upon to pay damages on behalf of the uninsured Ranjit, should the courts hold him liable. It should be noted that the MIB only pay for personal injury, not property damage. In this respect, Adam is will not receive damages for his phone, and will have to claim on his own insurance policy should he require a replacement.

LOOKING FOR EXTRA MARKS?

- Consider discussing policy issues, particularly the role of children as tortfeasors. Would Manjit be treated differently if she was 18?
- Likewise you may find an overlap with aspects of criminal law.

TAKING THINGS FURTHER

There have been several recent books and articles published which consider defences to tortious actions, including:

- Dyson, A., Goudkamp, J., and Wilmot-Smith, F. (eds.) *Defences in Tort. Hart Studies in Private Law: Essays on Defences* (2015) Hart Publishing.
- Fulbrook, J., 'Alcohol and Third Parties—"Dram Shop Liability" and Beyond' [2007] JPIL 220.
- Herring, J., Wall J, The Nature and Significance of the Right to Bodily Integrity' [2017] 76(3) CLJ 566.
- Hudson, A. W., 'Contributory Negligence as a Defence to Battery' (1984) 4 LS 332.
- Law Commission No. 219, *Contributory Negligence as a Defence to an Action for Breach of Contract* (1993).

There are also articles written on specific areas. The following concentrate on the relationship of suicide and contributory negligence.

- O'Sullivan, J., 'Employer's Liability for Injured Employee's Suicide' (2008) 67 CLJ 241.
- Ritchie, A. and McAllister, R., 'Damages for Self Harm after Suffering Tortious Injury (Suicide and Contributory Negligence)' (2009) 1 JPIL 20.
- Sullivan, R., 'Private Rights versus Public Values' in Green, S. and Bogg, A. (eds) *Illegality after Patel v Mirza* (2018) Hart Publishing, 81.

Online Resources   www.oup.com/uk/qanda/

Go online for extra essay and problem questions, a glossary of key terms, online versions of all the answer plans and audio commentary on how selected ones were put together, and a range of podcasts which include advice on exam and coursework technique and advice for other assessment methods.

Damages

12

KEY DEBATES

If you look at the various categories of damages you will notice that the awards given do not always appear to match the damage received. This is particularly the case for personal injury and loss of future earnings. Has the case of *Simmons v Castle* [2012] EWCA Civ 1288 helped to rectify this position? How might awards of damages be improved in the future?

QUESTION | 1

Jamie, aged 35, is badly injured in a road traffic accident caused by the admitted negligence of Chas. Jamie's car, valued at £10,000, is written off. The extent of his injuries is such that prior to the date of trial Jamie incurs private medical expenses of £12,500, but has also spent a number of

⊙

weeks in an NHS Trust hospital at public expense, with the result that the household costs incurred by Robert, Jamie's partner, are less than usual for part of the time, but greater than usual once Jamie returns home for convalescence. During the period of hospitalization and medical treatment, Jamie is unable to work as a research chemist at a salary of £40,000 per annum.

The extent of Jamie's injuries is such that for the future he will be unable to continue in his employment for a further three years after the trial and will be unable to continue his pastime as an amateur cricketer. Moreover, there is a distinct prospect that his injuries may worsen in years to come, although this is by no means certain. Jamie took out a personal accident insurance plan a number of years ago, which will pay substantial benefits following the accident. Moreover, Jamie has also received state benefits and will continue to do so after the date of the trial.

Advise Jamie.

CAUTION

- To answer this you need to be able to consider a 'mathematical' approach to the facts, as well as applying your legal knowledge.
- Make sure you draw a distinction between pre-trial expenditure and future loss.
- There is also a minor issue in relation to damages for harm to property.

DIAGRAM ANSWER PLAN

Identify
What are the heads of damages in this scenario?
Where might there be double recovery?

Relevant law
Dixon v John Were Ltd [2004] EWHC 2273 (QB).
Collett v Smith [2009] EWCA Civ 583.
Social Security (Recovery of Benefits) Act 1997.

Apply the law
How will the court deal with future losses and loss of amenities?
Can Jamie have his insurance payout in addition to other damages?

Conclude
The car is recoverable, and so is loss of earnings up to the trial date. Awards for loss of future earnings and household expenses will be more problematic. The court will need to deduct tax and social security benefits to reach a fair conclusion.

[1.] If you are told that one of the parties admits negligence, you do not need to discuss the duty issue or whether there is a breach of duty.

[2.] The issue of time is important to consider. Several cases are lost before they are begun as a result of being out of time.

[3.] It is useful to subdivide your categories to help you assess each aspect.

[1.] The facts of the question inform us that Jamie has been the victim of negligence, and has suffered both personal injury and financial loss as a result. Provided Jamie has issued his claim within the relevant time frame ([2.] three years for personal injury (Limitation Act 1980, s. 11)), he will be awarded damages for his personal injuries and financial losses. There is nothing in the facts to suggest that Jamie has not started his action in time. The aim of a damages award is 'to place the person who has been harmed by the wrongful acts of another in the position in which he or she would have been had the harm not been done' (*Knauer v Ministry of Justice* [2016] AC 908). [3.] To attempt to reach a fair solution, all financial categories will need to be assessed.

The Car

Jamie's car is damaged in the accident caused by Chas's negligence. The question states that it has been written off and that it is valued at £10,000. Where a vehicle has been written off, it is considered un-economic to repair it and the court is likely to treat this as a case of constructive total loss (*Darbishire v Warran* **[1963] 1 WLR 1067**). In the circumstances there is said to be no difference between the cost of repair and the reduction in market value of the damaged chattel. It follows that an award of damages will represent the replacement value of the damaged article; in Jamie's case, £10,000.

Private Healthcare

In an action for damages for personal injury, there are two distinct heads of damage. The first is expenditure incurred as a result of the tort, and the second is loss of earnings. Any expenditure prior to the trial is recoverable if actually and reasonably incurred. This will in-clude private medical expenses such as the £12,500 paid by Jamie, provided that Jamie could not receive the adequate level of services from the NHS. If he has chosen private healthcare without considering any other options provided by the state, this may be reflected in the amount awarded.

Household Costs

Whist Jamie is in hospital, Robert sees a reduction in their usual household expenses. [4.] A deduction in respect of the reduced expendi-ture due to Jamie's absence may be made (*Harris v Empress Motors Ltd* **[1984] 1 WLR 212**). However, the facts indicate that after Jamie returns home for convalescence, household expenses increase. In these circumstances this increase in expenditure may be taken into account. This will be a relatively straightforward figure to calculate. However, Robert may feel morally obliged to give up work in order to

[4.] Your examiner will wish to see that you have identified that the claimant is not overcompensated.

look after Jamie. In this case, there may be an application for a recognized pecuniary claim following the decision in ***Hunt v Severs* [1994] 2 All ER 385**. Jamie will hold any award in this respect on trust for Robert as a provider of the services.

Loss of Earnings

Provided that Jamie pleads 'special damages' in his claim (*Ilkiw v Samuels* [1963] 2 All ER 879), Jamie will be able to recover the amount he would have earned between the date of the tort and the date of trial, subject to deductions in respect of tax liabilities (***British Transport Commission v Gourley* [1956] AC 185**).

[5.]The award will take into account his loss of future income, by calculating his net annual loss multiplied by a figure which, as far as possible and if properly invested, will produce an overall amount equivalent to the lost income. This can be a substantial amount if the claimant has very good job prospects (***Dixon v John Were Ltd* [2004] EWHC 2273 (QB)**), but this is variable depending on individual factors (*Collett v Smith* [2009] EWCA Civ 583).

The fact that Jamie's injuries may worsen in years to come may affect his earning capacity in the future. This is a factor which may be considered when assessing damages if it is likely to serve as a handicap in the job market (***Moeliker v A Reyrolle & Co* [1977] 1 WLR 132**). However, the rule seems to be confined to complete loss of job prospects, whereas Jamie will be unable to work for three years, but may be able to work thereafter. Nonetheless, a person who is out of work for three years may find it difficult to find replacement employment after that period.

A problem with the lump sum system of paying damages is that it is not easy to deal with future uncertainties, but an award of provisional damages may be made to allow the claimant to return later to recover an additional payment, if warranted: **Senior Courts Act 1981, s. 32A**. There must be a reasonable chance that, at some definite or indefinite time in the future, the injured person will develop some serious disease or suffer some serious deterioration that is capable of measurement (***Wilson v Ministry of Defence* [1991] 1 All ER 638**).

There is no certainty that Jamie's injuries will worsen, so a court may feel unable to make an award of provisional damages under **s. 32A.** [6.]Moreover, continuing deterioration, such as the onset of osteoarthritis after injuries consisting of broken limbs, will not fall within the ambit of **s. 32A** (***Wilson v Ministry of Defence***).

The lump sum method of compensation can be ineffective if it fails to accurately reflect the claimant's loss if his condition worsens in the future. To cover this possibility, a court has a power to make a periodic payment order in relation to future income loss (see **Courts Act 2003, ss. 100 and 101** and **Damages Act 1996, s. 2(1)**). Where

[5.] This section can be enhanced by giving clearer information regarding multiplier and multiplicand.

[6.] Can you find any type of injury that may be allowable, in terms of a claim?

such an award is made, the court will determine the frequency and the amount of the payments, based on current needs at the time of the order, without regard to longevity. Moreover, the court should have regard to the best interests of the claimant rather than give effect to what the claimant (or his family) wants (*Thompstone v Tameside & Glossop Acute Services NHS Trust* **[2008] EWCA Civ 5**).

When an award of damages is made in respect of pecuniary loss, the court must take account of any relevant offsets, so that the award does not overcompensate the claimant. The question states that Jamie has received and will continue to receive state benefits and that he is due to receive a payment under a personal accident insurance plan. The insurance policy moneys will not be deducted from the award of damages (*Bradburn v Great Western Railway* **(1874) LR 10 Ex 1**), since the claimant has paid for the benefit and courts do not wish to discourage the making of insurance provision.

The rule on state benefits is different since these and tort damages are designed to compensate the same losses. [7] The **Social Security (Recovery of Benefits) Act 1997** now provides that the amount of any relevant benefit paid or likely to be paid to or for the claimant is to be disregarded, but the compensator is not permitted to pay any compensation until the Department for Work and Pensions has issued a certificate detailing the total amount of benefit. Once this has been issued, the amount certified must be deducted for a period of five years following the date of the accident, and is payable to the Secretary of State. The deduction is made from the whole of the award, which includes any element in respect of non-pecuniary loss, such as pain and suffering, which is not compensated by social security benefits.

Other Issues

In addition to pecuniary losses, an award of damages may also cover less easily quantifiable losses such as pain and suffering and loss of amenity (*H West & Son Ltd v Shephard* **[1964] AC 326**). Provided it can be assumed that the claimant has endured pain, an award of damages for pain and suffering may be made. [8] The one instance in which such an award is unlikely is where the claimant is and will remain permanently unconscious. Here there is nothing to suggest that Jamie is comatose, in which case the award of damages may include an element in respect of pain and suffering.

Jamie is unable to continue his pastime as an amateur cricketer. This is a factor which may be reflected in any award of damages. Thus if the claimant loses the joy of life and cannot ride a bicycle or kick a football, he is entitled to damages representing his loss of enjoyment of life (*Heaps v Perrite Ltd* **[1937] 2 All ER 60**).

[7] You may like to consider section 8 of the Act and schedule 2 to the Act here. This might be an opportunity to consider introducing academic literature, in order to consider policy decisions.

[8] Consider whether this really helps to answer your question. If you start writing in the abstract you will run out of time. Here, though, you have made your comments relevant by referring to the facts.

LOOKING FOR EXTRA MARKS?

- Be more specific in explaining the meaning and approach to multipliers and multiplicands. Consider using *Wells v Wells* [1998] UKHL 27, if you should wish to discuss lump sum payments.
- If your question allows it, explore policy elements present.

QUESTION | 2

Callum, through his admitted negligent driving, damages a vintage Bentley car owned by Vijay. The car is so badly damaged that in normal circumstances it would be written off by an insurance company, but Vijay is so attached to it that he wants to have it repaired. Vijay has a badly paid job and has maintenance commitments to the children of his first marriage. He cannot afford to arrange necessary repairs straight away, so he waits for six months before doing anything. In the meantime he takes advantage of a credit hire arrangement in order to be able to obtain a replacement vehicle. The credit hire company have agreed to present an account when Vijay's tort action against Callum is concluded. The charge for this credit facility and the replacement car is the equivalent of paying £50 per day for a hire car, when the normal daily charge for an equivalent hire car would be £33.

Subsequently Vijay discovers that the specialist in Bentley cars who is to carry out the necessary work has raised the cost of the work by £1,250 to a total charge of £4,500. This amount is £500 more than a general car repairer would charge for the same work.

Advise Callum of his potential liability in damages.

CAUTION

- Concentrate on the rules concerning an award of damages for property damage. You will not score highly if you discuss damages in a general way.

DIAGRAM ANSWER PLAN

| Identify | What are the heads of damages in this scenario? Where might there be double recovery? |

| Relevant law | *O'Grady v Westminster Scaffolding Ltd* [1962] 2 Lloyd's Rep 238. *Liesbosch (Owners) v Edison* (Owners) [1933] AC 449. |

| Apply the law | What is the legal situation regarding repair costs and diminution in value in respect of damage to chattels and when the different measures apply? Should Vijay be compensated on the basis of repair costs or diminution in value? |

| Conclude | As a private individual, Vijay may be awarded his full damages claim. However, a number of factors would need to be assessed before a final award was made. |

SUGGESTED ANSWER

¹·Explain what you have been asked to do in your opening paragraph.

¹·We have been informed that Callum has admitted to driving negligently, therefore our next step is to assess Callum's liability in damages for the harm suffered by Vijay.

Vijay's car is so badly damaged that in normal circumstances it would be written off by an insurance company. This is known as a constructive total loss (***Darbishire v Warran* [1963] 1 WLR 1067**) and the award of damages will be based on the replacement value of the vehicle. On rare occasions, the claimant may be allowed the cost of repair where the damaged property is unique: ***O'Grady v Westminster***

²·Consider how much detail is needed regarding the facts of cases. We do not want to read a precise of a case, just why you are discussing it.

***Scaffolding Ltd* [1962] 2 Lloyd's Rep 238.** ²·Vijay seems to be faced with the same difficulty as the claimant in *O'Grady*, in having an old, well-maintained car which would be difficult to replace. In this case, the cost of repair might be the appropriate measure of damages.

Consequential losses suffered as a result of the damage inflicted by the defendant, such as the cost of hiring a substitute, may also be recovered (***Darbishire v Warran***). Although Vijay has incurred no immediate cost in hiring a replacement, he will receive an account under the credit hire agreement later.

³·Is it fair that the defendant may pay greater damages due to claimant's lack of financial resources? Consider academic critique here.

³·The difficulty is that the hire charges are greater than the normal cost of hiring a car. However, Vijay may argue that he has been forced into doing this because of

lack of resources as he cannot pay the 'up-front' cost of hiring a car on a daily basis.

In *Liesbosch (Owners) v Edison (Owners)* **[1933] AC 449** it was held that losses resulting from the impecuniosity of a claimant are too remote to be recovered, despite the normal rule that the defendant has to take the claimant as he finds him. In the context of motorists who enter into credit hire arrangements, the House of Lords has considered the status of the *Liesbosch* principle twice, in *Dimond v Lovell* **[2002] 1 AC 384** and *Lagden v O'Connor* **[2003] UKHL 64**.

In *Dimond v Lovell* the House of Lords held that a claimant should mitigate his or her cost, and that any damages in respect of the hire of a replacement car should be restricted to the normal daily hire rate, and nothing more.

Vijay's position is different, since he is badly paid and has maintenance commitments towards his children. Because of this, he may not have the resources immediately to hand to be able to pay the standard daily hire rate for a replacement car while his own vehicle is off the road. In *Lagden v O'Connor* a similar, but not identical, position prevailed. The unemployed claimant's car was damaged by the defendant's negligent driving, but he could not afford to hire a replacement without using a credit hire company, so that there was no initial outlay. A replacement car was a convenience, but not an absolute necessity for the claimant. A majority of the House of Lords departed from the *Liesbosch* principle because it conflicted with the rule that a defendant should take the claimant as he finds him. Accordingly, provided the extra cost incurred by the claimant was not unforeseeable, the claimant's financial position was a factor that a court could consider in determining what damages should be awarded against a defendant and his insurer. [4.] A further reason given for departing from the *Liesbosch* principle was that it was decided before the case of *Overseas Tankship (UK) Ltd v Morts Dock and Engineering Co Ltd (Wagon Mound (No 1))* **[1961] AC 388**. (The *Liesbosch* principle was a consequence of the old directness of damage test applied in *Re Polemis & Furness, Withy & Co Ltd* **[1921] 3 KB 560**.)

In *Lagden*, the majority concluded that, given the claimant's lack of means, they were not constrained by the decision in *Dimond v Lovell*. It was reasonably foreseeable that the claimant would require a replacement car. Since he was not in a position to make any initial outlay on hiring a replacement on the daily hire spot market, it was foreseeable that he might take advantage of a credit hire arrangement, even though this would increase the claim for damages against the defendant.

Here, Vijay has chosen to own a vintage Bentley car, which in normal circumstances might be written off by an insurer. He could have sold the Bentley to another Bentley enthusiast with the means to pay

[4.] Damages may appear on your examination paper in essay form. Consider how you might change your material into an essay point here.

5. You are not expected to calculate a damages award as part of your LLB examinations, but you will need to be able to identify all the categories that need to be considered.

for its restoration and so get more than the scrap value. **5.** There may also be other reasons for his lack of means, albeit not mentioned in the facts of the problem. Does he take regular holidays abroad, smoke cigarettes, and drink alcohol? As Lord Nicholls observed, lack of financial means is a question of priorities (*Lagden v O'Connor* **UKHL 64** at [9]). It is arguable that Vijay may have made an unreasonable choice in the circumstances and may be confined to the measure of damages applicable in *Dimond v Lovell* and *Liesbosch*, namely, the market cost of a replacement vehicle, rather than the actual cost.

The *Liesbosch* principle only applies to the impecuniosity of the claimant, but if there are other reasons for the increased cost, they may be relevant. Thus in *Martindale v Duncan* **[1973] 2 All ER 355**, a taxi driver whose cab had been damaged due to the negligence of the claimant chose to wait until he had obtained authorization from his insurers before he had his vehicle repaired. Since there was another reason for the delay, namely that the claimant was awaiting the decision of his insurers, the *Liesbosch* principle was held not to apply. Similarly in *Perry v Sidney Phillips & Son* **[1982] 1 WLR 1297**, the claimant was able to recover damages for anxiety and inconvenience even though this anxiety arose principally from the claimant's inability to pay for the cost of repairs to the property concerned.

Apart from Vijay's impecuniosity, the question also indicates that Vijay has waited for some time before arranging to have his vehicle repaired, during which time the cost of repair has risen. Given the age and value of the car, it would appear perfectly reasonable to employ the services of a specialist in Bentley cars, even though they are more expensive than general car repairers. It would be reasonable to assume that the extra cost may be taken to represent the specialization in this type of vehicle. On the matter of the delay itself, it may be that the reason can be traced to the defendant and his insurer in seeking to delay the commencement of proceedings or taking their time in the process of agreeing a settlement. In this case the delay may be regarded as something brought about by the defendant rather than the claimant, in which case the *Liesbosch* principle does not apply: see *Alcoa Minerals of Jamaica Inc v Broderick* **[2000] 3 WLR 23**.

6. Remember your fundamental principles of tort law, particularly in relation to negligence. It has to be a fair award.

6. Applying all of this to Vijay, the main issue appears to be whether or not he has acted reasonably in delaying the process of repairing the vehicle and in obtaining a hire car in the way he has done.

Vijay is a private individual, who appears to be treated differently from businesses. In such a case, it may be foreseeable that such a person might not immediately be able to rectify the damage caused by the defendant's negligence. Assuming the delay in effecting repairs is reasonable, the cost incurred by Vijay in hiring a replacement will be recoverable and this may even include the additional charges incurred through taking out a credit hire agreement, depending upon whether

Vijay is taken to have no practical choice other than to acquire the car in this way due to his financial plight. Moreover, the additional cost in employing the services of a specialist in Bentley cars does not seem out of the way, given the value of the vehicle.

LOOKING FOR EXTRA MARKS?

■ Consider the issue of damages from the 'fair, just, and reasonable point'. The examiner will wish to see that you have explored various categories of damages and have reached a firm-policy driven conclusion, if there is any doubt.

QUESTION | 3

Consider the defects, if any, in the fault system of accident compensation and the case for reform of the means of accident compensation.

CAUTION

■ This is a very broad question on initial glance so it might be easy to stray away from essential arguments. Make sure you underline key words and consider them before starting your answer.

DIAGRAM ANSWER PLAN

Criticisms of the tort system based on cost, delay, the lump sum method of compensation, and general unpredictability of outcome.

▼

Alternatives to the tort system such as state insurance, no-fault accident compensation schemes, and private insurance.

¹· There are many ways to address this question. Consider what you want to incorporate before looking at the answer below.

²· In your introduction you have given the parameters of your answer. Check, on completion, whether you have actually covered everything stated.

The law of torts is concerned with compensating the victim of the defendant's wrongdoing by providing a remedy (damages) for the claimant's injuries, rather than punishing the defendant. **²·**The same objective can also be achieved through private insurance although, as will be discussed later, there are difficulties with this. The compensation objective may also be achieved through state social security payments, which tend to be lower than awards of damages.

If an accident victim can successfully pursue a tort action, he or she stands to recover more than a person with no such claim, since English law adopts a system of 'full compensation' that takes account of the actual earnings of the claimant, both pecuniary loss (eg expense incurred) and non-pecuniary loss (eg pain and suffering). However, the number of successful tort claims is relatively small because the claimant must be able to prove that the defendant caused the 'accident' (including disease or disability where man-made) by committing an actionable tort and, if there is no fault, no matter how serious the injury, no action will lie in tort and the victim will have to rely on such state benefits as might be available (see eg *Tomlinson v Congleton Borough Council* **[2003] UKHL 47**).

³· Rather than talk in general terms, I might be better to choose a specific example and back it up with case law or academic literature.

³·Other criticisms of the tort system as a means of accident compensation are those of cost, delay, unpredictability of outcome, the unbalanced way in which payments are made, and the problem of how compensation payments are used by the claimant after an award has been made.

⁴· Examiners are really looking for evidence of reading, so take the opportunity to display this.

In 1977, the administrative cost of tort compensation was said to be 85 per cent of the total amount paid out **⁴·**(Report of the Royal Commission on Compensation for Personal Injuries, Cmnd 7054, 1978). In contrast, the equivalent cost of the social security system came to only 11 per cent. Moreover, since a tort litigant must commence proceedings against the defendant, funds must be available at the outset. The development of 'no win, no fee' schemes for some personal injury cases, in which the legal adviser is only remunerated if the action succeeds, was allowed in order to facilitate the commencement of proceedings. These schemes appear to encourage settlements between the claimant's lawyer and the defendant's insurer. **⁵·**It is a popular conception that 'no win, no fee' arrangements may lead to the development of a 'compensation culture'. In reality, a claim has to have a very good chance of success in order to be taken on by a firm.

⁵· Although it may be an accurate statement, think how you could improve on this. Find statistics and incorporate those into your answer.

Proving fault is a major cause of the cost of the tort system as the claimant must show who is to blame for the harm he has suffered. The assessment of damages requires the preparation of expert reports, and because of the adversarial system of trial legal costs are duplicated as both parties require their own experts and lawyers.

The tort system is also very slow in delivering compensation, especially in complicated cases in which obstacles thrown in the path of claimants might tempt them to give up the process.[6] The Civil Justice Review (Cm 394, 1988) revealed that in 1987 an average High Court case took five years and a county court case three years. The Civil Justice Review (*Access to Justice*, 1996) or 'Woolf Report' suggested radical reforms designed to speed up the whole system of dispensing civil justice.

The unpredictability of the tort system is notorious. Even where the claimant can show that he is owed a duty of care, he must also establish breach of that duty and factual causation, and hope that the loss he has suffered is not too remote and that the court does not regard his losses as having been exaggerated: *Painting v University of Oxford* **[2005] EWCA Civ 161**. Even where the claimant is successful, the final award may be less than was anticipated, which must be offset against the cost of bringing the action in the first place. Because of this pressure, claimants will often settle out of court, resulting in undercompensation in more complicated cases. At the same time, the cost incurred by insurance companies in processing smaller claims may lead to an overgenerous settlement. The lump sum method of paying damages has been criticized as it requires the court to guess at what the future might bring and may fail to take account of events that exacerbate the claimant's loss.

If a claimant is successful, the decision to allow courts to order a means of compensation other than that asked for by the claimant is controversial. The periodic payment system also has, as its focus, the annual financial needs of the long-term accident victim. This different focus is argued to result in increased compensation in many cases that will have to be funded by the defendant's insurers [7] (see Lewis, 'The Politics and Economics of Tort Law' (2006) 69 MLR 418, 442). The advantages of the structured settlement fall on both sides. Not only does the annuity system avoid payment of tax by accident victims (**Taxes Act 1988, ss. 329A and 329B**, added by the **Finance Act 1995, s. 142**), but it also results in substantial savings over the normal lump sum system so far as insurers are concerned.

A very limited scheme was also introduced by the **NHS Redress Act 2006**, which applies to low-value medical negligence claims in order to avoid litigation, while also providing for a full investigation of the incident alleged to have caused the harm, so that lessons can be learned and improvements to procedures implemented.[8] Countries such as New Zealand and Sweden have a 'no-fault' liability system for personal injury. This is successful at reducing time delay and upfront court costs, but a detailed examination of cases shows that there are flaws with these systems, notably that a tortfeasor does not get 'punished' for his wrongdoing.

---

6. Good evidence, but can you look at more recent material?

7. Be precise with your referencing, even under examination conditions.

8. If you know this area in detail, this could have formed the main part of your answer. As always, use the knowledge you have, but ensure it is relevant.

Some types of accident damage can be insured against by means of life, permanent health, and personal accident policies. Moreover, some employers will take out occupational sick pay policies which go beyond state provision for short-term income replacement. The prevalence of such policies depends on the social class into which the accident victim falls and the nature of his employment. Before private insurance can replace the tort system, there must be a change in taxation policy so that all members of society are paid in such a way that they can afford to take out private insurance, and the problem remains that the low paid will not have the resources to cover themselves adequately. The fact that private insurance policies exist does not, at present, make any difference to an award of tort damages since the courts do not wish to discourage thrift, so payments out of privately arranged insurance will not be deducted from an award of tort damages (***Bradburn v Great Western Railway* (1874) LR 10 Ex 1**).

The present social security system provides for payment in respect of a number of injuries which may or may not result from the fault of an identified defendant and some of which are based on nothing more than the means of the claimant (eg income support and housing benefit). Payments, generally, are based on subsistence levels rather than the total loss suffered by the claimant and, as such, will be considerably less than an award of tort damages.

[9.] This paragraph does not refer to cases or statute. This is OK but a better piece would refer to academic literature to back up arguments.

[9.] Roughly, benefits can be divided into those relating to non-industrial injuries and those relating to injury suffered at work. The former include statutory sick pay, which is replaced by incapacity benefit after 28 weeks of illness, provided there have been sufficient contributions to the national insurance scheme. Claimants not qualifying for the latter, however, may claim severe disablement allowance. In severe cases, where constant care is required, a claim for disability living allowance may be permitted. In respect of industrial injuries, disablement benefit may be awarded to an injured employee. The important consideration concerning these benefits is that, at present, they are deductible from an award of tort damages, but they are not based on the principle of full compensation since the amount payable is based on average earnings rather than on the actual earnings of the accident victim. However, as has been observed, the social security system is more efficient in terms of the cost of making payments to individuals, and can be geared to the needs of the claimant as and when new financial difficulties might arise.

LOOKING FOR EXTRA MARKS?

■ Use the information you have learnt to be the central platform of an essay question. As long as it is relevant, and backed up with recent authorities, the examiner will be interested/excited to read a novel answer.

TAKING THINGS FURTHER

■ Atiyah, P. S., *The Damages Lottery* (Hart Publishing, 1997), ch. 8.

This is an important work, which proposes different solutions to awards of damages, such as introducing a no-fault liability scheme.

■ Government Consultation Paper, The Law on Damages (CP 09/07, May 2007).

This paper considers specific areas of the law on damages with the aim to provide a more coherent system in relation to valid claims.

■ Law Commission No. 257, *Damages for Personal Injury: Non-pecuniary Loss* (1999).

This investigates the effectiveness of the remedy of damages for monetary and non-monetary loss.

■ Lewis R., 'The Politics and Economics of Tort Law' (2006) 69 MLR 418.

This looks at the impact of legislation on personal lump sum payments.

Online Resources   www.oup.com/uk/qanda/

Go online for extra essay and problem questions, a glossary of key terms, online versions of all the answer plans and audio commentary on how selected ones were put together, and a range of podcasts which include advice on exam and coursework technique and advice for other assessment methods.

Mixed-topic Questions

13

QUESTION | **1**

Korkies, construction contractors, are engaged by Slapshire County Council to resurface a 10-mile stretch of the Ontown ring road. Korkies hire a surface-stripping machine in order to facilitate the work.

Dhillon, a surveyor employed by the County Council but on loan to Korkies, decides he is capable of using the surface-stripping machine but sets the controls in such a way that too deep a cut is made, so that the machine severs a water main which floods the road and a nearby power generator. The following parties claim damages for negligence:

(a) Petra, a successful businesswoman, was driving on the ring road at the time of the incident and claims she has been prevented from attending a meeting at which she had high hopes of securing a £500,000 contract with another business.

(b) Quantum-Green Ltd, owners of the generator engulfed in water from the severed main, claim the cost of repairing their damaged generator and the profit they would have made had the generator been operative during the five days it takes to effect repairs.

(c) Rubric Ltd, the beneficial owners of a factory on an industrial estate supplied with electricity generated by Quantum-Green's incapacitated generator, complain that their operations were

⊙

interrupted for five days. Rubric Ltd occupy these premises pursuant to a contractual arrangement with the legal owners, Property Holdings Ltd, a subsidiary company in the same group of companies as Rubric Ltd. Rubric say they had to dispose of a batch of plastic plates, valued at £10,000, as the plastic congealed when the power supply failed. The cost of cleaning congealed plastic from their machines is assessed at £2,500. Rubric Ltd also claim damages for loss of business profit on operations they could have carried on during the remainder of the five-day interruption to their power supply.

Advise Korkies of their potential liability in tort.

CAUTION

■ You are asked to advise Korkies on their potential liability to several parties.

■ You will need to address the issue of economic loss, and also assess the relationship between Korkies and the principal tortfeasor Dhillon.

■ Plan your time carefully.

DIAGRAM ANSWER PLAN

Identify	Economic loss for a negligent act Vicarious liability
Relevant law	*Spartan Steel & Alloys Ltd v Martin & Co (Contractors) Ltd* [1973] 1 QB 27. *Mersey Docks & Harbour Board v Coggins & Griffith (Liverpool) Ltd* [1947] AC 1. *Lister v Hesley Hall* [2001] UKHL 22.
Apply the law	Consider the categories of economic loss: are they 'consequential' or 'pure'? Is Dhillon an employee? If so, is he acting in the course of his employment?
Conclude	Dhillon is likely to be considered an employee acting in the course of his employment. If so, Korkies will be liable to some of the claimants. However, Petra is unlikely to be successful.

[1] Although you may be tempted to discuss general principles of negligence here, if you do so you may not have time to cover all the issues raised.

[2] If you are looking for extra marks, this section would be an opportunity to incorporate academic literature on pure economic loss.

[1] This question considers economic loss caused by a negligent act. Dhillon's actions clearly result in physical damage to the water main, and, on a straightforward application of *Caparo Industries plc v Dickman* [1992] UKHL 2, he will owe a duty of care to those who own the water main itself. [2] However, others suffer economic losses that may not be recoverable for policy reasons which will be discussed in what follows. Those whose claims are deemed to have merit will seek compensation. In this respect they are likely to sue Korkies, if it can be proved that Dhillon was their employee at the relevant time.

Petra

Petra's failure to secure a lucrative contract is 'pure economic loss' which is not directly related to the severance of the water main (*Murphy v Brentwood DC* [1991] UKHL 2). Further, the loss suffered by Petra is speculative, so that all she has lost is the chance to secure a lucrative contract. In *Hotson v East Berkshire Health Authority* [1987] 2 All ER 909 it was held that a claimant must prove, on a balance of probability, that the defendant was the cause of the harm complained of. Petra may find it difficult to discharge the onus of proof.

Furthermore, Petra's problem is that many other motorists could be affected in the same way, so there may be an indeterminate class

[3] Here the 'candidate' has taken the opportunity to display their knowledge of case law.

of claimants. This raises a 'floodgates' problem, or [3] 'liability in an indeterminate amount to an indeterminate class for an indeterminate time' (*Ultramares Corp v Touche* (1931) 174 NE 441 *per* Cardozo J).

[4] If you are planning to answer a question on economic loss you would be wise to study and learn this case. It appears frequently in questions.

In [4] *Spartan Steel & Alloys Ltd v Martin & Co (Contractors) Ltd* [1973] 1 QB 27 the Court of Appeal held that a defendant will be liable for negligently causing physical harm to the claimant's property and for economic loss directly consequent on that physical harm; there is no liability for pure economic loss which flows indirectly from a negligent act, that is from damage to property owned by a third party. The loss of the £500,000 contract must be regarded as falling within this principle and is therefore loss in respect of which no duty of care is owed. It is unlikely that Petra will be successful in her claim.

Quantum-Green Ltd

Quantum-Green Ltd have suffered physical damage to their generator, so, applying ordinary principle from *Caparo v Dickman*, Dhillon will be liable for that damage. The loss of profit flowing directly from the damage to the generator that is owned by Quantum-Green Ltd

[5] As you have discussed it at length before, you only need to touch on it briefly a second time.

falls squarely within the [5] *Spartan Steel v Martin* principle, so the duty of care should extend equally to that loss.

Rubric Ltd

Rubric's batch of plastic plates that congealed when the power supply was interrupted is another example of physical harm caused by Dhillon's negligence. This also resulted in the additional cost of cleaning plastic from their machine, which will be classified as physical harm, similar to the additional labour costs incurred in *Muirhead v Industrial Tank Specialties Ltd* **[1985] 3 All ER 705**. Moreover, any economic loss directly consequent on this physical damage, such as the resale value of the plates in process at the time of the interruption to the electricity supply, will be recoverable: *Spartan Steel v Martin*. However, Rubric Ltd must have a sufficient possessory or proprietary interest in the property affected by Dhillon's negligent act to be able to sue. In *Leigh & Sillavan Ltd v Aliakmon Shipping Ltd* **[1986] AC 785**, due to the terms of the contract he had made with a seller, the claimant was neither the owner nor the possessor of property damaged by the defendant carrier's negligence and, as a result, was unable to sue. In the present case, if Rubric Ltd are not the legal owners of the affected premises this might affect their ability to sue. However, in *Shell UK Ltd v Total UK Ltd* **[2010] EWCA Civ 180** it was held that the beneficial owner of a pipeline damaged by the defendant's negligence could sue by joining the legal owner of the pipeline as a party to the proceedings either as an unwilling defendant or as a willing joint-claimant. [6.] As Rubric Ltd and Property Holdings Ltd are part of the same group of companies, it seems likely that Property Holdings Ltd will agree to lend their name to any action brought by Rubric Ltd.

Both Quantum-Green and Rubric sue in respect of loss of general business profits resulting from the inability to continue operations following the power cut, but these losses are indirect and therefore not recoverable under the *Spartan Steel v Martin* principle.

[6.] Your examiner has set the question to assess how comprehensive your knowledge of a specific area is. You should look for a different aspect to discuss for each claimant.

[7.] **The Vicarious Liability Issue**

[7.] You should spend roughly half of your allowed time discussing this issue.

The discussion above assumes that Dhillon is personally responsible for his negligence, but if he is an employee acting in the course of his employment his employer may be vicariously liable for the torts committed by Dhillon.

Dhillon is normally employed by the County Council but has been 'lent' to Korkies, so who is Dhillon's employer? Relevant factors will include the terms of the contract between the Council and Korkies, but the onus of proof lies on the permanent employer: *Mersey Docks & Harbour Board v Coggins & Griffith (Liverpool) Ltd* **[1947] AC 1**. In *Viasystems (Tyneside) Ltd v Thermal Transfer (Northern) Ltd* **[2005] EWCA Civ 1151** and *Hawley v Luminar Leisure Ltd* **[2006] EWCA Civ 18** it was held that it has to be ascertained which of the two employers was best positioned to prevent the tort from being committed and that there is a presumption that the lending employer still remains responsible (*Hawley*), but this can be displaced if the employee was so much under the control of the borrowing employer that the latter can prevent the employee from committing the tort (*Viasystems*). Assuming sufficient control has passed to Korkies, they may be the responsible employer, which appears to be a reasonable assumption if the Council has no obvious means of preventing any tort from being committed.

Dhillon acts on behalf of Korkies, but they will only be liable for his acts if he is an employee rather than an independent contractor. Although this rule departs from the fault principle, it is justified on the basis that employers rather than employees are best positioned to bear the loss through insurance (see *British Telecommunications plc v James Thomson & Sons (Engineers) Ltd* [1999] 1 WLR 9).

Traditionally, the test for determining who is an employee is based on the concept of control, so that an employee can be told by his employer what to do and how to do it (*Collins v Hertfordshire County Council* [1947] KB 598), whereas an independent contractor is employed to do work but has a discretion as to the mode and time of doing the relevant work (*Honeywill & Stein v Larkin* [1934] 1 KB 191). However, this test does not work well with professional employees, such as Dhillon, a surveyor, as his skill is such that the employer may have little knowledge of how the work is done. Nevertheless, the control test can be helpful but other factors such as the method of payment, the provision of equipment, the power of dismissal, and the 'employee's' personal investment may also be relevant.

If Dhillon is to be regarded as an employee, Korkies, as employers, may be vicariously liable for Dhillon's torts committed in the course of employment. As a surveyor, he is unlikely to be employed to operate a surface-stripping machine. However, he may have been employed to supervise and give orders to those who do. The classic 'Salmond' test for determining when an employer is vicariously liable for an employee's tort was to ask if the employee had used a wrongful mode to carry out work he had been authorized to do or whether he had done some unauthorized act for which the employer would not be liable. However, since the decision in [8.] *Lister v Hesley Hall* [2001] UKHL 22 the appropriate test to apply is whether the wrongful conduct is so closely connected with the acts the employee was authorized to do that the wrongful conduct may fairly and properly be regarded as done by the employee in the ordinary course of the employer's business. This has been added to in later years by the case of *The Catholic Child Welfare Society and ors v Various Claimants and The Institute of The Brothers of The Christian Schools and ors* [2012] UKSC 56. In light of these recent cases, Dhillon's actions may well be viewed as being 'in the course of employment'.

[8.] Even if you decided that Dhillon is not an employee, it would still be worth your while discussing this case, as it is an important test in its own right.

LOOKING FOR EXTRA MARKS?

- Weave in your knowledge of case law at appropriate places.
- Keep focused on the question throughout. You are asked to advise Korkies. If they are not liable for Dhillon's actions, they will not be liable to any of the claimants.

 QUESTION | **2**

Steve has been warned by his doctor that he must not drive, but when his wife has been taken seriously ill, he decides to drive her to hospital rather than wait for an ambulance. On the way to the hospital, Steve collapses at the wheel, and the car swerves off the road. Matt, who is painting a second-floor window, believes the car will crash into his ladder, so he jumps of it, injuring himself. The car comes to a halt after smashing into a shop owned by Sascha.

Twenty minutes later, while the police are attempting to remove the car, part of a wall unexpectedly collapses on Jazz and Amy, two spectators. Amy, who has recently been divorced from her husband, Imran, is crushed to death in the space of three minutes and Jazz is so badly injured that she suffers from depression and commits suicide three months later. Jazz's live-in lover, Kali, is distraught at the death of her partner. Amy's ex-husband, Imran, seeks to recover damages in respect of Amy's death, including damages for the pain and suffering endured by her before she died.

Advise Matt, Sascha, Kali, and Imran.

 CAUTION

- You are asked to advise multiple parties, so time management will be important.
- This question requires a knowledge of damages. If you are not confident in this area, you would be wise not to tackle it, even if the rest of the question looks straightforward.

DIAGRAM ANSWER PLAN

Identify
Who is the potential tortfeasor?
What remedies will be sought?
Who is a dependant and what damages may be recovered in respect of such dependency?

Relevant law
Nettleship v Weston [1970] 2 QB 691.
Fatal Accidents Act 1976.
Reeves v Commissioner of Police for the Metropolis [2000] 1 AC 360.

Apply the law
Have all the requirements of negligence been met?
What actions might constitute a *novus actus interveniens*?

Conclude
Steve appears to be the tortfeasor and will be liable for damages.

A

SUGGESTED ANSWER

1. There is not time to discuss duty of care in depth here, so keep moving forward with your answer.

2. Regardless of what you believe the answer to be, make sure your answer is balanced all the way through.

3. Remember the criteria for negligence. You have to prove all the aspects.

1. All road users owe a duty of care to other road users (***Nettleship v Weston* [1970] 2 QB 691**), so Steve will owe Matt and Sascha a duty of care in respect of the physical injury and property damage they suffer. But we need to consider whether he has breached his duty of care. As a rule, if Steve has not behaved as the reasonable man (*Blyth v Birmingham Waters*) would have done in the circumstances, he will be deemed to have breached his duty.

2. Here we must balance up whether the failure to heed a warning not to drive can be defended by the necessity to potentially save a life. In ***Watt v Hertfordshire County Council* [1954] 1 WLR 835** (see also *S (a child) v Keyse* [2001] EWCA Civ 715) a relevant factor in deciding that the defendant was not in breach of duty was the objective of the journey (to save life).

However, Steve has taken a risk by driving a car; moreover, he has alternatives such as ordering a taxi or waiting for an ambulance. Whether these alternatives are feasible depends on the risk to his wife's life, but it is generally accepted that the defendant must take only reasonable precautions to guard against the risk, not all possible precautions (***Latimer v AEC Ltd* [1953] AC 643**). **3.** On balance it is submitted that he has breached his duty of care—but has this breach of duty caused the injuries?

Matt

Matt jumped from the ladder to avoid being struck by an oncoming vehicle. In *Jones v Boyce* **(1816) 1 Stark 493** it was held that a person who risks harm to himself to avoid reasonably perceived greater harm created by the defendant's actions may still hold the defendant responsible. If Matt reasonably believes that Steve's car is about to strike the ladder, it may be reasonable for him to jump, even though this may result in injury.

Whether Steve or the police are liable for the death of Amy and the injuries to Jazz will depend on whether the actions of the police amount to a *novus actus interveniens*. It has been held that the police should not be subject to a duty of care in relation to the conduct of investigations (*Hill v Chief Constable of West Yorkshire* **[1988] 2 All ER 238**), but it does not follow that the police cannot be liable for their negligence in the course of ordinary operations (*Rigby v Chief Constable of Northamptonshire* **[1985] 2 All ER 985**). Although Steve's negligent driving caused the car to collide with the wall of Sascha's shop, the way the police act subsequently may break the chain of causation, but not if the response is perfectly reasonable: *The Oropesa* **[1943] P 32**. Where the act of the third party is reckless, it is likely to be viewed as a *novus actus interveniens*: *Wright v Lodge* **[1993] 4 All ER 299**. [4] In *Knightley v Johns* **[1982] 1 All ER 851**, it was held that it should be asked whether the whole sequence of events is a natural or probable consequence of the defendant's negligence and whether it was more than just foreseeable as a mere possibility.

In the case of the accident caused by Steve, there does not appear to be any evidence of a negligent act on the part of the police, and the initial damage to the wall has resulted from Steve's driving. This might seem to suggest that the actions of the police do not amount to a *novus actus interveniens* and that Steve will also be responsible for the death of Amy and the injuries to Jazz. In this respect, there are likely to be two actions for dependency damages; one will be brought by Jazz's lover, Kali, and another is likely to be brought by Imran.

Imran

By virtue of **s. 1 of the Fatal Accidents Act 1976**, there is the right of action for wrongful act causing death. This action arises in situations where had deceased person survived from their injuries, they would have been able to maintain an action and recover damages for their injuries. The person liable for these injuries, had death not occurred, will be liable to an action for damages. The action for dependency damages is brought by the executor or administrator or the dependant personally.

[4] Try to embrace some of the technical aspects of the question, particularly if you are looking for higher marks.

5. As Amy's former husband Imran may have an action for dependency damages under the provisions of the **Fatal Accidents Act 1976**, even though he is no longer married to Amy. This is because the list of dependants set out in **s. 1(3)(a) of the Act** includes spouses and former spouses, including those who have remarried (*Shepherd v Post Office* (1995) *The Times*, 15 June).

The purpose behind the **Fatal Accidents Act 1976** is to give the dependant sufficient damages to represent the loss of a breadwinner. In order to be considered for dependency damages, the dependant must show financial loss as a result of the death, and will include the value of any 'domestic services' provided as a partner. We are not informed of any financial aspects of the parties so it will not be possible at this stage to assess how successful such an action might be.

6. Awards can take account of pain and suffering. However, if the period between the tort and the time of death is short, no award will be made for pain and suffering: *Hicks v Chief Constable of South Yorkshire Police* [1992] 2 All ER 65. Therefore, the period of three minutes, between the collapse of the wall whilst the police are attempting to remove Steve's car from Sascha's shop and Amy's death, is likely to be too short to allow an award of damages for pain and suffering.

Kali

Kali will also be able to pursue a claim in line with **s. 1 Fatal Accidents Act 1976**. As a cohabitee, she will also be regarded as a dependant if she has lived with Jazz for at least two years in an equivalent relationship to being a civil partner (**s. 1(3)(b) of the Act**).

Assuming Kali represents Jazz's estate, it will have to be shown that had Jazz lived, she could have sued Steve. Jazz's suicide, brought on by depression resulting from the accident, may amount to a break in the chain of causation, preventing Kali from maintaining an action. It should be noted that the House of Lords in *Reeves v Commissioner of Police of the Metropolis* [2000] 1 AC 360 held that public policy should not deny a remedy, but that it should be asked whether the suicide was caused by the breach of duty using the 'but-for' test. In *Reeves*, however, the defendants were under a duty to prevent the deceased from committing suicide, as he was in police custody. Here Jazz's state of depression is traceable to the injuries she has suffered in the accident caused by Steve's careless driving.

In *Corr v IBC Vehicles Ltd* [2008] UKHL 13 it was held that all the claimant has to do is to show that if her husband suffered an injury at work those injuries might lead to depression. As the depression suffered by the claimant's husband was a logical consequence of the defendants' negligence, there was no break in the chain of causation. If Jazz's sight of the accident, caused by Steve's negligence, started

Jazz's depression, then the suicide will not be a *novus actus interveniens* and the death will not be regarded as damage that is too remote.

In *Reeves* the claimant's damages were reduced by 50 per cent for contributory negligence so as to take account of the fact that the deceased had committed suicide while of sound mind. [7.] However, in *Corr* Lords Bingham and Walker thought that no such deduction should be made, since, on the facts, Mr Corr was not really to blame for his own death. However, a majority of the House of Lords did agree that, in principle, it would be right to reduce damages payable to the next of kin under the **Fatal Accidents Act 1976** where the person committing suicide bears some responsibility for his own death. Accordingly, should the court decide that Steve was the prima facie cause of Jazz's death, and award of damages might be reduced to take into account the act of the victim. In the usual course of events, it would be expected that Steve's motor insurance will pay compensation. However, [8.] if by driving Steve has in some way invalidated his insurance, the Motor Insurance Bureau will pay damages for personal injury. They will not, however, pay for property damage. Sascha may find that he has to make a claim on his own buildings insurance.

[7.] Display your detailed knowledge of cases to argue your points.

[8.] Always consider who will pay. If a tortfeasor cannot pay, the claimant might be placed in the unenviable position of winning a pyrrhic victory in court.

➕ LOOKING FOR EXTRA MARKS?

- It is not sufficient just to discuss the tort of negligence in this question, particularly if you are looking for extra marks.
- Display a detailed knowledge of case law to argue your points successfully.

ℚ QUESTION | 3

'Economic analysis can never be an all-embracing explanation of the objectives of tort law ... efficiency must at some point yield before ... other guidelines.'

(Murphy and Witting, *Street on Torts*)

In light of this statement, discuss the extent to which efficiency and justice are objectives of the law of torts.

❗ CAUTION

- This question deals with the law of torts as a deterrent to harm-causing activities. An answer should consider the various objectives of tort law, in particular whether the compensation objective is ever sacrificed at the hands of arguments based on economic efficiency.
- A wide reading of the area will be required to tackle the question.

DIAGRAM ANSWER PLAN

> The primary objectives of economic analysis of legal rules.

> Efficiency versus justice as objectives of the law of torts.

> The distinction between loss shifting and loss distribution.

> The role of private first-party and third-party insurance.

> The different notions of justice across the whole range of tortious liability.

SUGGESTED ANSWER

Much of tort law concerns itself with accidents which result in physical harm. The law may deter wrongdoers from engaging in activities which harm others but it also provides a remedy for those who are harmed as a result of the defendant's wrongs.

On an economic analysis, the desire to deter a person from engaging in activities which cause harm to others is seen as a primary objective, since prevention is preferable to cure, as evidenced in academic literature [1] (Calabresi, *The Cost of Accidents* (1970), Posner, 'A Theory of Negligence' (1972) 1 J Leg St 29, and *The Economic Analysis of Law*, 6th edn (2003)). Consequently, a legal rule is perceived as efficient if it deters wrongdoing in a cost-effective manner. However, in applying legal rules, the courts have to reach a balance between efficiency and justice. If we have a rule that a claimant is entitled to sue a defendant for the losses caused by his wrongdoing, the costs and benefits of such a rule need to be balanced.

The conflict between efficiency and justice can be seen most clearly in negligence cases when deciding if the defendant is in breach of a duty of care. An efficiency-based rule is that an act is only negligent if reasonable precautions have not been taken by the defendant (*Latimer v AEC Ltd* **[1953] AC 643**), since it is clear that taking every possible precaution to guard against a minor risk of harm would be uneconomic. [2] Virtually every activity has some capacity for causing harm, but if its likelihood is minimal, such as damage caused by a cricket ball, when the evidence shows that only six balls have been hit from a cricket ground in 30 years, there is no need to take special precautions (*Bolton v Stone* **[1951] AC 850**). However, if the magnitude of

[1] Your lecturers will usually indicate key texts that they wish you to study, but there is no harm in searching out academic material for yourself.

[2] You will already know these cases. Essay questions require you to be more creative with your use of them.

risk created by the defendant is such as to expose a highly vulnerable claimant to increased risk of harm, greater care should be taken (*Paris v Stepney BC* [1951] AC 367), illustrating the importance of practical justice in special cases.

Risk assessment is an increasingly common practice in business and if a particular risk is a distinct possibility, precautions such as the provision of proper training for employees should be made (see *Davis v Stena Line* [2005] EWHC 420 (QB)). However, to require a defendant to take precautions to guard against the sheer stupidity of

3. There are numerous cases that you could use here.

the claimant would be to go too far; see for example [3.] *Tomlinson v Congleton BC* [2003] UKHL 47.

If the law imposes liability for certain acts, this appears to have a deterrent effect: people realize they will have to pay damages and as a result refrain from conducting themselves in that way. But there are instances in which there may be little the defendant can do to avoid causing harm to others. For example, since the test of liability is objectively based, the defendant who does his incompetent best may still be liable since he is judged by the standards of the reasonable man and not by reference to his own ability (*Nettleship v Weston* [1971]

4. Choose arguments that interest you, and build in further academic debate and/or case law.

2 QB 691). [4.] Moreover, in many cases the defendant's fault amounts to little more than inadvertence, so that the defendant may not have foreseen the danger he creates, but the law may state that he has not acted in the same way as a reasonable man would have acted and is therefore liable.

Modern tort law is now dominated by the presence of an insurance market and there has been a move towards a system of compensation based on loss distribution. The insurance market is such that major causes of accidents can be identified and those who engage in accident-causing activities, such as employers, drivers, and manufacturers, may be required or encouraged to take out insurance to cover potential risks of loss. Moreover, in most cases, the insured accident causer can pass on the cost of insurance to the consumers of his product or his service, thereby spreading the costs associated with the accident risk more broadly. Since the accident causer must be or ought to be insured, the problem is that it is not the wrongdoer who pays damages but his insurer, and this undermines the argument that tort rules serve a deterrent purpose, since it is rarely the defendant who

5. Consider whether this is a balanced conclusion. Can you find case law that helps you to argue this point?

foots the bill. [5.] Insurers might be able to deter tortious misconduct, but there is little evidence that they do.

It is arguable that the threat of liability based on the notion of fault is likely to result in the adoption of defensive practices which might prove detrimental to the interests of the client or patient in professional negligence cases. The possibility that disproportionate measures might be taken is often put forward as a reason for not imposing a duty of care. But the concept of defensive practices is not confined to cases of medical malpractice and may extend into other areas such as the exercise of statutory powers by a public authority charged with a responsibility for protecting others (see *X (minors) v Bedfordshire County Council* **[1995] 3 WLR 152**) or the police (see *Hill v Chief Constable of West Yorkshire* **[1988] 2 All ER 238**), or the Crown Prosecution Service [6] (see *Elguzouli-Daf v Metropolitan Police Commissioner* **[1995] 1 All ER 833**). In contrast, there is some evidence to suggest that the fear of defensive practices is now given less emphasis: see *Fairchild v Glenhaven Funeral Services Ltd* **[2002] UKHL 22**, Lord Bingham; *Gregg v Scott* **[2005] UKHL 2**, Lord Nicholls (dissenting).

The deterrence and economic efficiency arguments are closely related as, if an activity imposes costs on others, those costs should be reflected in the true cost of the harm-causing activity ([7] see Calabresi, *The Cost of Accidents* (1970), p. 69). This would mean that the cost of a car not fitted with seat belts, or one which is to be driven by a 17-year-old, would have to reflect the increased accident costs associated with the use of such a vehicle, but it is often difficult to identify the true cause of an accident. An efficient solution is not necessarily a fair solution, as it may result in a decision to the effect that an accident victim is the best risk-bearer where he should have been insured, but that will leave the victim uncompensated.

Fairness or justice is seen by lawyers as the underlying purpose of tort rules. This may be rights-based justice under which the claimant is entitled to protection against unjustifiable interferences with his civil rights, such as rules which protect against battery, assault, and false imprisonment. However, although there is no common law rule protecting privacy (see *Wainwright v Home Office* **[2003] UKHL 53**), there is a right to prevent the wrongful disclosure of private information based on the **European Convention on Human Rights (ECHR), Art. 8** (see *Campbell v MGN* **[2004] UKHL 22**; *McKennitt v Ash* **[2006] EWCA Civ 1714**; *Murray v Express Newspapers* **[2008] EWCA Civ 446**).

A second notion of justice is based on a balance of competing interests such as those of neighbouring landowners to be found in *Rylands v Fletcher* **(1868) LR 3 HL 330** and the tort of private nuisance. These torts seek to balance competing ownership rights and take account of the notion of give and take. What matters is whether the defendant's use of his land is reasonable, having regard to matters such as the location of his property; the duration of the nuisance; whether the claimant's land use is unduly sensitive; and, in relation to the remedy provided, whether the defendant's activity is socially useful.

Where a claimant is injured as a result of the defendant's tort, there is a primary need for the harm to be adequately compensated. It is

[6] This is a sophisticated point to raise. This is the detail that examiners require if they are to award you a good grade.

[7] You would not be expected to mention page numbers of articles in an examination answer, but if you can that will impress your examiner.

generally accepted that victims of modern social conditions should not be left to bear all the costs. Thus in addition to liability rules under which most of the costs are borne by insurance, there are public compensation schemes to deal with matters such as invalidity payments, sickness benefit, and other forms of social security payment. The principal issue has become not who is to blame for a particular variety of harm, but who is in the best position to pay for the consequences of that harm. Instead of simply shifting losses from the claimant to the wrongdoing defendant, modern tort law and its accompaniments work on the basis of loss spreading. This notion is reflected in modern rules on vicarious and product liability which recognize that employers and producers are in a position to spread the cost of accidents by charging higher prices for their goods and services or by other cost-cutting measures, combined with the secure knowledge that relevant insurance will cover any award of damages which might be ordered.

LOOKING FOR EXTRA MARKS?

- ▪ This question can be used to discuss several torts. Keep focused on the question, but play to your strengths.
- ▪ Demonstrate your detailed knowledge at every turn, and refer to cases and academic commentary wherever relevant.

QUESTION | 4

Adeel is crossing the road at a pedestrian crossing when, through no fault of his own, he is struck by a car driven by Beatrice. Adeel is knocked to the ground and staggers to his feet, but is concussed and temporarily blinded by blood from a head wound. He is then hit by a car driven by Cassandra, who was texting on her mobile at the time, and knocked to the ground again, unconscious. Beatrice and Cassandra have both been breath-tested by the police, and Beatrice has been found to be significantly affected by alcohol.

Adeel has serious injuries which will make it impossible for him to work again, but his doctors are not able to say which car caused which specific injuries. Adeel's laptop computer was also damaged, causing information to be destroyed which led to loss of business for his employers, FatCat Ltd.

Advise Adeel and FatCat Ltd whether they have any remedy against Beatrice and/or Cassandra.

CAUTION

- ▪ The question is about the tort of negligence. For a full answer, issues of duty and breach must be looked at but will, on these facts, readily be answered.

DIAGRAM ANSWER PLAN

Identify	Who are the tortfeasors? Does the criminal act of a third party amount to a *novus actus interveniens*?
Relevant law	*Barnett v Chelsea and Kensington Hospital Management Committee* [1969] 1 QB 428. *Baker v Willoughby* [1967] AC 467. *Jobling v Associated Dairies Ltd* [1982] AC 794.
Apply the law	Consider the components of negligence, in particular the issue of causation where there is more than one possible cause of the injury.
Conclude	It seems that both Beatrice and Cassandra will be liable for Adeel's injuries and will have to pay compensation on a pro rata basis. FatCat's claim is likely to be considered pure economic loss and therefore unsuccessful.

SUGGESTED ANSWER

Assuming Adeel's injuries have been caused by the traffic collision, it is necessary to consider the liability of Cassandra and Beatrice. **Nettleship v Weston [1971] 2 QB 691** is one of numerous cases recognizing the long-established duty of care owed by motorists to other road users, so there will be no dispute about the duty Beatrice and Cassandra owe to Adeel.

There is little to choose between Beatrice and Cassandra so far as their breach of duty is concerned. Nevertheless, it is possible that Cassandra may argue, in terms of causation, that she was not to blame (or not solely to blame) for the second collision with Adeel because he stumbled unpredictably into her path. This would involve focusing the whole of the allegation of negligence against Beatrice on the basis that Adeel was still suffering from the effects of the first collision at the time.

¹· If you are looking for extra marks, discuss how factual causation works before moving onto legal causation.

¹· Using this approach, and applying the but-for test from **Barnett v Chelsea and Kensington Hospital Management Committee [1969] 1 QB 428**, it would have to be shown that Adeel would not have suffered any injury but for Beatrice's negligence. At first sight, this reasoning looks quite promising, but Beatrice will argue that

Cassandra's negligence constitutes a *novus actus interveniens*—an intervening act which breaks the chain of causation and frees her from liability in respect of the second batch of injuries. [2] The test identified in ***Knightley v Johns* [1982] 1 All ER 851** states that third party acts will break the chain unless they were a natural and probable consequence of the defendant's negligence. Several aspects of the question will make the application of this test problematic, not least the fact that it is impossible to attribute individual injuries to either car.

Although the second collision caused more serious injuries than the first, this case is not to be likened to ***Baker v Willoughby* [1967] AC 467**, in which there was a pre-existing disability caused by one tortfeasor and a subsequent worsening of that disability caused by another tortfeasor. In ***Baker*** there was no connection between the two tortfeasors or between the two incidents giving rise to the successive disabilities. [3] Moreover, there were also important policy considerations since the later injury was caused by a criminal who shot the claimant in the leg, causing that leg to be amputated, although this later event was held not to affect the claimant's existing claim for damages against the first defendant for injuries caused to the same leg in a road traffic collision. Ignoring the but-for test, the first defendant (the negligent driver) was held liable for the loss resulting from the original incident but the additional damage caused by the criminal was discounted. Had the claimant sought to bring an action in respect of the later injuries caused by the criminal, it was considered that the pre-existing injuries to the leg would have to be taken into account, thereby reducing the claimant's quantum of damages. However, since the criminal would not have been insured in respect of the damage he had caused, there was probably little likelihood of the criminal being able to pay the damages even if the claimant had chosen to sue him.

[4] As an alternative to the ***Baker v Willoughby*** approach, it was held in ***Jobling v Associated Dairies Ltd* [1982] AC 794** that a court should take account of the vicissitudes of life, such as (in that case) the subsequent development of a disease, which reduced the claimant's projected working lifespan and hence his overall claim for damages against the defendant in respect of a negligently caused work injury. However, it may be argued that the second road accident in the problem is not a 'vicissitude of life' but a separate tortious act, and therefore rather more like ***Baker***. In any case, in both ***Baker*** and ***Jobling*** the supervening event—whether tortious or natural—occurred well after the original negligence, whereas here the events occurred in very close proximity.

The present case should also be distinguished from the situation which arises when the claimant **must** have been injured by one of

[2] Consider using academic literature to argue the merits of/against the ruling of this case.

[3] If you are short of time, you do not need to go into this aspect in depth, but if you are hoping to do well consider discussing policy issues in your answer.

[4] Do not forget that we are looking for arguments for and against a particular situation.

two defendants, but it cannot be determined which of the two is responsible. This type of scenario came under scrutiny in *Fairchild v Glenhaven Funeral Services Ltd* **[2002] UKHL 22** in the context of mesothelioma caused by exposure to asbestos, where the damage had to have been caused by one of a series of negligent defendants. Ordinarily, a claim would fail wherever the claimant was unable to satisfy the but-for test and prove that a specific defendant had caused the injury. In *Fairchild*, however, the House of Lords, in recognition of the injustice that would result were the test to be applied too rigidly, agreed the circumstances called for an alternative approach. This was a scenario better dealt with by an application of the approach previously applied in *McGhee v NCB* **[1973] 1 WLR 1**, namely that if the defendant had negligently exposed the claimant to a material risk of injury and the injury actually suffered fell within the foreseeable range, causation is made out. 5. At least in respect of mesothelioma claims, this approach has more recently been endorsed by the Supreme Court in *Sienkiewicz v Greif (UK) Ltd* **[2011] UKSC 10**.

5. Does this advance your argument? If not, you do not need to incorporate it.

The House of Lords has held that, in cases where damage might have been caused by one tortfeasor or by natural causes, the tortfeasor cannot be held responsible unless it can be shown that the tortfeasor's negligence is, on the balance of probabilities, the most likely cause of the damage (*Wilsher v Essex AHA* **[1988] AC 1074**). When there is doubt as to whether a particular defendant caused certain damage to the claimant, or whether it was caused by a *novus actus interveniens*, English law seems to dictate that there is no substitute for proof, except in certain very narrow circumstances when public policy and notions of justice might promote a modified approach.

In practice, it is most likely that Beatrice and Cassandra will both be regarded as causes of the harm suffered by Adeel, as in *Fitzgerald v Lane* **[1989] AC 328**, where a careless pedestrian was hit by two cars at a pelican crossing. If this is the case, the issue of contribution between joint tortfeasors will arise. 6. Such argument is permissible under the **Civil Liability (Contribution) Act 1978 s. 1**.

6. Under exam conditions, do not write out big sections of the statute.

So far as this Act is concerned, it will make no difference whether Beatrice acted deliberately and Cassandra only negligently, since they will both be regarded as joint tortfeasors. Both may be required to make a contribution under the terms of the Act, and it will not be a defence for the merely negligent to argue that the degree of fault of the other tortfeasor was greater. 7. However, the greater degree of fault of one joint tortfeasor will clearly be a relevant consideration in determining what share of responsibility should be allocated to each defendant.

7. What do you think the apportionment should be?

Finally, the question arises whether FatCat Ltd can successfully sue Beatrice or Cassandra for the loss of business that was due to the destruction of data on Adeel's computer. Such a claim would face two possible problems. First, a negligent motorist may not owe a duty of care to the employers of a pedestrian who is injured as a result of the motorist's negligent driving, since, arguably, they would not meet the *Caparo* requirements of foreseeability; proximity; and fair, just, and reasonable. Secondly, the employers have suffered pure economic loss, since their loss of business is not connected with any physical damage to FatCat's property *Spartan Steel & Alloys Ltd v Martin & Co (Contractors) Ltd* [1973] 1 QB 27.

LOOKING FOR EXTRA MARKS?

- If your question appears relatively straightforward, your examiner will require detailed attention to the facts to award you a good grade.
- Do not be afraid to give a firm conclusion, if it is a logical conclusion from your survey of legal provisions in your answer.

Online Resources
www.oup.com/uk/qanda/

Go online for extra essay and problem questions, a glossary of key terms, online versions of all the answer plans and audio commentary on how selected ones were put together, and a range of podcasts which include advice on exam and coursework technique and advice for other assessment methods.

Skills for Success in Coursework Assessments

In Chapter 1, we looked at some of the challenges of taking your examination in tort law. In this chapter we look at structuring your answers to coursework questions and expose common errors that students make when undertaking coursework. You may be surprised to find how basic some of these errors are. As we discussed in Chapter 1, the starting point for obtaining a good grade in your examination is to answer the question set. It is even more important that you do so for coursework questions, as you are usually given plenty of time to plan and prepare your answer, and to ask for additional support if needed.

Whether you are answering a problem question or an essay question, you will be required to produce a convincing argument using 'evidence' from case law, statutory provisions, and academic literature. This means careful research and composition. Your examiners will assess your coursework, not only on your legal relevance and accuracy, but also on your clarity, depth of analysis, and overall production.

In terms of structure and content, answering coursework questions in tort law is no different to answering examination questions. However, whereas minor omissions in an examination answer are unlikely to have a significant impact on your marks, you may find that you are more heavily penalized if you make a similar error in your coursework.

Where to Begin?

Students are often daunted by the prospect of starting their coursework, especially when they are new to law. We all work in different ways, but rather than rushing to your keyboard, spend time reading and researching your question.

Consider: What is the overall theme of your question? Can you break down your question into smaller sections? For example, if you are set a general question on negligence, do not try to tackle all the components at once. You may prefer to start by investigating causation. This is **your** research, and you should feel empowered to do it in any order that best suits you.

As you are researching, make a note of any current legislation and seminal cases that you want to incorporate in your answer. Keep a comprehensive account of the research trail that you have conducted, to ensure that you have the full details of academic literature that you intend to use to give weight to your arguments. If you find a useful quote (whether from a case or an academic essay) make sure that you write down precisely where it came from, including the page or paragraph number. You will need to reference quotes fully in your answer (more on this later).

Putting Ink to Paper

When you have completed your initial research, make sure you understand the question that has been set. What form does your question take? An essay question will often contain terms such as 'critically evaluate/assess', 'outline', 'discuss', and 'analyse'. Make sure you do what the question is asking you to do. In an essay-style question, you will need to back up your arguments with evidence. If the question set is a problem question, use the IRAC method to help you structure your answer.

Although you will want your final submission to be well organized and presented in a logical order, it does not matter how you achieve this. Your first draft does not need to be perfect, either in terms of its content or its structure. Unless you are naturally gifted in writing, and most of us are not, your first draft will not be your last. In fact, if you submit your one and only draft, you are not likely to achieve the good mark that you are hoping for.

Most academic writers will tell you that the introduction is usually the last aspect of their work that is drafted, so do not feel compelled to write your introduction straight away. Having completed most of your answer, you can go back and write your introduction.

When you have produced your first draft, look at your question again—does your work **really** answer the question that you have been given? One of the most frequent comments made by examiners on coursework is 'discusses irrelevant issues in part', or, worse still, 'complete failure to answer the question set'. If you are not convinced that **all** of your answer is relevant, now is the time to rethink, and redraft.

When you are satisfied that your answer addresses the correct issues, and is correct in law, consider how much analysis you have given. If you have written out the facts of the cases but not focused on their importance, you have not analysed sufficiently. For example, in the context of an essay question, your examiner will want to know why you have mentioned a particular case, and will want to assess your thoughts on whether you have found it a satisfactory/unsatisfactory legal authority. This is where academic literature will assist you. You may not feel that you are in a position to criticize a legal authority, but there will be a number of academics who will are prepared to do so. If you have read differing opinions on the subject, you can specify, 'I agree with the arguments put forward by . . .'. Remember: look at an argument from all sides, and reach a conclusion.

Once you have ensured that your answer is relevant, accurate, analytical, and well structured, you are on the way to completion, but you will be surprised how long the 'finishing touches' take to achieve.

Final Submissions

There are a number of errors that students regularly make during their coursework composition/submission. Employing the following five measures will help prevent such errors taking place:

1. Submit on Time

    Make sure you know the date and time of your deadline. Do not try to submit your work at the last minute. It is no myth that online submission systems will malfunction one hour before the submission deadline. ... With this in mind, be ready to submit well in advance of the final hour—just in case something does not go to plan. In the words of Denning MR in *Spartan Steel & Alloys v Martin & Co (Contractors)* [1973] QB 27, '[t]he cutting of the supply of electricity . . . is a hazard which we all run'. You will not find a sympathetic lecturer's shoulder to cry on if this happens to you. Nor will we be very supportive if we hear that the reason for your non-submission is 'computer malfunction', or 'flash drive lost on the bus', or 'gerbil died this morning'. (We will of course be sympathetic and try to assist you if you are experiencing genuine and substantial difficulties.)

2. Correct Word Count

   Do pay attention to your word limit. Each institution has its own rules in this respect, but some will award you an automatic cap of 40 per cent if you have only **one** word more than you should in your answer, whilst other institutions will deduct 10 per cent of your final grade. You may find that you are awarded an instant 'fail'. It is important to check your own regulations on this.

3. Referencing

   You will be expected to follow a set style of referencing for footnotes, bibliographies, and tables of statutes and cases. The reason for this is to ensure academic integrity.

   One of the most frustrating aspects of students' coursework is their lack of respect for referencing. The role of referencing is to inform your reader where to find the original source, should we wish to find it for ourselves. This promotes academic integrity by attributing the ideas to the author, and more significantly for you, it protects you from any allegations of plagiarism. **It is essential that you provide full and accurate references and citations for your sources.** Make sure you know which system you are asked to use **before** starting your coursework. The recognized citation system for academic law writing is the Oxford Standard for the Citation of Legal Authorities (OSCOLA). The guide to OSCOLA is available for you to read online, at

   https://www.law.ox.ac.uk/sites/files/oxlaw/oscola_4th_edn_hart_2012.pdf.

   Some students master footnoting, but then fail to adhere to the requirements for bibliographies. Whichever system of referencing you are asked to adopt, make sure that you allow yourself enough time to perfect it. Referencing can be very time-consuming. This is not something to leave until the day of submission.

4. Proofreading

   A key part of any writing process is the checking and proofreading at the end. Does each point flow naturally to the next, or does the text appear disjointed? Put your work through a spellcheck, but be careful here, as the spellcheck cannot distinguish between wrong word choices (to/too, there/their, etc). Look at your final piece. Does it look professional? Does it have your student number on it, if appropriate? Is your font size big enough for us to read it?

5. Submit the Final Version of Your Work

   After all the work you have done, make sure that you have submitted your final version. I have had many students emailing me, telling me they have submitted the wrong version … sometimes we can help you—but only sometimes …

   If in doubt, ask your tutors for advice—but do not leave this until the last day, as we will not be able to assist you at this stage.

COURSEWORK PROBLEM QUESTION

[1.] Asif is working as a maintenance assistant for Shaky Boats Ltd. His main job is to ensure that the jetty is kept safe and clean. He uses an electric pressure hose to perform this duty. [2.] All of Shaky Boats' equipment is maintained by Gorust plc. One month ago, whilst Asif was using the hose, an electrical fault occurred, causing a power surge. There was a large bang and flames sparked out of the electrical pump. Asif sustained a severe burn to his right hand. [3.] Asif is convinced that the outside of the pump appeared to be in perfect condition when he commenced his duties that day. Pritpal, a customer, was buying tickets for herself and her son when the power surge occurred. [4.] Her son was near the flames and Pritpal screamed as she thought her son had been burnt. He was, in fact, unharmed, but Pritpal has suffered depression after the incident.

[5.] Advise Asif and Pritpal.

[1.] Asif is in an employee.

[2.] Who might be responsible for the injuries? What is the relationship between Shaky Boats Ltd and Gorust plc? Consider the role of the Employers' Liability (Defective Equipment) Act 1969 s. 1.

[3.] Is Asif responsible, or partly responsible, for his own injuries?

[4.] What is Pritpal's cause of action? The term 'depression' should indicate your starting point.

[5.] Inform your examiner what area of tort law we are looking at. Discuss the components of this tort.

ANSWER GUIDANCE

The question requires a consideration of employers' liability, and liability for psychiatric harm, which fall under the tort of negligence. In your introduction you may consider discussing the basic formula involved with an action in negligence, that is duty of care, breach and causation, and remoteness of damage. However, do not spend too much time discussing this; move quickly to the individual advice.

Can Asif sue his employers for the injuries he has received, under employers' liability? Consider the case of *Wilson and Clyde Coal Co v English* [1938] AC 57 which made the duty on the employer non-delegable at law. Assuming that Asif is competent for his employment, assess the defective equipment.

The employers, Shaky Boats, are under a duty to inspect equipment. However, they will argue that Gorust were employed to service the equipment. If the mechanical fault occurred due to inadequate servicing, then Gorust will be at fault. This does not matter for Asif as, under the Employers' Liability (Defective Equipment) Act 1969 s. 1, the injury is held to be attributable to the employer also. (It will matter for Pritpal, though.)

Is this an issue of contributory negligence? Remember you need to raise an issue, even if you believe that the outcome is clear.

Pritpal has suffered depression, therefore consider psychiatric damage. What does she have to prove to be successful in her action? Is she a primary victim or secondary victim? Use cases to justify your answer, namely *Page v Smith* [1995] UKHL 7, *White v Chief Constable South Yorkshire Police* [1998] UKHL 45, and *Alcock v Chief Constable of South Yorkshire Police* [1991] UKHL 5, [1992] 1 AC 310. If she is a secondary victim, spend some time looking at the three-point test in *Alcock*—a close tie of love and affection, proximity, and normal fortitude.

The final part of your answer should address the issue of who Pritpal can sue. In this respect, you will need to consider the relationship between Shaky Boats and Gorust. Are Gorust actually 'employees' or 'independent contractors?' (*Ready Mixed Concrete (South East) Ltd v Minister of Pensions* [1968] 2 QB 497).

COURSEWORK ESSAY QUESTION

'In its ruling on *Coventry v Lawrence* [2014] UKSC 13[1], the Supreme Court made fundamental changes to long-established principles of the law of nuisance,[2] but the changes are not radical enough.'
Critically analyse this statement.[3]

[1] Make sure you read the case.
[2] Develop your understanding of the tort, and what changes were made.
[3] The examiner is asking you to argue with the statement, for and against its accuracy; it is not enough just to 'discuss'.

ANSWER GUIDANCE

In approaching a question like this, it is imperative that you read the case. It would be unwise of you to answer an examination question without reading *Coventry v Lawrence*, but it will be fatal for you if you try to answer coursework questions without reading the case concerned—and yet many students try to do just this. ...

If the examiner specifies that you 'critically analyse' a statement, we are looking to read your arguments relating to the statement. Your conclusion is not as important as the logical thought that you put behind it. To be able to analyse the statement, you will need to fully understand the effect of the ruling.

In your introduction, discuss what the tort of nuisance is. A quick overview is all that is needed here. Do not go through all the finer points of the tort. If you can find a suitable quote from the case itself, write it in.

Your next step will be to focus on the case itself. What did the ruling say? How and why (if at all) did the case change the law? Look for support from academic literature, Law Commission reports, Hansard, etc. Discuss previous contradictions in cases which needed clarification. Blend all these points into your answer.

Reach a firm conclusion in your mind—then go back to the quote. Do you agree with the quote? If so, why? If not, why not?

Whichever side of the argument you choose to back, make sure you have justified your arguments by reference to legal or academic authorities.

Sum up your thoughts in a neat conclusion.

Then go back and do all the footnoting. ...

Good luck!

 Online Resources www.oup.com/uk/qanda/

Go online for extra essay and problem questions, a glossary of key terms, online versions of all the answer plans and audio commentary on how selected ones were put together, and a range of podcasts which include advice on exam and coursework technique and advice for other assessment methods.

Index